T0275112

U.S. Citizenship

2nd Edition

by Jennifer Gagliardi

for dummies®

A Wiley Brand

U.S. Citizenship For Dummies®, 2nd Edition

Published by: **John Wiley & Sons, Inc.**, 111 River Street, Hoboken, NJ 07030-5774, www.wiley.com

Copyright © 2022 by John Wiley & Sons, Inc., Hoboken, New Jersey

Published simultaneously in Canada

For general information on our other products and services, please contact our Customer Care Department within the U.S. at 877-762-2974, outside the U.S. at 317-572-3993, or fax 317-572-4002. For technical support, please visit https://hub.wiley.com/community/support/dummies.

Wiley publishes in a variety of print and electronic formats and by print-on-demand. Some material included with standard print versions of this book may not be included in e-books or in print-on-demand. If this book refers to media such as a CD or DVD that is not included in the version you purchased, you may download this material at http://booksupport.wiley.com. For more information about Wiley products, visit www.wiley.com.

Library of Congress Control Number: 2022937792

ISBN 978-1-119-76673-5 (pbk); ISBN 978-1-119-76688-9 (ebk); ISBN 978-1-119-76689-6 (ebk)

SKY10034527_052022

Contents at a Glance

Table of Contents

Introduction

So you want to live in America? You're in good company. Between 2015 and 2019, approximately 1.1 million people per year became permanent legal residents of the United States. Sixty percent of these new immigrants came to reunite with family members who had already made the move to the unparalleled freedom and opportunity the United States offers her people. Fourteen percent specifically came here to offer their skills to help keep the U.S. workforce strong. Still others came to escape persecution and tyranny in their homelands.

Many permanent residents choose to take living in the United States a step further by becoming naturalized United States citizens. By becoming a naturalized citizen, these immigrants will experience nearly all the benefits granted to citizens born in the U.S. (the only exception is that they can't become president or vice president of the United States).

Despite pandemic-related closures, the U.S. Citizenship and Immigration Services (USCIS) welcomed 625,400 new citizens in fiscal year (FY) 2020 during naturalization ceremonies held across the United States and around the world. Among the top five countries of birth for people naturalizing in FY 2020, Mexico was the lead country, with 13.3% of all naturalizations, followed by India (7.7%), the Philippines (5.3%), Cuba (5%), and the People's Republic of China (3.7%). The top five countries of birth comprised 35% of the naturalized citizens in FY 2020. For some, the process of immigrating to the U.S. and becoming a citizen was simple and straightforward. For others, the journey through the immigration and naturalization process became an endless parade of obstacles, delays, forms, and paperwork.

This book will help you get through this often confusing process, from determining how best to qualify to live permanently in the United States to gaining a green card to become a naturalized citizen of the U.S. Along the way, we point out the important requirements you need to meet and give tips and insights into dealing with USCIS, as well as other government agencies you'll come into contact with while attempting to immigrate to the U.S. or become a citizen.

We wish we could tell you the immigration process is always simple, but each case is different and there are many special circumstances and exceptions to the rules that can come into play. In the aftermath of the tragic events of September 11, 2001, the complications have only increased. The U.S. immigration system has been under unprecedented public scrutiny. In most immigration cases, the services of a competent immigration attorney are highly recommended. Sometimes an attorney's help is absolutely necessary in order to protect your immigration chances and help you through the process. Often, you can get free or low-cost help from nonprofit immigration services, designed to help immigrants legally live in the United States.

About This Book

In this book, we let you know things you can do to make the immigration and naturalization process easier and less stressful, as well as where to find additional help in case you need it. You'll discover how to be proactive and stay a step ahead of the USCIS by anticipating which forms and paperwork you'll need in advance. We also alert you to important points that can help you protect your immigration case throughout the proceedings.

If you plan on becoming a citizen, we also get you ready to pass the English, civics, reading, and writing portions of the naturalization interview. This part, more than any other, seems to fill potential citizens with fear. But you really shouldn't worry. The USCIS is not expecting you to be an expert. In this book, we show you how to find out what you need to know. In fact, you'll probably find practicing for the tests enjoyable, if not fun.

Why does a book on citizenship spend a fair amount of space on how to immigrate to the United States? Because you must first be a lawful permanent resident for a designated amount of time before you even qualify to try to become a naturalized citizen. So lawful immigration truly is the first step to naturalization.

Still, you will note this book is not called *U.S. Immigration For Dummies.* We'll help you identify potential ways to immigrate, but this book isn't long enough to cover actual petitioning and visa processing. We also avoid detailed discussion of non-immigrant visas.

In all cases, we've kept the chapters *modular,* meaning you'll find all the information you'll need on a given subject, or we'll refer you to other chapters in the book for further detail, and you don't have to read the book from start to finish to understand the topic at hand.

Foolish Assumptions

Because you bought this book, we assume you are interested in living permanently in the U.S. or are a friend or relative of someone else who does. You (or your friend or relative) probably want to take the immigration process all the way to the end — naturalization — but regardless of your immigration goals, this book can help.

We don't assume that you have a legal background or any familiarity with U.S. immigration. As such, we have made every attempt to explain the complicated legal process of immigration and naturalization in simple, easy-to-understand language. Nonetheless, we still strongly urge you to seek the advice of a competent attorney or immigration service to help you pursue your goals. Don't worry, we also tell you how to find reliable help.

Icons Used in This Book

Icons are the pictures you'll see in the margins throughout this book. Although they're mighty fun to look at, they're there to serve a purpose: flagging your attention to key pieces of information. Here's what the various icons mean:

REMEMBER

This icons calls your attention to information we cover elsewhere but that's so important we think it's worth repeating (and worth remembering).

TIP

The Tip icon points out practical advice that will make your naturalization and immigration process easier.

WARNING

This icon highlights key points that can save you trouble, money, or in the worst-case scenario, forced removal from the country.

TECHNICAL STUFF

This icon points out more information than you technically need, but provides interesting facts that explain the hows and whys of immigration.

Beyond the Book

For quick tips about immigrating to the United States and taking the first steps toward citizenship, go to www.dummies.com and type "U.S. Citizenship For Dummies Cheat Sheet" in the search box. You can find information on determining your eligibility for citizenship along with advice on how to become a lawful permanent resident of the United States.

Where to Go from Here

Depending on your goals and where you are in the immigration process, you can dive right into Chapter 1 and read the entire book or skip to the chapters that best apply to your unique situation.

If you already hold an alien registration card and are now interested in gaining U.S. citizenship, you can easily skip over the chapters that deal with visas and gaining lawful permanent residence — although if you have friends or family members who also want to immigrate, you can certainly help them with this information.

If you're just beginning the process, you won't need to concern yourself with studying for the naturalization interview yet. But when that time comes, the information will be waiting for you in Parts 2, 3, and, 4.

1

Pursuing Immigration and Citizenship

Plan your immigration and path to U.S. Citizenship

Find out about U.S. Citizenship and Immigration Services, the Department of Homeland Security, the Department of State, and other agencies that affect immigration and citizenship.

Safeguard your future immigration plans with the appropriate visa.

Fill out the USCIS Form N-400 Application for Naturalization.

Chapter **1**

The Joys of Becoming a U.S. Citizen

The decision to become a U.S. citizen is one of the most important choices you can ever make. Before you can become a U.S. citizen, however, you first must be a lawful permanent resident of the United States. For this reason, before you begin the process, you need to know what you want to achieve — legal immigration or naturalization — and whether you can expect to qualify for it.

This chapter gives you an overview of your immigration options, helps you understand the benefits and disadvantages of becoming a U.S. citizen, and shows you what to expect during the process. Although we go into more detail later in the book, this chapter helps you determine what your immigration and citizenship goals are and shows you how best to pursue them.

Determining Whether You Really Want to Become a U.S. Citizen

Becoming a U.S. citizen carries important duties and responsibilities as well as rights, rewards, and privileges. Before you make the decision to pursue U.S. citizenship, you need to be aware of what you stand to lose and what you stand to gain and be sure that you're ready to fulfill all the obligations of a good citizen.

Naturalization refers to the process by which immigrants become citizens. In most cases, if you were not born in the United States, you must be *naturalized* to become a U.S. citizen.

What you lose

When you become a U.S. citizen, you must give up all prior allegiances to other countries. Although nobody will care if you root for your birth country in a soccer match (actually, some soccer fans may care, but the U.S. government certainly won't), you won't be able to defend that country against the United States in times of conflict or war. You must also be willing to serve your new country, the United States of America, when required. What this means is that if the United States is at war or in the midst of some other type of crisis, you need to be willing to take up arms or otherwise aid the U.S. military effort in whatever capacity is needed.

Giving up your allegiances to other countries doesn't necessarily mean you have to give up your citizenship in other countries. You may be able to maintain your original citizenship(s) *and* hold U.S. citizenship (having citizenship in more than one country is known as *dual citizenship*). The United States allows dual citizenship (though it is disfavored). Some countries do not allow dual citizenship. If you are a citizen of such a country, you will likely give up your citizenship upon naturalizing to U.S. citizenship. This information may affect your decision to apply for U.S. citizenship. To find out if your citizenship can be affected, check with the embassy of each country where you have or are considering citizenship.

Furthermore, giving up your allegiance to other countries does not mean that you must stop speaking your native language, teaching your children about your culture, or practicing your religion. These are gifts to be shared not only with your friends and family but also your fellow Americans.

What you gain

The United States Constitution, the country's most important document and essentially the rulebook for how the U.S. government runs, guarantees all people living in the United States, whether U.S. citizens or not, certain rights. Freedom of religion and speech, the right to peaceable assembly, and the right to a fair trial if you're ever accused of a crime are all important freedoms guaranteed to everyone in the United States.

8   PART 1 **Pursuing Immigration and Citizenship**

U.S. citizens, both born and naturalized, however, are eligible for many additional benefits based on their status as U.S. citizens. These include the following:

>> The right to vote and, therefore, to have a voice in government

>> The right to hold elected office (except for the offices of president and vice president, which are reserved for natural-born citizens)

>> Certain government jobs

>> Scholarships and/or grants

>> The ability to petition for immediate relatives to join you in the United States without being subject to visa limits

>> Protection from forced removal from the country

>> Certain types of public assistance

Your rights and responsibilities as a U.S. citizen

When you become a naturalized U.S. citizen, you must take the *Oath of Allegiance.* The Oath of Allegiance is your promise to the government and the people of the United States that you will

>> Give up any prior allegiances to other countries.

>> Support and defend the Constitution and the laws of the United States against all enemies.

>> Support, defend, and obey the laws of the United States.

>> Serve the United States, if required, in times of war or national emergency. You may be called to serve in the military or help U.S. military efforts in some capacity.

>> Swear allegiance to the United States.

In addition to the responsibilities outlined in the Oath of Allegiance, U.S. citizens have other important duties:

>> **Serving on a jury:** One of the most important rights in the United States is the right to a trial by a jury in most cases. Serving on a jury when asked is an important obligation of U.S. citizens in order to protect the U.S. system of justice, in which the power still rests with the people.

Although there is a small chance you may never be called to report for jury duty, know that if you do receive a notice to report, you're legally compelled to do so. Failure to report for jury duty can result in a fine, jail time, or both.

>> **Voting:** The United States has a government of the people, by the people, and for the people. The ultimate political authority is not in the hands of the government or of any single government official — instead, the ultimate political authority is in the hands of the people. Citizens of the United States have the right to change or abolish the government or to amend the Constitution. U.S. citizens exercise their power by voting for elected representatives.

>> **Being tolerant of others:** Some people say that the United States is a "melting pot," the assimilation of many different peoples to create one people; others say that the United States is more like a "tossed salad," a medley of different cultures — each separately identifiable — while still enhancing the common culture. People living here need to be tolerant of all races, religions, and cultures.

Although you aren't legally compelled to perform some of these duties — for instance, no one will take you to jail if you don't exercise your right to vote — you will deprive yourself of the important benefits of living in the United States if you don't participate.

Mapping Your Way to America: Typical Ways People Immigrate to the U.S.

Before you can even think about becoming a naturalized citizen of the United States, you must be a lawful permanent resident of this country. A *lawful permanent resident* is a foreign national who has been granted the privilege of permanently living and working in the United States. Most adult applicants (those 18 or older) must have been lawful permanent residents of the United States for the five years prior to applying for citizenship. If you're married to and living with your U.S. citizen spouse, and your permanent residence is based on that marriage, the residence requirement drops to three years, as long as your spouse has been a citizen for the three years prior to your application. (We go over the eligibility requirements for naturalization in further detail in Chapter 3.)

If you were admitted or paroled into the United States by an immigration officer, you were issued or received a Form I-94, Arrival/Departure Record, which shows a specific date when you are required to leave. People who stay in the United States illegally for over 180 days past the I-94 Departure Date and then leave the United

States can be barred from reentering the country for at least three years. If the period of unlawful presence was less than a year, then the bar applies for three years (unless you leave voluntarily after removal proceedings start). If the period of unlawful presence was for a year or more, the bar is for ten years.

U.S Citizenship and Immigration Services (USCIS) won't count time you spent here illegally before April 1, 1997. Asylees (with pending cases), minors under the age of 18, Family Unity beneficiaries, and battered spouses/children and victims of trafficking (who can prove a connection between the status violation and abuse) do not accrue unlawful presence.

For further information, USCIS.gov has a detailed web page about Unlawful Presence and Bars to Admissibility with a link to the USCIS Adjudicators Field Guide (ch.40.9.2), which describes special circumstances and remedies. Please consult with an immigration legal service representative about lawful presence issues.

WARNING

Bottom line: Don't overstay your welcome. If you're in the United States on a temporary visa and you stay after your visa expires, you're putting your future chances for lawful permanent residence at risk. Being in the country illegally is grounds for removal and for denial of future immigration benefits. If you are currently in the country illegally, you should seek competent legal advice before leaving the United States to try to secure a visa.

TIP

To check whether your immigration status is currently legal, rely on your I-94 (Arrival-Departure Record). You receive this document from U.S. Customs and Border Protection (find out more about the CBP in Chapter 2) upon entering the country, or from the USCIS if you extended your immigration status while already in the United States. Many people believe the visa is what determines the amount of time you can stay in the United States, but this isn't the case.

The CBP is supposed to give a person the amount of time for which a visa petition is approved, rather than the amount of time the visa is valid — which is sometimes less than the amount of time granted in the petition. Likewise, the CBP can approve entry for a lesser amount of time than the visa would indicate.

REMEMBER

If you stay in the United States for more time than your I-94 allows, you are out of status, even if your visa indicates a longer period.

Your visa can say it expires tomorrow, but the airport inspector can stamp your I-94 for six months. On the other hand, your visa can say it's valid through 2010, but the inspector can stamp you for only one month. The stamp is always your guide.

HOW IMMIGRATION LAW DEFINES CHILDREN

The definition of a child has specific meaning in immigration law. When you read government documents that say, for instance, that you're able to sponsor "children," that means you can sponsor an unmarried son or daughter under the age of 21 who was born in wedlock or is your legally recognized stepchild or adopted child. If, on the other hand, an immigration document refers to a "son or daughter," this refers to a child age 21 or older.

How can you achieve legal permanent residence? Although there are other ways, which we go into in Chapter 3, most people immigrate for one of two reasons:

>> To reunite with family members already living in the United States

>> To pursue a permanent employment opportunity in the United States

Reuniting with your family

In order to use family connections to immigrate to the United States, you must have a *close* relative already living here who is willing to sponsor you. So how close is close? If your relative is at least 21 years old and a U.S. citizen, born or naturalized, they may sponsor you if you are their

>> Husband or wife

>> Unmarried child under age 21

>> Unmarried son or daughter over age 21

>> Married son or daughter

>> Brother or sister

>> Parent

Citizens may *not* sponsor their grandparents, grandchildren, aunts, uncles, cousins, or anyone else.

Legal permanent residents, or green-card holders — those legally living and working in the United States who have not become naturalized citizens — may only sponsor their

>> Husband or wife

>> Unmarried children of any age

Legal permanent residents (green-card holders) may *not* sponsor brothers or sisters, parents, grandparents, grandchildren, aunts, uncles, cousins, or anyone other than their spouse and children.

But wait, it's not so easy. Beyond having a willingness to sponsor you, your relative must meet certain criteria in order to be eligible to become a sponsor:

>> Your relative must be able to provide documentation of their own immigration status — as a lawful permanent resident or as a United States citizen (born or naturalized).

>> Your relative must be able to prove that they can financially support you (and any other family members they are financially responsible for) at 125 percent above the government-mandated poverty level. In other words, in order for a sponsor to bring a relative to live permanently in the United States, the sponsor must be both willing and able to accept legal responsibility for financially supporting that family member. You can find more information about how to meet this qualification in Chapter 3.

Pursuing employment opportunities

If you want to immigrate to the United States based on the fact that you have a full-time, permanent employment opportunity waiting for you here, both you and your prospective employer must meet a list of specific qualifications. Although one of the goals of the USCIS is to provide the United States with a strong and stable workforce, the USCIS also wants to be sure that immigrants aren't taking jobs that would otherwise go to unemployed U.S. citizens.

REMEMBER

Before you even get started, keep in mind that your prospective employer has to first certify the position with the Department of Labor. This *Labor Certification* is required to show there are no qualified, available U.S. workers to fill the job.

The USCIS grants permanent residence based on employment skills in one of five categories:

>> **Priority Workers (category EB-1)** have extraordinary ability in the arts, education, business, science, or athletics, or are considered to be outstanding professors or researchers. Notice the superlatives: *extraordinary, outstanding.* This category is one of the most difficult ones to qualify for unless you're a

Nobel Prize winner or hold other such prestigious and public accolades in your given field. You may qualify, however, by presenting extensive documentation proving your professional or academic achievements in one of the listed fields as well as evidence of your financial success in your field and your ability to substantially benefit the United States. Another way to qualify for the Priority Workers category is if you happen to be a manager or executive of a company that has transferred you to one of its branches in the United States.

» **Professionals with Advanced Degrees or Persons with Exceptional Ability (category EB-2)** are members of their professions holding advanced degrees, or their U.S. equivalent, or persons with exceptional ability in business, sciences, or the arts who will benefit the interests or welfare of the United States. In order to qualify for this category, be prepared to show how becoming a legal permanent resident will be good for the economy or culture of the United States or how you can help meet the academic needs of the country. You may also qualify for this category if you're a qualified physician and you agree to practice medicine in an area of the United States that is medically underserved.

» **Skilled or Professional Workers or Other Workers (category EB-3)** have less stringent requirements for qualification than people who qualify under the EB-1 and EB-2 classifications, but this category sometimes has a much longer backlog of people waiting for visas, especially in the Other Workers category. You can qualify for a classification EB-3 employment visa in three ways:

- **As a Skilled Worker:** If you can fill an open position that requires at least two years of experience or training, you can qualify as a Skilled Worker. The Department of Labor determines which jobs are considered skilled, as opposed to unskilled, labor.

- **As a Professional:** Professionals must hold a U.S. baccalaureate degree or the foreign equivalent degree normally required for the profession. Education and experience may not be substituted for the actual degree.

- **As an Other Worker:** Those who fall into the category of Other Workers have the skills to fill jobs that require less than two years of higher education, training, or experience. This category receives the most petitions, so if you fall in this group, you may have to wait many years before being granted a visa.

» **Special Immigrants (or category EB-4)** primarily are members of religious denominations that have nonprofit religious organizations in the United States. You must be able to prove that you have been a member of this organization and have worked for the organization for at least two years before you applied for admission, and you must be coming to the United

States to work as a minister or priest or other religious vocation that helps the organization. You may also qualify if your work helps the organization in a more professional capacity; however, this means that a U.S. baccalaureate degree, or the foreign equivalent, is required to perform the job.

» **Immigrant Investors (or category EB-5)** must agree to make a "qualified investment" in a new commercial enterprise. All Immigrant Investors must demonstrate that their investment will benefit the United States economy, as well as create a specified number of full-time jobs for qualified U.S. citizens.

This category is often known as the "million-dollar visa" because the minimum investment (which is subject to change) is, you guessed it, a million dollars. You can invest less and still qualify if you invest in a *targeted employment area* (a rural area or an area of high unemployment).

A special pilot program allows an investor within an approved regional center to receive an EB-5 visa by showing that their investment will create jobs indirectly through revenues generated from increased exports, improved regional productivity, job creation, or increased domestic capital investment resulting from the new commercial enterprise. As of December 31, 2021, legislation to re-authorize the EB-5 program is pending. For updates, check out www.uscis.gov/working-in-the-united-states/permanent-workers/eb-5-immigrant-investor-program.

There are several categories of visas for nonimmigrants that allow the visa holders to temporarily live and work in the United States. Of special note are the following categories of essential workers:

» H-1B Specialty Occupations (and their H-4 family members)

» H-2A Agricultural Workers

» H-2B Non-Agricultural Workers

» L-1A Intracompany Transferee Executive or Manager

» L-1B Intracompany Transferee Specialized Knowledge

Corporations or research facilities can sponsor a visa-holding employee with exceptional merit and skills to apply for an "Adjustment of Status," allowing the employee and their family to become U.S. lawful permanent residents, putting them on the path toward naturalization in five years. For further details, see the USCIS Temporary (Nonimmigrant) Worker page at www.uscis.gov/working-in-the-united-states/temporary-nonimmigrant-workers.

Winning the visa lottery

Even if you qualify for one of the visa categories listed in the preceding section, entering the Diversity Visa (DV) Lottery Program makes sense because it can speed up your process of receiving a visa, especially if you find yourself in one of the lower preference categories.

Natives of countries with historically low rates of immigration to the United States may be eligible to enter. Those born in any territory that has sent more than 50,000 immigrants to the United States in the previous five years are not eligible to receive a diversity visa.

SURPRISE! YOU MAY ALREADY BE A U.S. CITIZEN

TECHNICAL STUFF

If you were actually born in the United States — including, in most cases, Puerto Rico, Guam, and the U.S. Virgin Islands — you're considered a U.S. citizen at birth. Your birth certificate serves as proof of your citizenship. The one exception to this rule is if one or more of your parents was a foreign diplomat at the time of your birth (you would be considered a permanent resident in that case).

Are there ways to be born abroad and still be a U.S. citizen? Yes, under certain specific conditions. If you were born abroad but both your parents were U.S. citizens, and at least one of those two parents lived in the United States at some point prior to your birth, then you are considered a U.S. citizen in most cases.

If you were born abroad but only one of your parents was a U.S. citizen and the other parent was an alien, you will be considered a citizen in most cases if, before you were born, your citizen parent lived in the United States for at least five years. In order to qualify, at least two of those five years had to have taken place after your citizen parent's 14th birthday.

Notice how we keep saying "in most cases"? The previous explanation is current law, and it's a generalization. Whether you acquired U.S. citizenship at birth depends on the law that was in effect at the time of your birth. This is one of the toughest areas of immigration law, filled with loopholes and exceptions, so getting expert help in these cases is always a good idea. Be sure to seek and get competent legal help *before* you need it. (You can get more information on finding legal help in Chapter 7.)

Entering the visa lottery is easy. You can file online at `https://travel.state.gov/content/travel/en/us-visas/immigrate/diversity-visa-program-entry/diversity-visa-submit-entry1.html`. Submitting more than one application disqualifies you from the lottery.

If you receive a visa through the Diversity Visa Lottery Program, you'll be authorized to live and work permanently in the United States, as well as bring your husband or wife and any children under the age of 21 along with you.

Each year 50,000 immigrant visas become available to people who come from countries with low rates of immigration to the United States. The Department of State randomly selects about 100,000 applicants from among the qualified entries. Why do they pick 100,000 when only 50,000 visas are available? Because they know that not all the applicants will be able to successfully complete the visa process. When 50,000 applicants have qualified and completed the immigration process, no further Diversity Lottery visas are issued for that year.

Documenting Your Immigration Status

Your entry document (such as an I-94 card for nonimmigrants) or a green card (if you're a permanent resident) serves as the important documentation you need to prove that you're in the United States legally and that you're entitled to all the rights and privileges that come with that status. As long as you hold a valid USCIS entry document or green card, are maintaining lawful status, and have not committed a removable offense, you don't have to worry about being forced to leave the country. For naturalized citizens, a Certificate of Naturalization or a U.S. passport serves as the same proof of immigration status.

Depending on where you are in the immigration process, you'll need various forms and documentation.

Just visiting

A *nonimmigrant,* or temporary, visa allows you to legally stay in the United States for a given length of time, after which you must leave the country. In order to qualify for a temporary visa, you'll usually need to prove that you have a residence outside the United States, as well as binding ties to your home country, such as a family or a job. The U.S. government wants to be sure that you'll return home at the end of your visit. In most cases, you'll also need to show that you have enough money to support yourself while in the United States.

The type of temporary visa you get will depend on the reasons why you want to visit the United States. You can gain temporary access to the United States in many ways, including the following:

>> As a visitor or tourist

>> For business

>> To seek medical treatment

>> As a temporary worker or to receive work training

>> As a student, either for academic or vocational training

>> By participating in an educational or cultural exchange program

>> As a fiancé(e) of an American citizen

>> As a NAFTA professional

TECHNICAL STUFF

Qualified citizens of Canada and Mexico may obtain temporary TN (Trade NAFTA) status. This status is available to certain professionals under the North American Free Trade Agreement (NAFTA). These citizens are *visa exempt*, meaning they don't have to obtain visas at a U.S. consulate in order to enter the United States in this status. Through the agreement, a citizen of a NAFTA country may work in a professional occupation in another NAFTA country, providing they can meet the following conditions:

>> The profession is on the NAFTA list.

>> The person has the necessary skills and qualifications to fill the position.

>> The position requires someone in a professional capacity.

>> The person will be working for a U.S. employer.

Under this particular status, you will be allowed to bring your spouse and unmarried children under 21 with you, although they will not be allowed to work in the United States unless they qualify for work authorization on their own.

TIP

Travelers from certain eligible countries also may be able to visit the United States (for business or pleasure only) without a visa through the Visa Waiver Program. Check with the Department of State (www.travel.state.gov/vwp.html) to see if your home country qualifies. See the full list of visa categories at https://travel.state.gov/content/travel/en/us-visas/visa-information-resources/all-visa-categories.html.

Here to stay

To become a lawful permanent resident, an alien must first be admitted as an immigrant. Most people get their immigrant visas because a qualified relative or employer has sponsored them as follows:

1. The employer or relative filed a petition with the USCIS.

2. The USCIS approved the petition and then forwarded it to the National Visa Center for further processing.

3. The State Department issued a visa after an immigrant visa number became available.

If you're already living in the United States, you may be eligible to adjust your immigration status from temporary to lawful permanent resident without leaving the country. And here's some good news: As an applicant, you may apply for a work permit while your case is pending. (You can find out more about this in Chapter 3.)

WARNING

If you plan to leave the United States while applying for adjustment to permanent resident status, you must receive advance permission, called *advance parole,* to return to the United States. If you do not apply for advance parole *before* leaving the United States, the USCIS will assume that you have abandoned your application and you may not be permitted to reenter the United States.

In most cases, as an alien applying for permanent residence, you will need to provide

>> A valid passport

>> Three photographs

>> Birth and police certificates

>> Marriage, divorce, or death certificates of your current and/or prior spouse(s)

>> Proof of financial support

>> Proof of medical examination

TIP

You can get more-specific details about what to provide at the National Visa Center (NVC); requirements vary slightly from consulate to consulate. Submit online immigrant visa case inquiries at https://nvc.state.gov/inquiry. You can visit the NVC website at https://nvc.state.gov for more information.

Customer Service Representatives for Immigrant Visa inquiries only are available at (603) 334-0700 from 7 a.m. to midnight Monday through Friday, excluding federal holidays. You can see the current status of your case or make updates by logging into the Consular Electronic Application Center at `https://ceac.state.gov`.

Customer Service Representatives for Nonimmigrant Visa inquiries only are available at (603) 334-0888 from 7 a.m. to midnight Monday through Friday, excluding federal holidays. Please note only English-speaking representatives are available on this line.

WARNING

The NVC is not open to the public. Unfortunately, some people have traveled long distances to inquire about their case in person, only to discover that NVC staff is unable to meet with them.

REMEMBER

Seek competent legal help if you have been in the United States illegally. If you leave the United States to obtain an immigrant visa abroad and the unlawful presence accrued after March 31, 1997, you will be barred from reentering the United States for three years (if the continuous unlawful presence was from 181 days to one year) or ten years (if the continuous unlawful presence was for more than one year).

Joining the club: Naturalization

Naturalization, the process by which lawful permanent residents become U.S. citizens, is the next step in the immigration process. Many lawful permanent residents stop before achieving citizenship, but if you bought this book, chances are you're interested in going all the way.

TECHNICAL STUFF

As a naturalized citizen, a person has the exact same rights, responsibilities, and benefits of natural-born U.S. citizens, with one exception: Only natural-born citizens may become president or vice president of the United States.

In most cases, naturalization applicants must prove they can meet these requirements:

>> A designated period of continuous residence in the United States (usually three or five years immediately prior to applying) as a lawfully admitted permanent resident.

>> Physical presence in the United States for at least half the designated time.

>> Residence in a particular USCIS district prior to filing, usually for at least three months. Districts are geographical areas serviced by local USCIS offices. You can get up-to-date information about districts at www.uscis.gov/about-us/find-a-uscis-office/field-offices.

>> The ability to read, write, and speak basic English.

>> A basic knowledge and understanding of U.S. history and government.

>> Good moral character. Applicants for naturalization must be "of good moral character," meaning that the USCIS will make a determination based on current laws. Conviction for certain crimes will cause you to lose your eligibility for citizenship. If you have ever been convicted of murder or convicted of an aggravated felony (committed on or after November 29, 1990), you may never become a citizen of the United States. Other lesser crimes may delay your immigration or citizenship goals because they prevent you from applying until a specified amount of time has passed since you committed the crime. In 2014, USCIS added additional questions about violent activities and war crimes as per U.S. national security laws. These additional questions doubled the size of the N-400 Application for Naturalization from 10 to 20 pages' worth of questions that will be asked during your naturalization interview! In determining good moral character, however, the USCIS can consider conduct that would have been a crime even if you were never arrested, charged, or convicted. (You can find more on good moral character in Chapter 3.)

>> Attachment to the principles of the U.S. Constitution and a favorable disposition toward the United States. This means that you must be willing to take the Oath of Allegiance to the United States of America, giving up any prior allegiances to other countries.

SERVING YOUR WAY TO CITIZENSHIP

If you served honorably in the U.S. armed forces for at least one year at any time, you may be eligible to apply for naturalization. Currently, you must be a permanent resident at the time of your interview. In times of war or other declared hostilities, members of the U.S. armed forces may naturalize without even being lawful permanent residents. Such periods are designated by law or by Executive Order of the president and have included World War I, World War II, the Korean War, the Vietnam police action, and the Gulf War. Most recently, the War on Terror was added, allowing all active-duty military personnel honorably serving on or after September 11, 2001, until a date to be determined, to be naturalized without regard to prior permanent resident status. For further information about eligibility based on military service, see www.uscis.gov/military/naturalization-through-military-service.

Don't worry if this sounds like a lot. The purpose of this book is to help get you ready to successfully complete your immigration goals all the way to becoming a U.S. citizen. We go into greater detail on all these requirements later in the book.

Making Sense of the Immigration Process

If you bought this book, you're obviously interested in being more than just a temporary visitor to the United States. You want to be a U.S. citizen. But first you must become a lawful permanent resident (with one exception — see the "Serving your way to citizenship" sidebar, earlier in this chapter).

Doing the paperwork

The type of application you file will depend on your path to immigration — in most cases, through family or through employment. (You can find more details on specific forms and paperwork in Chapter 4.)

After the USCIS approves your sponsor's immigrant visa petition, the Department of State must determine if an immigrant visa number is immediately available to you or if you will be on a waiting list. When an immigrant visa becomes available to you, you can process your immigrant visa through a U.S. consulate.

TIP

If you're already in the United States, you may only apply to change your status to that of a lawful permanent resident *after* a visa number becomes available for you.

Proving your identity

In order to gain your Permanent Resident Card, if you're adjusting your status while in the United States, or to become a naturalized citizen, you're going to have to prove your identity. Be prepared to be fingerprinted and provide the USCIS with at least two photographs, in addition to documents and paperwork that must be included with your application (you can find more information on this in Chapter 4).

Even if you have a Permanent Resident Card, you'll have to be fingerprinted and photographed when applying to become a naturalized citizen. After you've filed an application with the USCIS, you will receive a fingerprinting appointment letter, usually advising you to go to a local application support center or police station. The USCIS will do a criminal background check, cross-referencing your fingerprints with the Federal Bureau of Investigation (FBI). In some cases, the quality of the fingerprints is not sufficient for the FBI to read. If this happens, the USCIS will notify you of another fingerprinting appointment. Don't worry — you'll only have to pay a fingerprinting fee ($85 as of this writing) once.

WARNING

If the FBI rejects your fingerprints twice, you'll most likely be asked to provide police clearances for every place you've lived since you were 16 years old. Contact the local police departments in those cities or towns to obtain the clearances. If you're processing through an overseas consulate, as opposed to adjusting your status while in the United States, you'll need to provide police clearances for every place you have lived (for your country of nationality if you lived there six months or more; for all other countries, if you lived there for at least one year).

TECHNICAL STUFF

In some cases, especially if you live far away from the nearest fingerprinting station, a mobile fingerprinting van will travel to perform the process.

Being Interviewed by the USCIS

Presuming you plan on following the immigration path all the way to the final step of naturalization, you can plan on interviewing with the USCIS at least twice: once to qualify for your permanent resident status or green card, and again when you become a naturalized U.S. citizen (unless your visa processing took place at an overseas consulate, in which case you'll only interview with USCIS once — for naturalization).

The interviews fill many potential immigrants and citizens with terror. "How will I ever remember everything?" they worry. Relax. Passing the USCIS interview is easier (you are The Expert of your own life) *and* more difficult (uncommon vocabulary related to violent activities and war crimes) than you think. For some people, the biggest challenge is learning how to speak a new, crazy language, English. Don't worry; study! In fact, you probably already have most, if not all, of the skills and information you need. And if you don't, this book has you covered.

Interviewing for a green card

You need to live in the United States as a lawful permanent resident for at least three to five years before you can qualify for naturalization. Look at obtaining your green card as taking the first step toward citizenship.

TECHNICAL STUFF

Wives or husbands of U.S. citizens who die while honorably serving in the U.S. military (not necessarily during a time of hostilities) do not need to meet the residence or physical presence requirements; they just need to be a legal permanent resident at the time they file for naturalization.

For example, assume you're a qualified applicant for permanent residence and you have a qualified sponsor — usually your employer or a spouse or other family member. You can prove these facts and have sent the USCIS all the necessary applications and documents covered in Chapter 4. You've prepared your case and have kept careful records of all the paperwork you've ever sent to the USCIS. Because immigration laws can be complicated, you've probably consulted an attorney or received other professional help in preparing your case up to this point. It's been a long road, but you've done the work and now you're ready to take the final step toward lawful permanent residence — interviewing with the USCIS (if you're adjusting your status while in the United States) or interviewing with a consular officer (if you're applying at an overseas consulate).

TIP

In many employment-based cases, the USCIS does not require an interview. If you receive an interview notice, however, don't be nervous about your interview. Be prepared! Here's what to expect: At the beginning of the interview, the USCIS officer will place you under oath. This means that you swear to tell the truth at all times during the interview. The officer will then review your file and ask you questions about the answers you gave on your application. Be prepared to answer questions about whether you have a criminal record or have ever been involved in deportation proceedings or any of the other permanent or temporary bars to immigration outlined in Chapter 8.

The USCIS officer will also review your medical examinations. The officer will ask if there is anything you want to correct about the background and biographical information you provided the USCIS. If anything has changed or you feel your documents contain inaccurate information, now is the time to speak up.

If your case is based on employment, the officer may also review your Department of Labor paperwork. They may ask questions about your job to determine whether you really worked in the occupation you claim when you lived in your native country. The officer may also want to know whether you have the necessary skills to perform the job in the United States.

Be prepared to answer questions designed to determine whether you've been working illegally while waiting for your green-card application to be approved.

REMEMBER

Some applicants aren't allowed to work in the United States while waiting to get their green cards — and working illegally provides grounds for the USCIS to deny your application. As long as you're truthful and have followed the rules, you should have nothing to worry about.

If your case is based upon your marriage to a U.S. citizen, the interviewing officer will ask questions about your marriage and life together. The USCIS wants to feel confident that yours is a true marriage and not a union of convenience designed to get you into the country. The USCIS will require your spouse to come to the interview, and they can choose to interview you separately or as a couple.

In some cases, the officer will need additional information and paperwork in order to make a decision. If this happens in your case, the USCIS officer will reschedule you to return with the requested items another day.

If all goes well and the officer doesn't need any more documentation, they will issue you an approval and you'll be asked to return to the USCIS to get your passport stamped — as a lawful permanent resident. If you've been married to your U.S.-citizen spouse for less than two years, your passport will be stamped as a *conditional permanent resident* — conditioned on your still being married after two years. At that time, you may have the condition removed to become a full lawful permanent resident, which may require another interview with the USCIS. In either case, you won't actually receive the green card itself for several months, although your new immigration status takes effect with the stamping of your passport.

TIP

All applicants for adjustment of status are entitled to work authorization. If you're in the United States waiting to go to an overseas consulate to process, you have to maintain a status that permits employment (see Chapter 3 for more information) and only work pursuant to your status.

Obtaining U.S. citizenship

Assume you've been a lawful permanent resident of the United States for at least five years or, if your permanent resident status is based on marriage, you've been married to and living with your U.S.-citizen spouse for at least three years. If you're a man between the ages of 18 and 26, you've registered for the draft with Selective Service. You've properly completed and filed your Application for Naturalization Form (Form N-400) and supplied the USCIS with all the necessary documents and paperwork (you can find more on this in Chapter 4). Now comes the final step in the process of becoming a citizen: the USCIS interview.

Although it only takes about 10 to 15 minutes, the interview fills many prospective citizens with fear and dread. After all, you not only have to be prepared to answer questions about yourself, you also have to prove that you know how to read and write one dictated sentence in English plus answer six out of ten questions correctly from a list of one hundred U.S. history, government, and civics questions.

We know it sounds intimidating, but if you do your homework, you'll have nothing to worry about. USCIS examiners don't expect you to know *everything* about the United States. Nor do you have to be an English professor to pass the language test. If you can read and understand this book, you can pass the English text. If you're having trouble, don't worry. We give you some fun and easy ways to improve your skills.

REMEMBER

USCIS officers are required to give "due consideration" to your education, background, age, length of residence in the United States, opportunities available, and efforts made to acquire the requisite knowledge, along with any other elements or factors relevant to appraising your knowledge and understanding. As far as U.S. history and civics are concerned, the USCIS wants to know you understand the principles that the United States stands for. Finding out about history helps you understand how the United States became the great nation it is today. Parts 3, 4, and 5 of this book help you prepare for the history and civics test, but we predict that you already know more than you think you do.

After your interview, you'll get a USCIS Form N-652, which simply tells you whether your application was granted, denied, or continued. Here's an explanation of what each of these three possibilities means:

>> **Granted:** Congratulations! If your application was granted, you'll soon receive a notice of when and where to go for your swearing-in ceremony, where you'll take the Oath of Allegiance. You don't become a U.S. citizen until you attend this ceremony and take the Oath of Allegiance.

>> **Denied:** If the USCIS denies your application for naturalization, you'll receive a written notice telling you why. If you feel you were wrongly denied, you can ask for a hearing with another USCIS officer to appeal your case. On the back of your denial letter, you'll find USCIS Form N-336 "Request for Hearing on a Decision in Naturalization Proceedings." You'll also conveniently find full instructions on how to file and what fees you'll need to pay. If your application is again denied at your second hearing, don't give up — you still have one more chance: You can file to have your application reviewed in U.S. district court.

WARNING

Keep in mind that you only have 30 days after receiving your denial letter to file for an appeal hearing. After 30 days, the case is considered closed, and you'll have to start the entire process over again if you want to reapply.

>> **Continued:** Cases are most often *continued,* or put on hold, because the applicant didn't provide all the documents the USCIS needed or because the applicant failed the English or civics test. If the USCIS requires more information, they will give you a Form N-14, which explains exactly what information or documents they're looking for. The form will also tell when and how you should provide these papers.

WARNING

You're close to gaining citizenship, and details count. Follow the instructions on Form N-14 carefully. Not paying attention to details can result in your application being denied. If you don't understand the instructions, ask for help and make sure that you deliver what's asked for on time. (See Chapter 7 for information about finding competent and ethical help.)

If you failed the English test and/or the civics test, the USCIS will give you a time to come back and try again in another interview. Study hard, because if you fail the tests a second time, your application will be denied. Don't worry — you'll have plenty of time to prepare for your second test (usually between 60 and 90 days).

Recognizing Permanent and Temporary Bars to Naturalization

Are there any situations in which you can be automatically disqualified from ever becoming a U.S. citizen? You bet. Having committed certain crimes may cause you to lose your chance at citizenship — these are known as *permanent bars to naturalization.* A murder conviction on your record is a permanent bar to naturalization. If you were convicted of an aggravated felony that was committed on or after November 29, 1990, you've also lost your chance of becoming a U.S. citizen.

Other crimes are *temporary bars to naturalization*, meaning you must wait a designated time after committing the crime before you can become eligible to apply for citizenship. In Chapter 8, you can find out more about other ways you can be disqualified for citizenship.

TECHNICAL STUFF

DISABILITY AND AGE EXCEPTIONS TO THE ENGLISH AND CIVICS REQUIREMENTS

In order to accommodate those with disabilities, certain applicants — those with a physical or developmental disability or mental impairment — may not be required to take the English and/or civics test. If you think you, or an immigrant you are assisting, may qualify for these exceptions, be prepared to file USCIS Form N-648 "Medical Certification for Disability Exceptions" along with the naturalization application. Don't send in the application until a licensed medical or osteopathic doctor or licensed clinical psychologist with knowledge of the case has completed and signed Form N-648. If you qualify for the English language proficiency portion of the test, be prepared to bring a qualified interpreter with you to your interview.

When it comes to gaining U.S. citizenship, age has its privileges in the form of easier English and/or civics test requirements:

- **If you are over 50 years old** and have lived in the United States as a lawful permanent resident for periods totaling at least 20 years, you won't have to take the English test. You will, however, be required to take the civics test in the language of your choice.

- **If you are over 55 years old** and have lived in the United States as a lawful permanent resident for periods totaling at least 15 years, you won't have to take the English test. You will be required to take the civics test in the language of your choice.

- **If you are over 65 years old** and have lived in the United States as a lawful permanent resident for periods totaling at least 20 years, you won't have to take the English test. You'll also be given a simpler version of the civics test in the language of your choice.

You must meet the age and permanent residency requirements at the time you file your Application for Naturalization in order to qualify for an age exception. Your time as a permanent resident need not be continuous, but it must total a period of at least 15 or 20 years. (We cover this topic in more detail in Chapter 4.)

WARNING

Failure to pay child support or support other legal dependents can present a bar to naturalization. Make sure that your legal financial obligations to any dependents are current and up-to-date before applying for citizenship.

Attending Your Swearing-In Ceremony

Assuming you pass your interview, you'll receive a notice of when to attend your swearing-in ceremony, where you'll take the Oath of Allegiance. (In some cases, the interviewing officer will give you the oath on the spot, and you'll become a naturalized citizen then and there, but most often you'll return another day for a ceremony.)

The Oath of Allegiance plays an important part in becoming a U.S. citizen, and it carries serious implications. The oath serves as your solemn promise to the government of the United States that you

>> **Give up loyalty to other countries**

You may still have feelings of respect and admiration for your former homeland. You may even have family and friends still living there. However, in order to take the oath, your government loyalty must be to the United States and only to the United States.

>> **Defend the Constitution and laws of the United States**

You promise to protect the Constitution and all laws from all enemies, from other countries, or from inside the United States.

>> **Obey the laws of the United States**

You promise to obey the Constitution, follow the rule of law, and support human rights.

Be loyal to the United States

You promise that your allegiance is to the United States only.

>> **Serve in the U.S. military (if needed)**

You promise to use a weapon as a member of the U.S. military to protect the country's safety and security (if the U.S. government asks you to do so).

>> **Serve (do important work for) the nation (if needed)**

You promise to do other non-military work that is important to the country's safety and security (if the U.S. government asks you to do so).

Taking the Oath of Allegiance is also known as *Attachment to the Constitution.* In this case, the word *attachment* means loyalty or allegiance.

Receiving your Certificate of Naturalization

After you've taken the Oath of Allegiance, you'll be presented with your Certificate of Naturalization. Congratulations! You are now officially a citizen of the United States of America, and you can use your certificate to prove it. This legal document is quite ornate in appearance, resembling a diploma — one personalized with your photograph.

TIP

Applying for a passport as soon as you receive your Certificate of Naturalization is a good idea. A passport can also serve as proof of your citizenship, and it's much easier to carry than the certificate itself. If you ever lose your certificate, getting a replacement can sometimes take up to a year. If the certificate serves as your only proof of citizenship, a year can feel like a mighty long time — especially if you want to travel. You can usually pick up a passport application at your swearing-in ceremony. If not, your local post office has passport applications, or you can download a DS-11 Passport Application from https://eforms.state.gov/Forms/ds11.PDF.

If it is not already in your seat at the ceremony, people from your county Registrar of Voters will hand you a voter's registration card on your way out. Don't wait another minute — register to vote and exercise your right to participate in democracy!

You should also update your record with the Social Security Administration by applying for a new Social Security Card: www.ssa.gov/forms/ss-5.pdf. Proudly check the "U.S. Citizen" box on Line 5 Citizenship.

If you have a U.S. driver's license or state-issued identification card (ID), take this opportunity to update your record with the agency that issues driver's licenses in your state. You may update your ID information and photo or apply for a REAL ID.

Now that you are a citizen, share this gift with others. Volunteer at your local adult school or community center and help people prepare for their citizenship interview. Find volunteer opportunities at `www.volunteer.gov/s/`.

TECHNICAL STUFF

MODIFYING THE OATH

We take freedom of religion seriously in the United States, which is why the USCIS allows the oath to be *modified,* or changed, in some cases, by leaving out these phrases:

- **". . . that I will bear arms on behalf of the United States when required by law":** In order for these words to be left out of the oath, you must provide evidence that your objection to fighting for the United States is based on your religious beliefs and training.

- **". . . that I will perform noncombatant service in the armed forces of the United States when required by law":** If you can provide enough evidence that your religious training and beliefs completely prohibit you from serving in the armed forces in any capacity, the USCIS will also leave out this portion of the oath.

- **". . . so help me God":** If your religious beliefs keep you from using the phrase *so help me God,* the USCIS will omit the words.

- **". . . on oath":** If you are unable to truthfully swear using the words *on oath,* the USCIS will substitute the phrase with *solemnly affirm.*

If you think you qualify to take a modified oath, you'll need to write the USCIS a letter explaining why and send it along with your Application for Naturalization. Be aware that the USCIS will probably ask you to provide a letter from your religious institution explaining its beliefs and declaring that you are a member in good standing.

If you have a physical or mental disability that prevents you from communicating your understanding of the oath's meaning, the USCIS will probably excuse you from this requirement.

Chapter **2**

Meeting the Officials Who Can Help You on Your Quest

Before you start your journey on the path to immigration, knowing whom you're dealing with is helpful. This chapter introduces you to the government agencies you may encounter and work with during the immigration and naturalization processes. Knowing the goals and missions of these government agencies can help you identify the ways they can impact you, as someone seeking lawful permanent residence or citizenship, and how to deal with them most effectively.

Understanding the Goals of the U.S. Immigration System

In 2002, Immigration and Naturalization Services (INS) was incorporated into the Department of Homeland Security (DHS) and INS functions were delegated to three separate agencies: U.S. Citizenship and Immigration Services (USCIS),

Immigration and Customs Enforcement (ICE), and Customs and Border Protection (CBP). USCIS performs many of the duties of the former INS, focusing on immigration cases, including applications for work visas, asylum, and naturalization. (See the sidebar "A day in the life of USCIS" later in this chapter.)

On Presidents' Day, 2018, USCIS updated its mission statement to reflect national security concerns and express the agency's commitment to core values of integrity, respect, innovation, and vigilance, as follows:

> "U.S. Citizenship and Immigration Services administers the nation's lawful immigration system, safeguarding its integrity and promise by efficiently and fairly adjudicating requests for immigration benefits while protecting Americans, securing the homeland, and honoring our values."

The U.S. immigration system works to achieve three main goals:

>> **Bringing and keeping families together:** U.S. immigration laws are designed to encourage families to stay together when possible. Immigrating through a family connection is the most common way people come to the United States.

>> **Supplying a qualified workforce to keep the United States prosperin:** Another of the USCIS's duties is to help supplement the U.S. workforce by ensuring that there are enough foreign workers to fill positions not filled by U.S. workers.

>> **Providing safe refuge and asylum:** The USCIS also exists to help those who are seeking a safe refuge in the United States from political, religious, or social persecution in their home countries.

Identifying the Major Players and Their Roles in the Immigration System

A popular American expression with its origins in baseball, the country's national pastime, says, "You can't know the players without a score card." And so it is with immigration. During the immigration and naturalization process, you'll work with several government agencies. This section is your "score card" of the major players in the immigration game.

The Department of Homeland Security (DHS)

Effective January 24, 2003, the new Homeland Security Act represents the most significant and extensive transformation of the U.S. government in over 50 years. In the aftermath of the terrorist attacks against the United States on September 11, 2001, President George W. Bush decided 22 domestic agencies could better serve and protect the country if they were coordinated into one department. The new department reorganized a patchwork of government agencies under the authority of the Department of Homeland Security (DHS).

TECHNICAL STUFF

The DHS encompasses a wide range of duties and responsibilities. Although you may only interact with one or two parts of the DHS, all the department's activities are ultimately aimed at accomplishing six primary missions:

>> Counter terrorism and security threats

>> Secure U.S. borders and manage safe, orderly, and humane immigration processes

>> Secure cyberspace and critical infrastructure

>> Preserve and uphold the nation's prosperity and economic security

>> Strengthen disaster preparedness and resilience

>> Champion the DHS workforce

One of the potential major advantages of the DHS is that it gives state and local officials one main contact instead of many when it comes to homeland-security needs. In theory, this will streamline the processes of efficiently obtaining necessary supplies and equipment, and training emergency personnel like police and firefighters, as well as medical personnel, to manage security emergencies. The DHS also manages federal grant programs, protects the U.S. borders, and more.

U.S. Citizenship and Immigration Services (USCIS)

Through the U.S. Citizenship and Immigration Services (USCIS), the DHS took over half of the INS's former duties, including the following:

>> *Adjudicating* (hearing and deciding on) immigrant and nonimmigrant petitions

>> Adjusting the immigration status of immigrants already in the United States

>> Issuing work authorization and other permits

>> Naturalizing qualified applicants for U.S. citizenship

>> Processing asylum and refugee cases

>> Deterring, detecting, and addressing vulnerabilities to the legal immigration system

>> Promoting lawful immigrants' assimilation into American society

A DAY IN THE LIFE OF USCIS

The following info comes directly from the USCIS. On an average day, the USCIS does the following:

- Adjudicates more than 28,000 requests for various immigration benefits.

- Processes 3,100 applications to sponsor relatives and future spouses.

- Analyzes nearly 600 tips, leads, cases, and detections for potential fraud, public safety, and national security concerns.

- Processes refugee applications around the world in support of the refugee admissions ceiling of 125,000 refugees for fiscal year 2022.

- Grants asylum to 25 individuals already in the United States.

- Screens 170 people for protection based on a credible fear of persecution or torture if they return home.

- Serves 800 people at in-person appointments for document services and other urgent needs.

- Fingerprints and photographs 12,000 people at 130 application support centers.

- Approves applications and petitions to help unite five foreign-born orphans with the Americans who want to adopt them.

- Grants lawful permanent residence to more than 2,000 people and issues nearly 5,400 green cards.

- Welcomes 3,200 new citizens at naturalization ceremonies — that's one every 27 seconds. Typically, about 35 of these new citizens are members of the U.S. armed forces.

- Ensures the employment eligibility of 100,000 new hires in the United States.

- Receives 50,000 phone calls to its toll-free phone line and more than 150,000 inquiries and service requests via online accounts and digital self-help tools.

- Receives 986,000 visitor sessions to its website.

- Conducts automated verifications on employment eligibility and immigration status for more than 136,000 cases in E-Verify and 66,000 cases in SAVE.

U.S. Customs and Border Protection (CBP)

United States Customs and Border Protection (CBP) is one of the Department of Homeland Security's largest and most complex components, with a priority mission of keeping terrorists and their weapons out of the United States. It also has a responsibility for securing and facilitating trade and travel while enforcing hundreds of U.S. regulations, including immigration and drug laws. Other duties include

» Securing the U.S. border

» Preventing aliens from entering the country unlawfully

» Preventing terrorists and other criminal aliens from entering the United States

» Conducting border and port-of-entry inspections

» Answering questions about and helping find solutions to immigration concerns brought by the public, special-interest groups, and other government agencies, as well as the U.S. Congress

TECHNICAL STUFF

Immigration and Customs Enforcement (ICE) enforces immigration laws, including removal, and Customs and Border Protection (CBP) protects and monitors the nation's borders.

U.S. Immigration and Customs Enforcement (ICE)

The U.S. Immigration and Customs Enforcement (ICE) is a federal law enforcement agency under the U.S. Department of Homeland Security. ICE's stated mission is to protect the United States from the cross-border crime and illegal immigration that threaten national security and public safety. ICE has two primary and distinct law enforcement components:

» **Enforcement and Removal Operations** (ERO) is responsible for enforcing the nation's immigration laws and primarily deals with the deportation and removal of undocumented noncitizens.

>> **Homeland Security Investigations** (HSI) is the primary investigative arm of the Department of Homeland Security and primarily deals with threats to national security such as human trafficking and drug smuggling.

The United States continues to welcome nonimmigrants and immigrants who seek opportunity in the country while excluding terrorists and their supporters. Under the heading of immigration enforcement, the mission of ICE is to

>> Detect and remove those who are living in the United States unlawfully

>> Detain and remove criminal aliens from the country

>> Apprehend and prosecute illegal aliens and workers, including performing worksite enforcement of immigration laws

>> Enforce laws regarding immigration document fraud

>> Decide matters of removal from the United States

The Department of State

As the leading U.S. foreign-affairs agency, the Department of State (www.state.gov) maintains diplomatic relations with about 180 countries as well as with many international organizations. With the primary mission of maintaining and improving relationships with these countries, the Department of State runs nearly 260 diplomatic and consular posts around the world, including embassies, consulates, and missions to international organizations.

To be sure, the State Department has many important duties, including providing support for U.S. citizens at home and abroad; helping developing countries grow strong, stable economies and governments; bringing nations together to address global concerns; and combating threats like terrorism, international crime, and narcotics trafficking. But the State Department also provides many services to U.S. citizens traveling and living abroad through many offices, including the State Department's Bureau of Consular Affairs and the Bureau of Population, Refugees, and Migration.

State Department Bureau of Consular Affairs

The State Department Bureau of Consular Affairs (CA) operates and maintain Travel.State.Gov, the one-stop website for travelers (immigrants and non-immigrants) to and from the United States. Its duties include

- >> Issuing passports (approximately 11.71 million U.S. passports were issued in 2020 alone)
- >> Providing information about safely traveling and living abroad
- >> Warning travelers of particularly dangerous areas
- >> Helping U.S. citizens traveling overseas to obtain emergency funds
- >> Checking on the whereabouts or welfare of U.S. citizens traveling or living abroad
- >> Helping families in the event a U.S. citizen's loved one dies while traveling overseas
- >> Aiding U.S. travelers who become sick while traveling overseas
- >> Providing assistance to U.S. travelers who get arrested overseas
- >> Assisting in international adoptions and custody disputes
- >> Protecting and assisting U.S. citizens living or traveling abroad during international crises
- >> Distributing federal benefits payments
- >> Assisting with oversees absentee voting and Selective Service registration

In addition to providing services to U.S. citizens, the Department of State issues visas for foreigners who want to enter the United States. In fact, they issued more than 240,000 immigrant visas and 4 million nonimmigrant visas in 2020 (down from a recent high of 617,000 immigrant visas and 10 million nonimmigrant visas in 2016). When it comes time for you to get a visa, whether it is a temporary visa or a permanent visa, you'll deal with the Department of State.

REMEMBER

The USCIS must first approve your immigrant visa before forwarding it to the National Visa Center (NVC), a processing facility of the U.S. State Department, for further processing. The NVC will issue more paperwork for you to complete, and when you've completed that paperwork satisfactorily, the NVC will assign you an immigrant visa number. The State Department issues a monthly guide called the *Visa Bulletin*, explaining the status of various classes of immigrant visas. The *Visa Bulletin* charts visa availability for both family- and employer-sponsored immigrants based on *priority date* (the date the sponsoring petition was filed). Some categories, such as the fourth preference for siblings of U.S. citizens, are usually several years behind, while other categories may be current. (You can find out more about preference categories in Chapter 3.)

TIP

To access the *Visa Bulletin* go to the State Department website (www.state.gov). You can obtain past issues of the *Visa Bulletin* at https://travel.state.gov/content/travel/en/legal/visa-law0/visa-bulletin.html.

HOW THE STATE DEPARTMENT HELPS ASYLUM SEEKERS

The State Department also has a huge impact on refugees and those seeking asylum — the millions of people each year who are displaced by war, famine, and civil and political unrest or those who are escaping persecution and the risk of death and torture in their home countries.

The difference between those seeking asylum and refugee admission is important. A *refugee* is someone who is living outside the United States *and* outside their home country who petitions the U.S. government for lawful permanent residence in order to escape intolerable conditions in their home country. An *asylum-seeker* is someone already in the United States or someone seeking admission at a U.S. entry point when they apply to the U.S. government for permission to stay.

State Department Bureau of Population, Refugees, and Migration

The Bureau of Population, Refugees, and Migration (PRM) is a bureau within the United States Department of State. It has primary responsibility for formulating policies on population, refugees, and migration, and for administering U.S. refugee assistance and admissions programs. It develops policy, coordinates funding, and manages refugee resettlement in the United States with the UN Refugee Agency (UNHCR), the International Committee of the Red Cross (ICRC), and other aid groups.

Each year, the State Department prepares a report to Congress on proposed refugee admissions. Congress then advises the president on the proposed *ceilings* (limits) on refugee admissions for that *fiscal* (financial) year. Asylum-seekers are not subject to the refugee admissions set by Congress — at least not until they become *asylees* (those granted asylum) and seek permanent residence.

TECHNICAL
STUFF

According to the Secretary of State, for the 2022 fiscal year (October 1, 2021, through September 30, 2022), the total ceiling is set at 125,000 admissions, divided among six geographic regions and a catchall unallocated category. Here's how those 125,000 admissions are divided:

>> **Africa:** 40,000

>> **East Asia:** 15,000

>> **Europe and Central Asia:** 10,000

>> **Latin America and the Caribbean:** 15,000

>> **The Near East and South Asia:** 35,000

>> **Unallocated reserve:** 10,000

The Department of Labor (DOL)

The U.S. Department of Labor (DOL) is responsible for protecting the nation's workforce by making sure that workers enjoy safe conditions and fair employment practices. If you're applying for immigration through employment, your potential employer and your employer's attorneys will need to interact with the DOL.

Before a U.S. employer can hire a foreign worker, the employer will usually have to first obtain a DOL-issued *labor certification.* The certification is the DOL's way of officially letting the USCIS know that there are no qualified U.S. workers available and willing to work at the prevailing wage in the occupation for which the employer wants to hire a foreign worker. For further information about the required labor certifications, visit the Foreign Labor Application Gateway at www.flag.dol.gov.

After a labor certification is obtained, the potential employer must petition the USCIS. For the proper forms, see the USCIS Working in the United States web page at www.uscis.gov/working-in-the-united-states. If everything passes USCIS approval, the case then goes to the National Visa Center (https://travel.state.gov/content/travel/en/us-visas/immigrate/national-visa-center.html) to await a visa number, or if you are in the United States, you may be eligible to apply for adjustment of status. Even if the DOL issues a certification, you aren't guaranteed a visa. Whether you get a visa is ultimately up to the USCIS or State Department and also depends on visa availability. Nonetheless, applicants for a labor certification must prove they're able to pass other necessary immigration qualifications, like those outlined in Chapter 3.

The Federal Bureau of Investigation (FBI)

The Federal Bureau of Investigation (FBI) is the national law-enforcement agency in the U.S. The FBI's headquarters in Washington, D.C., provides direction and support to 56 field offices, about 400 satellite offices, 4 specialized field installations, and more than 40 liaison posts. Each foreign liaison office is headed by a legal officer who works with both U.S. and local authorities abroad on criminal matters that fall under FBI jurisdiction, including cases of immigration and visa fraud.

Even if you're an immigrant already living in the United States, you'll have some dealings with the FBI, because applicants for all immigration benefits are required by law to have their fingerprints taken by the USCIS or a designated state or local law-enforcement agency. The fingerprints are then checked against the FBI's international database. Before allowing you to live here, the U.S. government wants to make sure you're not currently wanted for any crimes and that your record is free from crimes that present bars to immigration and naturalization (you can find more about this in Chapter 3). If your record has nothing to show, you may never realize you had a brush with the FBI, but rest assured that your USCIS-obtained fingerprints did.

For more information about fingerprints, see USCIS Preparing for Your Biometric Services Appointment (www.uscis.gov/forms/filing-guidance/preparing-for-your-biometric-services-appointment).

TECHNICAL STUFF

To obtain a copy of your FBI identification record, submit a written request via the U.S. mail directly to the FBI, Criminal Justice Information Services (CJIS) Division, ATTN: SCU, Mod. D-2, 1000 Custer Hollow Road, Clarksburg, WV 26306. This request must be accompanied by satisfactory proof of identity, which shall consist of name, date and place of birth, and a set of rolled-inked fingerprint impressions placed upon fingerprint cards or forms commonly utilized for applicant or law enforcement purposes by law enforcement agencies.

HELPING REFUGEES: THE UNITED NATIONS

The Office of the United Nations High Commissioner for Refugees (www.unhcr.org/en-us/) was established to lead and coordinate international action to protect refugees and resolve refugee problems worldwide. Striving to safeguard the rights and well-being of refugees, the agency has helped an estimated 50 million people restart their lives in the last 70 years. During the first half of 2021 alone, 142,900 refugees returned or were resettled.

Today, a staff of around 7,300 staff working in 135 countries continues to help an estimated 26.6 million people find safe refuge in other countries.

Chapter **3**

Finding Out about Immigrant and Nonimmigrant Visas

W hether you're just visiting the United States on a nonimmigrant basis or hoping to live here permanently, you'll need to know about visas and how to get them in order to remain in the country legally.

All visa applicants should be aware that having a valid visa does *not* guarantee you entry into the United States. Upon arrival in the United States, you'll receive a form I-94 "Arrival–Departure Record" from the Bureau of Customs and Border Protection (CBP). (You can find out more about this in Chapter 1.) This document states the amount of time you're allowed to remain in the United States legally.

Just Visiting: Nonimmigrant Visas

Nonimmigrants enter the United States for a temporary period of time, and their activities are restricted to the reasons their visas are granted. In other words, if you enter the United States on a tourist visa, you may not legally work because that would necessitate an employment visa.

TECHNICAL STUFF

Business travelers who stay for pleasure after their business concludes — provided they leave the country within the time period authorized when they are admitted to the United States — do not need to go through the paperwork of changing their status from visitor for business to visitor for pleasure.

Determining whether you need a visa

You may not need a visa to enter the United States if you're entering under NAFTA or the Visa Waiver Program (VWP). The VWP allows foreign nationals from certain designated countries to enter the United States as nonimmigrants for business or pleasure under limited conditions, and for no more than 90 days, without first obtaining a nonimmigrant visa.

MARRYING INTO THE UNITED STATES

In order for a U.S. citizen to bring their foreign-born fiancé(e) to the United States, the citizen must file a Form I-129F with the U.S. Citizenship and Immigration Services (USCIS). See Visas for Fiancé(e)s of U.S. Citizens at www.uscis.gov/family/family-of-us-citizens/visas-for-fiancees-of-us-citizens. After the form is approved, USCIS forwards the petition to the relevant U.S. embassy or consulate abroad. The embassy or consulate then contacts the fiancé(e) to schedule a visa interview. The U.S. citizen and their foreign-born fiancé(e) must marry within 90 days from the day the fiancé(e) enters the country.

If you have already married, plan to marry outside the United States, or your fiancé(e) is already residing legally in the United States, your spouse or fiancé(e) is not eligible for a fiancé(e) visa. Go to the Bringing Spouses to Live in the United States as Permanent Residents web page for more information about how to help your foreign spouse apply for a green card (www.uscis.gov/family/bring-spouse-to-live-in-US).

You and your fiancé(e) may be romantics, but the USCIS is not. They don't automatically assume you will actually marry. After the wedding, the U.S. citizen must again contact the USCIS to change their spouse's immigration status from nonimmigrant to lawful permanent resident.

The U.S. government believes that the countries accepted in the VWP are not likely to compromise U.S. law-enforcement or national-security interests — including the enforcement of immigration laws. Countries can be added or deleted from the program at any time, so be sure to consult the U.S. Department of State for the latest information (go to `https://travel.state.gov/content/travel/en/us-visas/tourism-visit/visa-waiver-program.html` for information). There are over 40 countries on the Visa Waiver Program list, including most European countries, Australia, Brunei, Chile, Japan, New Zealand, Singapore, South Korea, and Taiwan. Although not specifically listed as a Visa Waiver country, Canada's citizens and landed immigrants also can enter the Untied States for business or pleasure without visas.

TECHNICAL STUFF

In order to travel without a visa on the VWP, you must have authorization through the Electronic System for Travel Authorization (ESTA) prior to boarding a U.S.-bound air or sea carrier. ESTA is a web-based system operated by U.S. Customs and Border Protection (CBP) to determine eligibility to travel under the VWP to the United States for tourism or business. Visit the ESTA web page on the CBP website for more information (`https://esta.cbp.dhs.gov/esta`).

Discovering the common types of nonimmigrant visas

Most nonimmigrants in the United States fall under the categories of business or pleasure visitors:

>> **Business visitors:** The B-1 nonimmigrant category includes those coming to the United States to conduct business with a company here. Activities include consultation, negotiating a contract, and participating in short-term training. This type of visa does *not* allow the visitor to hold a job or work for pay in the United States. See B-1 Temporary Business Visitor at `www.uscis.gov/working-in-the-united-states/temporary-visitors-for-business/b-1-temporary-business-visitor`.

>> **Pleasure visitors:** The B-2 nonimmigrant category includes those visiting the United States for the pure enjoyment of the many attractions this country has to offer. It also includes those who come to this country for a number of other purposes, including seeking medical treatment. In our experience, most medical treatments are hardly pleasurable, but nonetheless, the government lumps them into the same category as pleasure visitors. See Tourism (B-2) at `travel.state.gov/content/travel/en/us-visas/tourism-visit/visitor.html`.

THE VISA WIZARD

TECHNICAL STUFF

The Visa Wizard is an online tool to help foreign citizens understand which visa category may be appropriate for their travel to the United States. See the Visa Wizard at `travel.state.gov/content/travel/en/us-visas/visa-information-resources/wizard.html`.

The results from this Visa Wizard do not guarantee that you will be eligible under law to receive a visa. You must meet all legal requirements of the visa for which you are applying. The consular officer at the U.S. Embassy or Consulate where you apply will determine your visa eligibility and the visa category suitable for your purpose of travel, based on U.S. immigration law.

Note: The Visa Wizard includes the most common visas but does not include every visa.

Students, temporary workers, crewmen, journalists, and all others planning to travel to the United States for a purpose other than business or pleasure must apply in a different visa category. The State Department issues a huge range of visas for all different types of circumstances. For additional detailed information about your unique visa needs, consult the State Department website (`travel.state.gov/content/travel/en/us-visas.html`).

Changing or adjusting your nonimmigrant status

Certain individuals who are already legally in the country may qualify to *change* or *adjust* their immigration statuses. They may be eligible to *change* from one category of nonimmigrant status to another or may even have the opportunity to *adjust* from nonimmigrant to lawful permanent resident status.

TECHNICAL STUFF

Petitioning in one nonimmigrant status for change to another nonimmigrant status is referred to as *changing status* (example: change from a tourist to a student); applying for permanent residence while in the United States as a nonimmigrant is referred to as *adjusting status* (example: noncitizen spouse to lawful permanent resident).

WARNING

Unlawful presence in the United States can have serious consequences, so be sure your immigration status always remains legal. For example, sometimes a noncitizen spouse in the first family preference category assumes that because the noncitizen spouse is married to a U.S. citizen, they can stay in the United States. Marriage to a U.S. citizen does not protect a noncitizen spouse from deportation.

A problem may occur while the noncitizen spouse is waiting for the adjustment of status petition to be processed. If the noncitizen spouse overstays the original visa, they are "out-of-status" and are unlawfully residing in the United States. Therefore, the noncitizen spouse is not eligible for adjustment of status. Upon leaving the United States after having been unlawfully present for more than 180 days or a year, the noncitizen spouse is barred from reentering the United States for three or ten years (depending upon how long they were in the country). There are some exceptions and some waiver provisions, which is why we stress the importance of consulting a qualified immigration attorney or legal services if you have any unlawful presence time in the United States.

REMEMBER

To check whether your immigration status is currently legal, rely on your I-94 "Arrival-Departure Record" — the document you received from the CBP (find out more about them in Chapter 1) upon entering the country, or from the USCIS if you extended your immigration status while already in the United States.

Switching nonimmigrant visa categories

If you want to change the purpose of your visit while you're in the United States, then you, or in some cases your employer, must ask the USCIS to change your nonimmigrant status. Not all requests will be honored. For instance, if you're a tourist who wants to become a student in the U.S., you should state that you're looking into schools when you first enter the United States on a tourist visa. Otherwise, you'll need to first leave the country before being able to obtain a student visa.

If you were admitted to the United States in one of the following visa categories, you may *not* apply to change your nonimmigrant status (you will first need to leave the country in order to change your immigration status):

>> C (Alien in Transit)

>> D (Crewman)

>> K-1 or K-2 (Fiancé[e] or Dependent of Fiancé[e])

>> K-3 or K-4 Certain Husbands and Wives of U.S. Citizens and their Dependent Children

>> S (Witness or Informant)

>> TWOV (Transit without Visa)

>> WT or WB (Under the Visa Waiver Program)

If you were admitted in any of the following nonimmigrant categories, there are certain restrictions concerning your ability to request a change in your nonimmigrant status:

>> **J-1:** An exchange visitor subject to the two-year foreign residence requirement cannot change status, with certain exceptions.

>> **M-1:** A vocational student cannot change status to F-1. (Also, a vocational student cannot change status to any H classification even if the vocational training helped the student qualify for the H classification.)

TIP

For more information, see the USCIS FAQ M-577: "I am a nonimmigrant C-2: How do I change to another nonimmigrant status?" at www.uscis.gov/sites/default/files/document/guides/C2en.pdf

There's one exception to the rule that limits nonimmigrant visa holders to the activity stated on their visas: Business travelers may stay for pleasure after their business is over — providing they leave the country within the time period designated on their I-94 cards. Everyone else who wants to change the nature of their visit from the purpose stated on their visa must submit an application to change status to the USCIS. Failing to do so constitutes breaking U.S. immigration law, which in turn damages your chances of getting future temporary or permanent visas.

Adjusting status from nonimmigrant to immigrant

Providing that a visa number is available through the Department of State (unless you're in a category that is exempt from numerical limitations — you can find more on this later in this chapter), certain nonimmigrants may adjust their immigration status from nonimmigrant to immigrant. Immediate relatives of U.S. citizens usually are exempt from waiting for visa numbers and can adjust their status quickly.

If you have to wait for an immigrant visa number and are outside the United States when it becomes available, you'll be notified to go to the local U.S. consulate to complete the processing. This visa process is known as *consular processing*.

REMEMBER

If you are inside the United States and are waiting for an immigrant visa number to adjust your status, you must maintain valid nonimmigrant status while in the United States, or you risk encountering a three- or ten-year bar to naturalization.

Gaining Permanent Resident Status (or a Green Card)

As we discuss in Chapter 1, most people gain lawful permanent residence through a family connection or through employment. In the following sections, we explore these categories in more detail, as well as other ways people can legally live and work in the United States on a permanent basis.

Understanding the family preference categories

Family-based immigrant visa numbers are distributed according to preference categories. The higher you rank on the preference scale, the sooner you're likely to receive a number. The following are the four family-preference categories:

>> **First preference (F1):** Unmarried sons and daughters (21 years of age and older) of U.S. citizens

>> **Second preference (F2A):** Spouses and children (unmarried and under 21 years of age) of lawful permanent residents

>> **Second preference (F2B):** Unmarried sons and daughters (21 years of age and older) of lawful permanent residents

>> **Third preference (F3):** Married sons and daughters of U.S. citizens

>> **Fourth preference (F4):** Brothers and sisters of U.S. citizens (if the U.S. citizen is 21 years of age or older)

See USCIS Green Card for Family Preference Immigrants at www.uscis.gov/green-card/green-card-eligibility/green-card-for-family-preference-immigrants.

REMEMBER

After the visa petition filed for them by their sponsoring relative is approved by the USCIS, the immediate relatives of U.S. citizens — parents, spouses, and unmarried children under the age of 21 — usually don't have to wait for an immigrant visa number to become available.

Marrying your way to permanent residence

Although it's usually relatively easy for the foreign-born spouses of U.S. citizens or lawful permanent residents to come to the United States, the USCIS doesn't take kindly to folks who marry for the sole purpose of obtaining a green card. The countless TV sitcom and movie plots we've all seen on this subject are close to the truth. The USCIS wants to see evidence that yours is truly a marriage and not just a union on paper. You and your spouse should expect to answer questions about each other and about the marriage as well as provide physical evidence of the relationship. For this reason, in addition to important documents like your marriage certificate, be sure to save things like travel documents, vacation and family photos, billing statements, and other tangible evidence of your life together.

Marrying a U.S. citizen

If your spouse is a U.S. citizen, either born or naturalized, you are considered an immediate relative and are likewise usually eligible for an immigrant visa immediately, providing your I-130 Petition for Alien Relative (the form your sponsoring relative filed on your behalf) has been approved by the USCIS.

If you've been married less than two years when you gain lawful permanent resident status, that status is given on a conditional basis — conditional on your still being married after a full two years. At that time, you and your spouse will need to apply together to remove the condition.

WARNING

You must apply to remove conditional status within 90 days *before* the two-year anniversary of the date your conditional permanent resident status was granted. If you fail to file during this time, you'll be considered out of status as of the two-year anniversary, and you may be subject to removal from the country. Use USCIS Form I-751 to apply to remove the condition. For more information, see the following:

>> USCIS I am Married to a U.S. Citizen: www.uscis.gov/citizenship/learn-about-citizenship/citizenship-and-naturalization/i-am-married-to-a-us-citizen

>> Remove Conditions on My Status Based on Marriage: www.uscis.gov/forms/explore-my-options/remove-conditions-on-my-status-based-on-marriage

>> I-751, Petition to Remove Conditions on Residence: www.uscis.gov/I-751

Marrying a green-card holder

If you marry a lawful permanent resident of the United States, you aren't considered an immediate relative. Instead, you fall under the family second preference category. If your spouse's I-130 Petition for Alien Relative form is approved, the Department of State will notify you when a visa number becomes available.

If you were married before your husband or wife became a permanent resident, you cannot obtain permanent resident status along with your spouse without being subject to visa limits. If, for whatever reason, you did not physically accompany your spouse to the United States when they became a permanent resident, you may be eligible to receive *following-to-join benefits.* This means your husband or wife won't have to file a separate I-130 Petition for Alien Relative form, and you won't have to wait any extra time for an immigrant visa to become available. You may be eligible for following-to-join benefits, provided your marriage still exists and your husband or wife received their lawful permanent residence status in one of the following ways:

>> Through a diversity immigrant visa (winning the visa lottery)

>> Through an employment-based immigrant visa

>> Based on a relationship to a U.S. citizen brother or sister

>> Based on a relationship to U.S. citizen parents after you were already married

If you're a lawful permanent resident of the United States who marries a noncitizen spouse inside of the U.S., you can file Form I-130, Petition for Alien Relative. After a visa number becomes available, apply to adjust your spouse's status to permanent residency using Form I-485.

Legally marrying a green-card holder OUTSIDE of the U.S.

Although no exact document exists in the United States, all civil-law countries require proof of legal capacity to enter into a marriage contract. This means that the lawful permanent resident of the United States must obtain certification by competent authority that no impediments to the marriage exist. Unless the foreign authorities will allow such a statement to be executed before one of their consular officials in the United States, the parties of a prospective marriage abroad must execute an affidavit at the U.S. embassy or consulate in the country where the marriage will occur. This affidavit of eligibility to marry states that both parties are free to marry. Some countries require witnesses to these affidavits. Check the law where you plan to marry.

A lawful permanent resident of the United States who married an noncitizen spouse outside of the U.S. can bring the noncitizen spouse to the United States by filing Form I-130, Petition for Alien Relative. When Form I-130 is approved and a visa is available, it will be sent for consular processing and the consulate or embassy will provide notification and processing information.

Marrying a U.S. Service member

Noncitizen spouses of U.S. service members may be eligible for expedited naturalization outside the United States. Generally, noncitizen spouses need to have lawful permanent resident status before naturalizing. To apply for adjustment of status, the noncitizen spouse must file Form I-485, Application to Register Permanent Residence or Adjust Status, and the U.S. citizen service member must file Form I-130, Petition for Alien Relative, including the biometrics fee. See USCIS Citizenship for Military Family Members at `www.uscis.gov/military/citizenship-for-military-family-members`.

MAKING THE BEST OF A BAD SITUATION: THE VIOLENCE AGAINST WOMEN ACT

In order for an alien to qualify for family-based immigration, a U.S. citizen or lawful permanent resident must file a I-130 Petition for Alien Relative form with the USCIS on the alien's behalf. When, or even if, the petition is actually filed is strictly up to the relative petitioner.

Unfortunately, some people use their control of this process to abuse family members by threatening to report them to immigration authorities. As a result, most battered immigrants are afraid to report the abuse or their abusers.

Passed by Congress in 1994, the Violence Against Women Act (VAWA) allows the spouses and children of U.S. citizens or lawful permanent residents to self-petition for permanent legal immigration status. In order to protect the victims from their abusers, provisions of the VAWA allow certain battered immigrants (women or men) to file for immigration relief without their abusive relative's assistance or even knowledge. Children of these self-petitioners also receive *derivative benefits,* meaning they can gain lawful permanent residence along with their parents.

Under VAWA, you may be eligible to become a lawful permanent resident (get a green card) if you are the victim of battery or extreme cruelty committed by any of the following:

- A U.S. citizen spouse or former spouse
- A U.S. citizen parent
- A U.S. citizen son or daughter
- A lawful permanent resident (LPR) spouse or former spouse
- An LPR parent

You may self-petition under VAWA by filing a Petition for Amerasian, Widow(er), or Special Immigrant (Form I-360) without your abusive family member's knowledge or consent. A person who files a VAWA self-petition is generally known as a VAWA self-petitioner. If your self-petition is approved and you meet other eligibility requirements, you may be eligible to apply to become a lawful permanent resident.

For further information, see USCIS Green Card for VAWA Self-Petitioner at www.uscis.gov/green-card/green-card-eligibility/green-card-for-vawa-self-petitioner.

Remember: If you are a victim of domestic violence, help is available to you through the National Domestic Violence Hotline. Call 800-799-SAFE (7233) or 800-787-3224 (TDD) for information about shelters, mental health care, legal advice, and other types of assistance, including information about self-petitioning for lawful permanent residence. You can also text "START" to 88788 or chat online at www.thehotline.org/get-help/.

Using family connections

REMEMBER

Family connections provide the most common path to immigration, and family reunification is a primary goal of the U.S. immigration system. Nonetheless, immigrating through a family connection can be a complex and challenging proposition. Sponsoring relatives have significant obligations to meet before they can bring family members here.

In order to immigrate through a family connection, your relative must file on your behalf with the USCIS an I-130 petition (www.uscis.gov/i-130) that includes proof of your familial relationship. This petition can now be filed online through a USCIS account (https://myaccount.uscis.gov/).

REMEMBER

Born or naturalized citizens may sponsor their spouses, children, brothers and sisters, and parents. Lawful permanent residents may only sponsor their husbands or wives and children.

Assuming the USCIS approves the I-130 petition your relative filed for you, the State Department must determine if a visa number is immediately available. If you're an immediate relative of a U.S. citizen, a visa will be available at once. If you fall within a family preference category, you will be placed on a waiting list (you can find more information on preference categories in the earlier section "Understanding the family preference categories").

REMEMBER

You can check the status of a visa number in the Department of State's *Visa Bulletin*.

In order for your relative to be eligible to sponsor you to immigrate to the United States, they must meet the following criteria:

>> They must be a citizen or a lawful permanent resident of the United States and be able to provide documentation proving their citizenship or immigration status.

>> They must be at least 18 years old, in most cases, and at least 21 years old for U.S. citizen sons or daughters sponsoring a parent.

>> They must prove and document their relationship to you, the relative being sponsored.

>> Your relative must also document and prove that they can support you and any other financially dependent relatives at 125 percent above the mandated poverty line.

Your relative must prove they can support you by completing an Affidavit of Support (Form I-864) (www.uscis.gov/i-864) for you to file with the USCIS (if you're adjusting your status) or with a U.S. consulate (if your visa is processing — there is a filing fee in this case). To complete an Affidavit of Support, your relative must live in the United States as their primary residence. The Affidavit of Support states that the sponsoring relative accepts legal responsibility for financially supporting you. Your relative must be able and willing to accept this legally enforceable responsibility until you go through the entire immigration and naturalization process and become a United States citizen or until you can be credited with 40 quarters of work (which usually takes about ten years).

Your relative must also complete an affidavit of support if they have filed an employment-based immigration petition (Form I-140; www.uscis.gov/i-140) as the employer on your behalf or if they have a significant ownership interest (5 percent or more) in a business that filed an employment-based immigrant petition for you.

In determining their income amount, your relative can include in the count

>> Money held in savings accounts, stocks, bonds, and property

>> Your income and, in some cases, your assets

>> The income and, in some cases, the assets of members of your relative's household related by birth, marriage, or adoption or of those listed on your relative's most recent federal income tax return (whether or not they reside with your relative)

Not surprisingly, meeting the financial support qualifications presents an insurmountable obstacle to many otherwise willing and qualified potential sponsors. In some cases, if the relative visa petitioner's household income doesn't quite reach the minimum 125 percent above the government-mandated poverty level, a joint sponsor may also be allowed to sign an additional affidavit of support. A *joint sponsor* is someone, other than the family member who is sponsoring you for immigration, who is willing to share legal responsibility, along with your family member, for supporting you if for any reason you are unable to support yourself after immigrating to the United States.

A joint sponsor must meet the same sponsorship qualifications as the sponsoring relative with one important exception: The joint sponsor does *not* need to be a relative of any kind (they can be, but that isn't required in order for the person to qualify).

TECHNICAL STUFF

The joint sponsor (or the joint sponsor and their household) must meet the 125 percent income requirement on their own. You can't combine your income with that of a joint sponsor to meet the income requirement the way you can with your primary sponsor.

So how much is 125 percent above the mandated poverty level? The U.S. Department of Health and Human Services sets the annual poverty guidelines. For more information about financial support, visit the following resources:

>> USCIS document "How do I financially sponsor someone who wants to immigrate?" (www.uscis.gov/sites/default/files/document/guides/F3en.pdf)

>> USCIS I-864, Affidavit of Support Under Section 213A of the INA (www.uscis.gov/i-864)

>> USCIS I-864P, 2022 HHS Poverty Guidelines for Affidavit of Support (www.uscis.gov/i-864p)

>> HHS Poverty Guidelines (https://aspe.hhs.gov/topics/poverty-economic-mobility/poverty-guidelines)

Note the difference between the contiguous 48 states and U.S. territories compared to Alaska and Hawaii.

Identifying exceptions to the sponsorship requirements

As with all things related to U.S. immigration, there are exceptions to most rules, including the family member sponsorship requirements.

If you are the immigrant, and you can prove you've already legally worked in the United States a total of at least 40 qualifying quarters, as defined in Title II of the

Social Security Act, an affidavit of support is not required. Because rules related to means-tested public assistance benefits changed in October 2021, see the following instructions for updates: USCIS Form I-864W Instructions for Request for Exemption for Intending Immigrant's Affidavit of Support (www.uscis.gov/sites/default/files/document/forms/i-864winstr.pdf).

If the immigrant is the child of a citizen and if the immigrant, if admitted for permanent residence on or after February 27, 2001, would automatically acquire citizenship under the Immigration and Nationality Act, as amended by the Child Citizenship Act of 2000, they are exempt from sponsorship requirements. Approved in October 2000 by President Clinton, the Child Citizenship Act of 2000 states that a child born outside the United States automatically becomes a citizen of the U.S. when *all* the following conditions apply:

>> At least one parent of the child is a citizen of the United States, either born or naturalized.

>> The child is under 18 years old.

>> The child is living in the United States in the legal and physical custody of the citizen parent after being admitted as a lawful permanent resident.

It's important to realize that in order to qualify under the Child Citizenship Act, an applicant must have met all three of the preceding requirements on or after February 27, 2001. If an applicant meets all the requirements except that their 18th birthday fell *before* February 27, 2001, the applicant legally remains an alien until they can go through the normal naturalization process as outlined in this book.

Working for a Green Card

A second goal of the U.S. immigration system is to allow U.S. employers to hire citizens of other countries when no qualified U.S. citizens or legal residents can fill the positions. Each year, a minimum of 140,000 employment-based immigrant visas become available in five preference categories.

In most cases, you will need a solid offer of employment from a qualified employer who is willing and able to sponsor you for immigration. In addition to filing forms and guaranteeing employment, in many cases the employer should also be prepared to show evidence that no qualified U.S. citizens or lawful permanent residents are available to fill the position.

After determining if you qualify for an employment-based visa, you and your employer will usually be required to obtain a labor certification from the

U.S. Department of Labor (Form ETA 750), as well as file an Immigrant Petition for Foreign Worker (Form I-140) with the USCIS. As always, you'll probably have to file other forms and paperwork — you can find more on this in Chapter 4.

Making sense of employment preference categories

Just as with family-based visas, U.S. immigration laws allow people to gain lawful permanent residence legally through several preference categories. See USCIS Green Card for Employment-Based Immigrants (www.uscis.gov/green-card/green-card-eligibility/green-card-for-employment-based-immigrants) or Employment-Based Immigrant Visas (https://travel.state.gov/content/travel/en/us-visas/immigrate/employment-based-immigrant-visas.html).

First preference: Priority workers

Priority workers receive 28.6 percent of the yearly worldwide allotment of employment visas, plus any left over from the fourth and fifth preference categories. Within this preference category, you'll find three subgroups. Although qualifying for a first preference visa is quite difficult, none of these categories requires labor certification, which saves processing time.

PEOPLE WITH EXTRAORDINARY ABILITY

REMEMBER

In order to qualify in this category, be prepared to prove your extraordinary ability or past employment record to qualify.

If you can offer extensive documentation showing sustained national or international acclaim and recognition as a person of extraordinary ability in the sciences, arts, education, business, or athletics, you won't be required to have a specific job offer or a sponsoring employer to immigrate to the United States — provided you're coming here to continue work in your established field. An employer can petition for you, however.

Keep in mind that the first priority classification is reserved for those with *truly extraordinary* achievement (for instance, Nobel Prize winners). If you haven't yet won such a prestigious award, other documentation that can help you prove your case as a person of extraordinary ability includes

» Receipt of nationally or internationally recognized prizes or awards for excellence in your field

» Membership in associations that demand outstanding achievement of their members

- >> Published material about yourself in professional or major trade publications or other major media attention

- >> Evidence that you have judged the work of others, individually or as a member of a professional panel

- >> Evidence of contributions of major significance to your field

- >> Evidence of authorship of scholarly articles in professional or major trade publications or other major media

- >> Evidence that your work has been displayed at artistic, business, educational, scientific, or athletic exhibitions or showcases

- >> Evidence that you perform a leading or critical role in distinguished professional organizations

- >> Evidence that you command a high salary in relation to others in your field

- >> Evidence of your commercial successes in your field

- >> Other comparable evidence

OUTSTANDING PROFESSORS OR RESEARCHERS

No labor certification is required if you can prove to the satisfaction of the USCIS that you are an internationally recognized outstanding professor or researcher with at least three years' experience in teaching or research. You must be entering the United States in a tenure or tenure-track teaching capacity or in a comparable research position at a university or other institution of higher learning. If your prospective employer is a private company rather than an educational institution, the department, division, or institute of the private employer must employ at least three persons full time in research activities and have achieved documented accomplishments in an academic field in order to sponsor you for immigration.

You cannot self-petition in this category (an employer must petition on your behalf). In order to qualify as an outstanding professor or researcher, you also need to be able to document at least two of the following:

- >> Receipt of major prizes or awards for outstanding achievement

- >> Membership in associations requiring their members to demonstrate outstanding achievements

- >> Articles in professional publications written by others about your work in the academic field

- >> Participation, on a panel or individually, as a judge of the work of others in the same or allied academic fields

>> Your original scientific or scholarly research contributions to your field

>> Authorship of books or articles in scholarly journals with international circulation

CERTAIN FOREIGN EXECUTIVES OR MANAGERS

If you're a foreign executive or manager, and you were employed at least one of the three preceding years by the overseas affiliate, parent, subsidiary, or branch of a U.S. company, your U.S. employer can petition for you without having to file a labor certification application. Of course, you must be immigrating in order to continue work for that same company in a managerial or executive position.

Second preference: Professionals

Professionals holding advanced degrees, or persons of exceptional ability in the arts, sciences, or business, receive 28.6 percent of the yearly visa allotment, plus any leftover first preference employment visas. In most second preference category cases, you must have a firm offer of employment and your U.S. employer must file a USCIS petition on your behalf. In most cases, an employer must also obtain labor certification from the Department of Labor (DOL) before filing the petition.

The labor certification is the DOL's way of officially letting the USCIS or State Department know that there are no qualified U.S. workers who are willing and able to take the position. Working in conjunction with State Workforce Agencies (SWAs), the Department of Labor, through its Employment and Training Administration (ETA) reviews the proposed employment for compliance with U.S. wage and occupational practices and may guide the actual hiring process. The government wants to be sure that employing an immigrant under the terms described in the application will not adversely affect wages and working conditions of similarly situated U.S. workers.

For more information about labor certifications or for an online application, visit the DOL website at www.ows.doleta.gov/foreign.

REMEMBER

Even if the DOL issues a labor certification, this does not guarantee you a visa. Whether you get a visa is ultimately up to the USCIS or State Department and also depends on visa availability.

Because of labor certification backlogs, the standard procedure can take years. Measures to expedite the process, and a new process to be implemented after this book is published, promise to improve the situation in the future. This is a complicated area of immigration law that requires familiarity with how different positions are defined, their standard requirements and wages, and how to approach both DOL and USCIS processing. Your sponsoring employer should work with a qualified immigration attorney or legal organization (see Chapter 7 for more information about finding reliable help).

Members of the professions holding advanced degrees (professors and researchers) must be internationally recognized in their particular area and meet other requirements, including having earned a master's degree or a bachelor's degree with at least five years of post-baccalaureate, progressive experience in the specialty (such as advancing levels of responsibility and knowledge).

Regulations vaguely define exceptional ability as "having a degree of expertise significantly above that ordinarily encountered in the sciences, arts, or business." In order to document your qualifications as an alien of exceptional ability, be prepared to show at least three of the following:

>> An official academic record showing you have a degree, diploma, certificate, or similar award from a college, university, school, or other institution of learning relating to your area of exceptional ability

>> Letters documenting at least ten years of full-time experience in your chosen occupation

>> A license to practice the profession or certification for a particular profession or occupation

>> Evidence you have commanded a salary that demonstrates exceptional ability

>> Membership in professional associations

>> Recognition by peers, government entities, or professional or business organizations for your achievements and significant contributions to your field

Your employer may not need a labor certification before petitioning under the second preference category if one of the following is true:

>> Exemption from labor certification would be in the United States' national interest.

>> You qualify for one of the shortage occupations in the Labor Market Information Pilot Program, which defines up to ten occupational classifications in which there are labor shortages. For aliens within a listed shortage occupation, a labor certification will be deemed to have been issued for purposes of an employment-based immigrant petition.

>> You are employed in an occupation designated as Schedule A. In these cases, the Department of Labor delegates authority to approve labor certifications to the USCIS. Schedule A, Group I includes physical therapists and professional nurses. Schedule A, Group II includes aliens of exceptional ability in the sciences and arts (except the performing arts).

IMMIGRATION THROUGH THE NATIONAL INTEREST WAIVER

If you're a qualified physician who is willing to work in an underserved area of the United States or at a Department of Veterans Affairs (VA) facility, you may be able to skip the labor certification process. In some instances, you'll be allowed to self-petition for second preference classification, although a qualified employer may also file a national interest waiver on your behalf. In order to fulfill the obligations of obtaining this waiver, you'll be required to complete an *aggregate* (accumulated) five years of qualifying full-time clinical practice during the six-year period that begins when you receive the necessary employment authorization documents. You can find information on how to apply by visiting the USCIS Green Card Through a Physician National Interest Waiver (NIW) at www.uscis.gov/green-card/green-card-eligibility/green-card-through-a-physician-national-interest-waiver-niw. If you need more detailed information or have questions not answered on the website, consulting qualified legal counsel is a good idea — they can best help you prepare the documentation needed for your unique case and circumstances.

Another, very restrictive and therefore rarely used, national interest waiver is available on a case-by-case determination of whether foregoing labor certification is in the national interest. This type of waiver is available to nonphysicians also. Unlike the physician national interest waiver, however, approval of this type of national interest waiver waives only the requirement of labor certification, which means it also waives the requirement for a job offer. Therefore, in addition to proving all the elements needed for the national interest waiver, you (or the petitioning employer) also must prove that you hold an advanced degree or are an alien of exceptional ability, as described earlier in this chapter.

Third preference: Skilled or professional workers

This category receives 28.6 percent of the yearly worldwide employment visa pool, plus any unused first and second preference category visas. Unless the job qualifies for a Schedule A designation, or as one of the shortage occupations in the Labor Market Information Pilot, all third preference petitions must be accompanied by a labor certification.

REMEMBER

The Labor Market Information Pilot Program defines up to ten occupational classifications in which the United States has labor shortages. For aliens within a listed shortage occupation, a labor certification will be deemed to have been issued for purposes of an employment-based immigrant petition.

REMEMBER

The Department of Labor delegates authority to the USCIS to approve labor certifications to occupations in the Schedule A Group — Group I includes physical therapists and professional nurses; Group II includes aliens of exceptional ability in the sciences and arts (except the performing arts).

Within the third employment-based preference group are three subcategories:

>> **Skilled workers** are persons capable of performing a job requiring at least two years' training or experience.

>> **Professionals** must hold a U.S. baccalaureate degree or a foreign equivalent degree. Unfortunately, a combination of some education and experience cannot be substituted for the actual degree in order to qualify.

>> **Other workers** are those persons capable of filling positions requiring less than two years of training or experience.

Note that the third preference category usually generally becomes oversubscribed or backlogged before the higher categories. Also, the "other worker" subcategory of third preference generally becomes oversubscribed or backlogged before the skilled or professional worker categories.

TIP

You can track visa availability trends by referring to past issues of the *Visa Bulletin*. Find an online archive at `travel.state.gov/content/travel/en/legal/visa-law0/visa-bulletin.html`.

Fourth preference: Special immigrants

Special immigrants receive 7.1 percent of the yearly worldwide limit. Thirteen subgroups qualify as special immigrants, the most notable of which is the religious worker special immigrant. Other special immigrants include certain juveniles and battered spouses, certain overseas employees or retirees of the U.S. government, certain members of the U.S. armed forces, certain current and former employees of the Panama Canal Company, retired employees of international organizations, and certain dependents of international organization employees.

The religious worker category receives 5,000 of the allotted special immigrant visas. Religious workers are those who will work for a religious denomination that has a bona fide nonprofit religious organization in the United States and who are coming to work as ministers of religion, to work in a professional capacity in a religious vocation, or to work in a religious occupation. The worker must have been a member of this religious denomination and must have worked for the denomination for at least two years before applying for admission to, or adjustment of status in, the United States.

Fifth preference: Immigrant investors

Employment creation investors receive 7.1 percent of the yearly employment visa total. To qualify in this category, be prepared to invest about $1.8 million (or the U.S. dollars equivalent in your currency), depending on the employment rate in the geographical area where you will set up business. Your U.S. enterprise will also need to create at least ten new full-time jobs for U.S. citizens, permanent resident aliens, or other lawful immigrants, not including you and your family.

REMEMBER

If you plan on establishing a business in an area of high unemployment, you may only have to invest $900,000 to qualify for the fifth preference.

Discovering Other Ways to Qualify for Permanent Residence

What if you don't qualify for family- or employment-based immigration? Are there other ways you can gain lawful permanent residence in the United States? Thankfully, yes, but only under some specific conditions and restrictions.

Immigrating through asylum

If you are a potential immigrant already in the United States (legally or illegally) or you're applying for admission at its borders, you may petition the government for asylum by demonstrating you have a "well-founded fear of persecution" in your home country, based on race, religion, nationality, membership in a social group, or political opinion. Proving you belong in one of these protected categories can be complicated, because the legal definitions of *well-founded fear* and *persecution* are vague at best. We strongly recommend you seek the advice of a qualified immigration attorney. (You can find out more about hiring qualified and ethical help in Chapter 7.)

In most cases, if you're seeking to enter the United States and you indicate a desire to seek asylum, the Directorate of the Department of Homeland Security (DHS) places you in expedited removal, where an asylum officer from the USCIS determines whether you have a credible fear. If the asylum officer determines that you do have a credible fear, you're allowed to apply before an immigration judge (who is part of the Department of Justice).

Although the USCIS won't grant work authorization for the first 150 days after the filing of an asylum claim (unless, of course, asylum is granted in the meantime), work authorization is automatic for cases on the docket longer than 180 days — as long as you're not the one who caused the delay.

WARNING

Be sure to file your asylum application within one year after entering the United States. Failing to file the application on time can result in rejection of the claim and removal from the United States. After one year, applications will only be considered in certain cases of changed or extraordinary circumstances. You may still be eligible for withholding of removal, but it is only a temporary form of relief, from which you cannot gain permanent residence.

TIP

If you have held asylum status for at least one year, you may be eligible to adjust your status to lawful permanent resident by filing an application to adjust status (currently Form I-485). You will be required to provide evidence that you were physically present in the United States as an asylee for at least a total of one year prior to filing the adjustment of status application. For this reason, keeping important paperwork throughout the immigration process is essential. Examples of documents that can help prove physical presence include

>> A copy of your USCIS or DHS Arrival-Departure Record (Form I-94), obtained when you first entered the country

>> A clear copy of the letter granting your asylum status

>> Any documentation of the conditions being removed (if you were originally granted conditional asylum)

>> Copies of documents covering large periods of time, such as apartment leases, school enrollment records, or letters of employment

REMEMBER

If you arrived in the country before March 1, 2003, the former Immigration and Naturalization Service (INS) processed your Arrival–Departure Record. If you arrived any time after March 1, 2003, the Bureau of Customs and Border Protection (CBP), part of the Department of Homeland Security, administered your Arrival–Departure Record.

Looking for safe refuge

REMEMBER

Refugees are those living outside the United States and outside their home countries who petition the government for lawful permanent residence in order to escape intolerable conditions in their home countries.

Benefits the U.S. government provides for qualified refugees include

>> A no-interest travel loan to the United States

- » Eight months of Refugee Cash Assistance (RCA) and Refugee Medical Assistance (RMA)

- » Food stamps to help pay for groceries

- » Housing assistance, furnishings, food, and clothing

- » A Social Security card

- » School registration for children

- » Referrals for medical appointments and other support services

- » Employment services

- » Case management through community-based nonprofit organizations

- » Adjustment of status from refugee to lawful permanent resident for refugees who have been physically present in the United States as refugees for a total of at least one year prior to filing for adjustment (see "Immigrating through asylum" earlier in this chapter for more information about documenting your presence).

TECHNICAL STUFF

In your immigration proceedings, you may come across the word *parole*. In immigration-speak, parole is a way to gain legal entry into the country, although it is not an official admission under one of the visa categories. Parole serves a specific purpose — for example, humanitarian parole or parole for the purpose of proceeding with adjustment.

Investing in the United States

You don't necessarily need talent, family connections, a job, or sympathy to get a green card. Money talks. The Immigration Act of 1990 created the immigrant investor program as the fifth preference within the employment-based category (EB-5). For a minimum investment of $1.8 million — or as little as $900,000 in a *targeted area* (a rural area or area of high unemployment) — noncitizen entrepreneurs who employ at least ten U.S. workers may be eligible to immigrate based on their investment in the United States.

USCIS administers the EB-5 Immigrant Investor Program, created by Congress in 1990 to stimulate the U.S. economy through job creation and capital investment by foreign investors.

On March 15, 2022, President Biden signed a law that re-authorized the EB-5 Immigrant Investor Regional Center Program through Sept. 30, 2027. USCIS is reviewing the new legislation and will provide additional guidance. USCIS will provide additional information on the EB-5 Reform and Integrity Act of 2022 at a later date.

TIP

MAKING THE MOST OF YOUR BIRTHPLACE

If you're trying to come to the United States, where you come from may help your chances of obtaining permanent resident status if you qualify under special laws. These cases are often complicated, so seek the advice of a competent immigration attorney if you think you may qualify.

The Cuban Adjustment Act of 1966 (CAA) provides for a special procedure under which Cuban citizens and their accompanying spouses and children may obtain a haven in the United States as lawful permanent residents. This act gives the Attorney General discretion to grant permanent residence to Cuban nationals, admissible as immigrants, seeking adjustment of status if they have been present in the United States for at least one year after inspection and admission or parole. Because many of the rules on immigration do not apply to adjustments under the CAA, you don't have to be the beneficiary of a family-based or employment-based immigrant visa petition. The CAA may also apply to your spouse and children, regardless of their citizenship or place of birth, provided the relationship existed at the time you obtained lawful permanent residence and they are now living with you in the United States.

In ordinary circumstances, the arrival of a potential immigrant to the U.S. at a place other than an open port of entry is a ground of inadmissibility. However, a Cuban national or citizen who arrives at a place other than an open port of entry may still be eligible for adjustment of status, providing the Customs and Border Protection (CBP) has paroled them into the United States.

The Nicaraguan Adjustment and Central American Relief Act of 1997 (NACARA) provides various forms of immigration benefits, including relief from deportation to certain Nicaraguans, Cubans, Salvadorans, Guatemalans, and nationals of former Soviet bloc countries and their dependents.

The Haitian Refugee Immigration Fairness Act of 1998 (HRIFA) established procedures for certain Haitian nationals, who have been living in the United States, to become lawful permanent residents without having to first apply for an immigrant visa at a U.S. consulate abroad. The law also waives many of the usual requirements for immigration. Principal applicants wanting to apply for lawful permanent residence under HRIFA initially had until March 31, 2000, to file for the adjustment of status. After March 31, 2000, in most cases, only *dependents* of noncitizens who met HRIFA's requirements are able to apply for lawful permanent residence under HRIFA.

The Victims of Trafficking and Violence Protection Act of 2000 added two more categories of individuals eligible to apply for relief from removal under NACARA: Victims of Criminal Activities (U visa) and Victims of Human Trafficking (T visa).

The Central American Minors Refugee and Parole Program 2014 (CAM) allowed lawfully present parents in the United States the opportunity to request a refugee or parole status for their children residing in the Northern Triangle: El Salvador, Guatemala, and Honduras. This act was suspended in 2017, and On Sept. 13, 2021, the Department of State (DOS) and the Department of Homeland Security (DHS) announced that the U.S. Refugee Admissions Program is now accepting new applications as part of Phase Two of reopening the CAM program.

The Afghan Allies Protection Act of 2009 established visas for thousands of Afghans who have been admitted to the United States under the Special Immigrant Visa (SIV) program. Congress passed the Afghan Allies Protection Act of 2009, which was extended in 2014. Afghans who had put their lives at risk during the U.S.-led war in Afghanistan became eligible for SIVs. This program for Afghans created a legal pathway toward U.S. citizenship for the recipients and their immediate family members.

Since the fall of Kabul in August 2015, and the subsequent humanitarian crisis, information about visas extended to Afghan nationals has been constantly updated. See the following for more information:

- USCIS Information for Afghans: `www.uscis.gov/humanitarian/information-for-afghans`

- Special Immigrant Visas for Afghans - Who Were Employed by/on Behalf of the U.S. Government: `travel.state.gov/content/travel/en/us-visas/immigrate/special-immg-visa-afghans-employed-us-gov.html`

EB-5 Immigrant Investor Program basic requirement:

>> Create or preserve 10 permanent full-time jobs for qualified U.S. workers.

>> Invest the following amount of capital:

On or before 11/21/2019:

- $1,000,000 (Minimum Investment)

- $500,000 (Targeted Employment Area)

- $1,000,000 (High-Employment Area)

On or after 11/21/2019:

- $1,800,000 (Minimum Investment)

- $900,000 (Targeted Employment Area)

- $1,800,000 (High-Employment Area)

Each year, about 10,000 EB-5 visas are allotted to qualified investors and their spouses and children. At least 3,000 of the visa numbers are reserved for investments in targeted areas.

Immigrant investors are admitted for two years in conditional permanent resident status. During that time, they must invest the required capital and create the required employment. The condition may be removed if the investment was sustained throughout the period of the investor's residence in the United States.

If you're a prospective immigrant investor, you must petition for yourself on USCIS Form I-526 "Immigrant Petition by Alien Entrepreneur," which you file with the required fee and supporting documentation with the USCIS's Texas Service Center, depending on which office has jurisdiction over the area where the commercial enterprise will principally be doing business. The required documentation must show that you have invested, or are investing, the required lawfully gained capital in a qualifying commercial enterprise within the United States, and that you will create full-time (at least 35 hours per week) jobs for at least ten U.S. workers (U.S. citizens, lawful permanent residents, asylees, or refugees). At the end of the two-year period, you must file INS Form I-829 "Petition by Entrepreneur to Remove the Conditions" and demonstrate that the investment has been completed and sustained for the conditions to be removed.

The investment must be in a for-profit commercial enterprise. The business may be a

>> Sole proprietorship

>> Limited or general partnership

>> Holding company

>> Joint venture

>> Corporation

>> Business trust

>> Other public or privately owned entity

In addition, a new commercial enterprise may be established through

>> The creation of an original business

>> The purchase of an existing business and restructuring and reorganizing it into a new commercial enterprise

>> The expansion of an existing business through a 40 percent net increase in its net worth or in the number of employees

Check the USCIS website EB-5 Investor Program at www.uscis.gov/working-in-the-united-states/permanent-workers/eb-5-immigrant-investor-program for more information.

Winning the green-card lottery

Entering the Diversity Visa Lottery Program can speed up your chances of receiving a visa, especially if you find yourself in one of the lower preference categories. Even if you're currently on a waiting list, you have nothing to lose by entering the visa lottery — it's easy, and it costs nothing but your time and the price of a few USCIS-style photographs. (Find out more about taking a good photo USCIS-style in Chapter 4.)

If you receive a visa through the Diversity Visa Lottery Program, you will be authorized to live and work permanently in the United States, as well as bring your husband or wife and any children under the age of 21 along with you.

REMEMBER

Each year 55,000 immigrant visas become available to people who come from countries with low rates of immigration to the United States. The qualifying countries can change from year to year, so check with the Department of State (www.travel.state.gov) to get the latest list of qualifying countries and detailed instructions for applying.

The Department of State randomly selects about 100,000 applicants from among the qualified entries. They pick 100,000 applicants when only 55,000 visas are available because they know that not all the applicants will qualify to successfully complete the visa process. After 55,000 applicants have qualified and completed the immigration process, no further diversification lottery visas are issued for that year. The following year, the process starts all over again — so if you didn't win this year, try again next year, and if necessary, the year after that, and so on.

Visa lottery winners wanting to adjust their status must still meet the normal adjustment criteria, including lawful status at the time of adjustment.

WARNING

Many unscrupulous companies prey on the insecurities of noncitizens. They charge big bucks for the service of helping them fill out their visa lottery applications. Don't pay it! Filling out the visa diversification lottery application is one of the easiest things you'll do during the entire immigration process. If you have doubts about your ability to fill it out properly, you and an English-speaking friend or family member should be able to figure it out in less than 20 minutes.

REMEMBER

Even though filling out the form is easy, be sure to read and follow the instructions carefully. If you don't do everything as required in the instructions, your application will not be considered.

UNDERSTANDING THE PRIORITY DATE

In the case of a relative immigrant visa petition, the *priority date* is the date on which the petition was actually filed. In the case of an employer-sponsored petition, the priority date is the date the labor certification was filed with the Department of Labor or, if no labor certification is required, the date the petition was filed.

You can track changes in priority date availability with the *Visa Bulletin* `https://travel.state.gov/content/travel/en/legal/visa-law0/visa-bulletin.html`.

Waiting for a Visa

Several factors influence how long the process of getting an immigrant visa can take.

The U.S. government does not impose a limit on the number of immediate-relative visas that can be issued in any given year. Therefore, USCIS workload permitting, processing often begins upon receipt.

On the other hand, preference categories for both family and employment visas are numerically limited. A visa must become available before the Department of State can start to process the case or before you can apply to adjust status in the United States.

The reason for lengthy waits — priority dates that are months or several years away — is that each year many more people apply for immigrant visas than can be allowed to enter the country under the yearly preference limits set by law.

Chapter **4**

Filling Out the Forms

I n the immigration process, you'll encounter a form for just about every situation and purpose that can occur. In fact, forms, paperwork, and immigration documentation can be so complex that getting qualified help from an attorney or immigration service is usually a good idea. (You can find out how to get reliable help in Chapter 7.)

To give you an idea of the types of forms you may encounter, check out the document checklist in Appendix C of this book. This checklist, prepared by the USCIS, can show, at a glance, the immigration forms you'll need to include with your naturalization application.

Understanding the Process of Becoming a U.S. Citizen

This section presents an overview of the naturalization application process. Before you apply, confirm that you meet all eligibility requirements and check further to see if you qualify for any exceptions or accommodations during the interview.

Step 1: Are you already a U.S. citizen?

The USCIS Eligibility Tool (www.uscis.gov/citizenship-resource-center/learn-about-citizenship/naturalization-eligibility-tool) asks you a series of questions to help you determine whether you are eligible to naturalize. If you are not a U.S. citizen by birth, or you did not acquire or derive U.S. citizenship from your parent(s) automatically after birth, go to the next step.

Step 2: Are you eligible to become a U.S. citizen?

To apply for naturalization to become a U.S. citizen, you must

>> Be at least 18 years of age at the time you file the application

>> Have been a lawful permanent resident for the past three (based on marriage to a U.S. citizen) or five (based on lawful permanent residence) years

>> Have continuous residence and physical presence in the United States

>> Be able to read, write, and speak basic English

>> Have good moral character

>> Have basic knowledge of U.S. history and civics

>> Follow the U.S. Constitution and laws

>> Be willing to take the Oath of Allegiance

For detailed information and exceptions, including special provisions for those who have served in the U.S. military, please see USCIS Naturalization through Military Service (www.uscis.gov/military/naturalization-through-military-service).

Step 3: Prepare your Form N-400, Application for Naturalization

Read the instructions to complete Form N-400. Collect the necessary documents to demonstrate your eligibility for naturalization and submit the supporting evidence. See the USCIS Document Checklist (www.uscis.gov/sites/default/files/document/guides/M-477.pdf). You need the following items:

>> A copy of your permanent resident card

>> A check or money order for the application fee and the biometric services fee

>> A copy of your marriage certificate (if applicable)

>> Two passport-style photographs (if you reside outside the United States)

>> Further documents for naturalization based on military service or a foreign spouse applying under 319(b) — see M-477 at the military website noted earlier or the USCIS Military Service portal.

Step 4: Submit your Form N-400 and pay your fees

The purpose of USCIS is to oversee lawful immigration to the United States. A key component to the naturalization process is the submission of the N-400 Application for Naturalization form which is available at www.uscis.gov/n-400.

You generally have two options for filing your Form N-400: You can file with USCIS online or via the mail (for paper forms).

Transitioning from a paper-based environment to a digital environment is key to achieving the USCIS goal of continuous improvement of the immigration system. Processing applications in the order that they are received ensures fairness. As soon as you click the submit button, you are "in line."

The following are the main advantages of submitting your N-400 application online:

>> You securely upload your application and evidence.

>> You skip over the sections of the application that do not apply to you.

>> You can closely monitor your case status, alerts, and correspondence.

>> You can immediately update personal information (such as change of address).

Although applicants have been able to submit the N-400 online since late 2017, the advantages of online submission became more evident during the 2020 COVID-19 lockdown. Online applications were accessible to USCIS adjudicators to process, and applicants were called in for interviews with only slight time delays.

Furthermore, applicants who submit their applications online are thoroughly familiar with their own application and evidence, and are well prepared to answer any questions about their case during the naturalization interview. Some applicants hand off the chore of filling out the N-400 to a family member or legal representative (who usually submit the application online anyway). They then arrive at their interview fully prepared to answer all 100 civics questions but are woefully unprepared to answer any N-400 questions, which comprises the bulk of the naturalization interview.

If you prefer, you can download the application to your computer, complete the pdf, print out the completed application, write the check, gather the additional evidence, stuff everything into a large manila envelope, go to the post office, give the envelope a kiss for good luck, and send it off. And then you *wait*. In about 10 days, you will receive a receipt notice acknowledging that the application has been received at a secure USCIS lockbox facility.

For further advice about submitting the N-400 by mail, see the Form Filing Tips at www.uscis.gov/forms/filing-guidance/form-filing-tips. This process is also covered later in this chapter in the section "Submitting Your Application."

You may also pay your fees and submit evidence online or by mail.

At the time of this book's publication, the fee for Form N-400 is $640 plus $85 for Biometrics for a total of $725. See the USCIS fee calculator tool (www.uscis.gov/feecalculator) for further details. Here are two ways to pay the fee:

>> If you submit your N-400 online, you can pay your fee online using a credit/debit card or bank withdrawal.

>> If you submit your N-400 by mail, you can pay with a card, check, or money order.

- If you pay by check, write "U.S. Department of Homeland Security" (not "USDHS" or "DHS") on the "Pay to the Order of" line.

- If you pay by a credit card, complete and sign Form G-1450, Authorization for Credit Card Transactions (www.uscis.gov/g-1450).

You can also download, complete, and mail in Form N-400 with your fee and evidence. Once you submit Form N-400, USCIS will send you a receipt notice.

TECHNICAL STUFF

If you submit a Form I-942, Request for Reduced Fee (www.uscis.gov/i-942) or a Form I-912, Request for Fee Waiver (www.uscis.gov/i-912), you must mail it together with your Form N-400 and evidence. You cannot submit a Form I-942 or I-912 online.

Step 5: Go to your biometrics appointment, if applicable

USCIS will send you an appointment notice (Form I-797C) that includes your biometrics appointment date, time, and location. You must bring

- » Your ASC appointment notice (Form I-797C

- » Valid photo identification (such as your green card, passport, or driver's license)

Step 6: Complete the interview

Once your background check is complete, USCIS will schedule an interview with you to complete the naturalization process. Go to the USCIS field office at the date and time on your appointment notice. Please bring the appointment notice with you. During the interview, the USCIS officer will ask you oral questions in English based on your Form N-400, give you one sentence to read, dictate one sentence to write, and ask you ten U.S. civics and history questions. See Chapter 5 for more details about your interview.

Step 7: Receive a decision from USCIS on your Form N-400

After your interview, the USCIS adjudicator will give you a Form N-652, Naturalization Interview Results, that gives you the results of the interview. It will indicate one of the following outcomes:

- » **Granted:** USCIS may approve your case if you passed your interview during which you verified the information on your Form N-400, correctly read and wrote one out of three sentences, and correctly answered six out of ten civics and history questions correctly.

- » **Continued:** USCIS may continue your case if you need to provide additional documentation or failed any of the tests.

    If additional documentation is required (ex: marriage license or tax return form), a follow-up letter will be sent with specific details of the evidence that you must submit. Send only the specific documentation that is requested!

    If you failed your English and/or civics, reading, or writing tests, USCIS will reschedule you for a second examination approximately sixty to ninety days after your original interview. The appointment letter will note the date, time, and place of the re-examination, but will not note the actual test to be administered — that info is on the N-652 from your first interview which documented which tests you successfully completed and failed. At the second appointment, you will be given the opportunity to successfully complete the section of interview that you failed, and you will not have to repeat the test(s) that you successfully passed during the first interview.

If you fail the interview a second time, or simply skip the re-examination appointment, you have failed to satisfy the education requirement for U.S. citizenship and must re-submit the N-400 Application for Naturalization, fees, and evidence again. Use your time, money, and energy wisely to study and pass!

>> **Denied:** USCIS will deny your Form N-400 if your documentation shows that you are not eligible for naturalization or you failed English and/or civics, reading, or writing tests for the second time.

Step 8: Receive a notice to take the Oath of Allegiance

If USCIS approved your Form N-400 in Step 7, you may be able to participate in a naturalization ceremony on the same day as your interview. In most cases, the USCIS will mail you a notification with the date, time, and location of your scheduled ceremony. Depending on the location, this ceremony can be scheduled one to six months after your interview. Hold on! You're not a citizen just yet!

Step 9: Take the Oath of Allegiance to the United States

You are not a U.S. citizen until you take the Oath of Allegiance at a naturalization ceremony! Here's how that happens:

>> Complete the questionnaire on Form N-445, Notice of Naturalization Oath Ceremony (it includes several questions about changes in marital status, travel, and so on between the date of your naturalization interview and the date of your Oath Ceremony).

>> Go to your naturalization ceremony and check in with USCIS. A USCIS officer will review your responses to Form N-445.

>> Turn in your permanent resident card (green card — good-bye, old friend!).

>> Take the Oath of Allegiance to become a U.S. citizen.

>> Receive your Certificate of Naturalization (Hello, new U.S. Citizen!). Remember that passport photo you submitted? It's there on the certificate! Check it for errors and immediately notify USCIS of any errors you see on your certificate before leaving the ceremony site.

Step 10: Understanding U.S. citizenship

As a noncitizen, you enjoyed many rights. But as a new U.S. citizen, you can participate fully in the democratic process by

- >> Serving on a jury

- >> Voting in federal elections

- >> Applying for federal employment and scholarships requiring U.S. citizenship

- >> Running for elected office

- >> Petitioning for family member to immigrate to the United States

- >> Traveling on a U.S. passport

- >> Supporting human rights and the rule of law

- >> Belonging to a single people that includes every race, religion, nationality, social group, and political opinion

Using USCIS Tools and Forms

USCIS.gov, and specifically the USCIS Forms page (www.uscis.gov/forms), is your one-stop shop for all forms related to naturalization and immigration. Why is USCIS.gov such a great resource? For several reasons, including the following:

WARNING

- >> **When you get your forms from the USCIS.gov, you always get the latest version of the forms available.** Forms change from time to time, but you can rest assured that what you get from their website is always up-to-date.

  Many nongovernment websites — websites that do not carry a .gov suffix — offer downloadable immigration forms for a fee. Be aware that these sites are *not* affiliated with the Department of Homeland Security (www.dhs.gov), USCIS, or any other U.S. government entity. In many cases, these sites may have older versions of the forms — and using out-of-date forms can result in your case being rejected. You're much better off getting your forms from the official government website at http://uscis.gov/forms. It won't cost you anything, and you'll always get the latest versions of the forms available with the correct edition date, which you can find at the bottom of the form or instructions.

- >> **Downloading and printing the USCIS forms you need is free.** Why pay a fee when you don't have to?

>> **You can complete many USCIS forms on your computer.** You'll need Adobe Acrobat for this.

>> **You can submit some USCIS forms online.** Most notably, you can submit Form N-400 Application for Naturalization plus supporting evidence by creating an account at myaccount.uscis.gov/users/sign_up (see the later section "Creating a USCIS online account" for details). Other forms you can submit online include

- AR-11, Alien's Change of Address Card (www.uscis.gov/ar-11)

- I-90, Application to Replace Permanent Resident Card (www.uscis.gov/i-90)

- I-130, Petition for Alien Relative (www.uscis.gov/i-130)

>> **You can download forms 24 hours a day.** If you have a computer and an internet connection at home, you can even download forms in your pajamas, if you want, and your immigration officer will be none the wiser.

WARNING

Failure to follow the instructions on immigration and naturalization forms can result in your application being delayed or even denied. If you're not sure about something, ask for help (you can find more about this in Chapter 7).

TIP

When you have a choice in the matter, send copies and keep track of original documents in your own files (keeping copies of your original documents doesn't hurt — just store them someplace other than where you store the originals). Even when you're required to send original documents, make sure to always keep at least one paper copy and scanned copy of everything in your files for future reference.

TIP

You'll be required to include additional documentation with many immigration applications. If you don't have a required document and cannot obtain a certified copy of the original, you can try submitting a certification from the recording authority that explains why you cannot provide the documentation. In cases such as this, the USCIS will consider other evidence such as notarized affidavits. A good country-by-country resource as to what alternative documents are acceptable can be found in the State Department's Foreign Affairs Manual (FAM) (https://fam.state.gov/).

Your citizenship tool belt

USCIS online tools and resources (http://uscis.gov/tools) can deliver the information you need without having to call or visit a field office. Here are seven quick tools to help you get the job done:

>> **Ask Emma, the USCIS Virtual Assistant:** "Emma" is a computer-generated virtual assistant who can answer your questions and even take you to the right spot on the USCIS.gov website (http://uscis.gov/emma).

>> **Check Case Processing Times:** Select your form number and the office that is processing your case (https://egov.uscis.gov/processing-times/).

>> **Fee Calculator:** This tool asks questions to help determine your fee; however, it does not store answers to the questions or any other personal information. Currently, the fee for Form N-400 is $640; Biometrics $85; total $725. If you are 75 years old or older at the time you submit your Form N-400, your Biometrics is free! (http://uscis.gov/feecalculator)

>> **MyUSCIS account:** Create a USCIS account. File your form online and upload evidence. Get detailed case status. Send USCIS a secure message. Pay with a credit or debit card (http://myaccount.uscis.gov).

>> **Case Status Online:** Use this tool to track the status of an immigration application, petition, or request (http://uscis.gov/casestatus).

>> **Case Inquiry:** Use this tool to submit an online inquiry about a case outside of the normal processing time; a missing notice, card, or document; or service requests such as appointment accommodations or to correct a typo on a form (http://uscis.gov/e-request).

>> **USCIS Office Locator:** Field offices (within the United States) handle scheduled interviews on non-asylum-related applications. Application Support Centers provide biometrics collection services (http://uscis.gov/about-us/find-uscis-office).

Creating a USCIS online account

The best reasons to get a USCIS online account are that you can file forms online and track your case anytime from anywhere. If you work with an attorney or representative, they can also create their own account to manage your case, but they cannot use your account.

Filing a form online is better than mailing a paper form because you can

>> Enter your information using a phone, tablet, or computer

>> Avoid common mistakes (for example, you won't be able to submit without signing)

>> Save your draft application and finish it at your own pace

>> Easily and securely pay your filing fee

>> Receive immediate confirmation that your form has been received instead of waiting for the mail

After you file, you can use your account to

>> Get your current case status and the history of your case

>> Respond to Requests for Evidence (RFEs)

>> Access every notice that's sent to you

>> Send secure messages and get answers

Even if you file on paper, you can link your case to your account. You can then see your case status and history. For some forms, you can also do the same things listed previously as if you had filed online.

For a quick overview of the USCIS account creation process, watch the video: USCIS How to Create a USCIS Online Account: `https://youtu.be/c_5YDNyMJ30`. In late January 2022, USCIS released a another very helpful video on the USCIS YouTube Channel: Apply for Citizenship Online: How to File Your Application for Naturalization Online (`https://youtu.be/s15HbkUAVh4`). Here's a quick overview of the process of creating an account:

1. **Go to** `http://my.uscis.gov`.

2. **Click "Sign In"; then click the blue "Create Account" link.**

3. **The system will prompt you to enter your email address.**

   We suggest using an individual email address, not one that you share with others.

   When you create your account, the system will send you a notification to your email asking you to confirm your USCIS account request.

4. **Go to your email account and confirm your account request.**

   Click the blue "sign up" button in the email you receive from USCIS. The system will redirect you to the "create a password" screen.

5. **Create and confirm your password for the account.**

   Passwords must be between 8 and 64 characters and can contain letters, numbers, or special characters.

6. **Secure your account by opting for the two-step verification process for login.**

   Every time you log in, in addition to entering your password, you will also need to enter a short verification code.

   You need to select how you prefer to receive that code: text or email. Then you need to choose five security questions in case you ever need to reset your password.

7. **Now you need to select an account type.**

   You choose whether you are an applicant, petitioner, requestor, or legal representative.

8. **Once you make your selection, click the blue "Submit" button.**

Your new account will step you through the qualifications of naturalization. Next, you can then move on to actually answering Form N-400 applications. Unlike a paper application in which you must read every line and check every box, the online N-400 is similar to an online tax preparation program, using casual English to guide you through tricky, technical questions. If a section doesn't apply to you, such as Travel Outside of the U.S., you simply answer "no," and the program skips forward to the next Form N-400 section, Marital Status. Finally, you can save your work on your application and come back to work on it later.

Applying for Citizenship: Form N-400

Assuming you meet all the qualifications for becoming a United States citizen, you'll most likely apply for naturalization using Form N-400 Application for Naturalization.

Form N-400 is 20 pages long and divided into 18 sections. Part 12 is notorious for its questions about morality, violence, and crime. However, the form is well-organized and follows a logical sequence.

REMEMBER

You'll probably be asked about the answers you give on your Application for Naturalization at your citizenship interview, so remember what you say, be clear about what you mean, and be truthful. (You can find more information about the actual interview in Chapter 5.)

Some helpful info before you begin

Filing online is the best option. Or you can download Form N-400 and fill it out in Adobe Acrobat. Or you can print the form and type or print legibly in black ink on the hard copies. But filling out the form online is so much easier.

>> **If you need extra space to complete any item in this application,** use and attach a separate sheet of paper; include your Alien Registration Number (A-Number) at the top of each sheet; and indicate the page number, part number, and item number to which your answer refers. A common example is Part 9, seven or more trips outside the U.S., or Part 11, five or more children.

>> **Answer all questions fully and accurately.** If a question does not apply to you (for example, if you have never been married and the question asks "Provide the name of your current spouse"), write "N/A." If the question requires a numeric response, write zero (0).

>> **Do not write outside the area provided for a response.** If you must make corrections to your Form N-400, print out another copy of the affected page and swap it for the page of the damaged section. USCIS scanners may see through white correction tape or fluid. Submit a clean 20-page Form N-400 with no duplicate pages. Add extra pages of additional information (see the first bullet) to the end of the Form N-400.

>> **Provide your A-Number on the top right corner of each page (if any).** Your A-Number is located on your permanent resident card (formerly known as an alien registration card). If the A-Number on your card has fewer than nine digits, place enough zeros before the first number to make a total of nine digits on Form N-400. For example, print number A-1234567 as A-001234567.

>> **Your application must be properly completed, signed, and filed.** You must include all pages when you file Form N-400, even if the pages are blank. A photocopy of the application is acceptable as long as all signatures on the application are handwritten and original. USCIS will not accept a stamped or typewritten name in place of a signature on a mailed Form N-400. Digital signatures are acceptable on Form N-400 applications submitted online via your My USCIS online account.

>> **If you're actively serving in the military at the same time you're applying for naturalization,** the USCIS recommends that you go to your service's personnel office for information about, and help in, preparing your application, particularly if you are sponsoring a spouse or other dependents. See the USCIS military section (www.uscis.gov/military/military) for more details. Of course, if you feel more comfortable securing your own representation, you can do that too.

>> **Include any explanations you may need to give to the USCIS, such as absences from the United States greater than six months, prior criminal convictions on your record, failure to register for the draft, and so on.** You must file these explanations in the form of affidavits. The government may or may not accept your explanation, but you still need to include it. If you feel you need to explain something about your application, you should always seek out the services of a qualified immigration attorney (see Chapter 7).

N-400 Parts 1 to 11: Personal Information

This section of Form N-400 covers your identity and background, including name, birthplace, family history, education, and more.

Part 1: Eligibility

You may apply for naturalization when you meet all the requirements to become a U.S. citizen.

Part 2: Info about You

Item Number 1: Your Current Legal Name: Family Name (last name); Given Name (first name); Middle Name (if applicable). Traditionally, western women change their family name to their husband's last name (however, this is changing).

Item Number 2: Your Name Exactly As It Appears on Your Permanent Resident Card: Check carefully — initials sometimes shorten a two-part first name (Asian given names) or switch the order of Hispanic last names (which is composed of the father and mother's surnames).

Item Number 3: Other Names You Have Used Since Birth: Nicknames, aliases, maiden name, professional name, stage name, pseudonym (if applicable).

Item Number 4: Name Change (Optional): A court can allow you to change your name when you are naturalized. *Note:* USCIS cannot process name change requests for members of the military, or their spouses, who are naturalizing overseas.

Item Number 5: U.S. Social Security Number: Print your U.S. Social Security number. Type or print "N/A" if you do not have one.

Item Number 6: USCIS Online Account Number (if applicable): You can find your USCIS Online Account Number by logging in to your account and going to the profile page.

Item Number 7: Gender: Indicate if you are male or female. *Note:* In March 2021, the White House said it was open to putting a third gender option on government forms. Stay tuned!

Item Number 8: Date of Birth: Always use eight numbers to show your date of birth. Type or print the date in this order: Month, Day, Year (MM/DD/YYYY). For example, print May 1, 1958, as 05/01/1958.

Item Number 9: Date You Became a Lawful Permanent Resident: Check your green card! Provide the official date when your permanent residence began as shown on your permanent resident card (green card) — which may or may not be the date you arrived in the United States (especially if you adjusted your status). Provide the date in this order: Month, Day, Year (MM/DD/YYYY).

Note: You need both your USCIS A-Number and your permanent resident date to file Form N-400. Where applicable, if you do not have this information, you should apply for a replacement green card (www.uscis.gov/i-90) or contact USCIS (800-375-5283 [TTY 800-767-1833]) to schedule an appointment to obtain this information *before* you file your Form N-400.

Item Number 10: Country of Birth: Type or print the name of the country in which you were born. Use the name of the country at the time of your birth, even if the name of the country has changed.

Item Number 11: Country of Citizenship or Nationality: Print the name of the country as it currently exists. If the country no longer exists, type or print the current name of the country with current authority. See "A Guide to Naturalization" (Form M-476) for further details.

Item Number 12: Do you have a physical or developmental disability or mental impairment that prevents you from learning and/or understanding the English language and/or civics material for naturalization?

Select "Yes" if you are requesting an exception to the English language and/or civics tests based on a physical or developmental disability or mental impairment that prevents you from complying with the English language and/or civics requirements for naturalization. Submit Form N-648, Medical Certification for Disability Exceptions (www.uscis.gov/n-648), as an attachment to your Form N-400.

REMEMBER

Submitting a Form N-648 does not guarantee you will be exempted from the testing requirements.

Item Number 13: Exemptions from the English Language Test: Depending on your age and the length of time you have been a lawful permanent resident, you may not be required to take the English language test.

According to "A Guide to Naturalization" (Form M-476), you are not required to take the English language test if

> 1. At the time of filing your Form N-400, you are 50 years of age or older and have lived in the United States as a permanent resident for periods totaling at least 20 years. You do not have to take the English language test, but you do have to take the civics test in the language of your choice.
>
> 2. At the time of filing your Form N-400, you are 55 years of age or older and have lived in the United States as a permanent resident for periods totaling at least 15 years. You do not have to take the English language test, but you do have to take the civics test in the language of your choice.
>
> 3. At the time of filing your Form N-400, you are 65 years of age or older and have lived in the United States as a permanent resident for periods totaling at least

20 years. You do not have to take the English language test, but you do have to take the civics test in the language of your choice.

NOTE: If you qualify for an exemption from the English language test based on your age and how long you have lived in the United States as a lawful permanent resident, you should answer "Yes" to at least one question in Part 2, Item Number 13, of Form N-400.

Part 3: Accommodations

USCIS is committed to providing reasonable accommodations for qualified individuals with disabilities and/or impairments to help them fully participate in the naturalization process. See "A Guide to Naturalization" (Form M-476) for details and exceptions.

All domestic USCIS facilities meet the accessibility guidelines of the Americans with Disabilities Act, so you do not need to contact USCIS to request an accommodation for physical access to a domestic USCIS office. However, in Part 3, Item C, in Item Number 1 of Form N-400, you can indicate whether you use a wheelchair. This will allow USCIS to better prepare for your visit.

USCIS also ensures that limited English proficient (LEP) individuals are provided meaningful access at an interview or other immigration benefit-related appointment, unless otherwise prohibited by law. LEP individuals may bring a qualified interpreter to the interview.

WARNING

During the COVID-19 pandemic, there are restrictions about people accompanying the interviewee. Before the interview, consult the USCIS Visitor Policy guidelines at www.uscis.gov/about-us/uscis-visitor-policy or contact the local field office at www.uscis.gov/about-us/find-a-uscis-office/field-offices/.

WARNING

A USCIS interviewing officer can deny permission for an interpreter to participate in the interview because of safety protocol. Before the interview, review Form G-1256, Declaration for Interpreted USCIS Interview (www.uscis.gov/g-1256), which describes the responsibilities of an interpreter. Complete Form G-1256 and bring it with you to the interview, but do not sign it — Form G-1256 must be signed in the presence of the USCIS interviewer.

USCIS considers requests for reasonable accommodations on a case-by-case basis, and will make their best efforts to reasonably accommodate your disabilities and/or impairments. USCIS will not exclude you from participating in USCIS programs or deny your application because of your disabilities and/or impairments. Requesting and/or receiving an accommodation will not affect your eligibility for an immigration benefit.

Part 4: Contact Info

Provide your current telephone numbers as well as your current email address. Type or print "N/A" if an item is not applicable.

Part 5: Residence

List every address where you have lived during the last five years (including other countries) prior to filing your Form N-400. Start with where you live now, and then include the dates for each place you have lived in a month, day, and year format (MM/DD/YYYY). Include your mailing address if it is different from your current address.

Always keep your address up-to-date. If you move, you can file a free AR-11, Alien's Change of Address Card, at www.uscis.gov/ar-11.

If you are a victim of domestic violence, see the special instructions about address change that maintains the victim's safety and security under the Form AR-11 subsection Victims of Domestic Violence, Trafficking, and Other Crimes (www.uscis.gov/addresschange).

Part 6: Parents

If neither one of your parents is a United States citizen, skip this part and go to Part 7. If applicable, complete the information about your parents' U.S. citizenship.

Part 7: Biographical Info

Include info about ethnicity, race, height, weight, and eye color.

Part 8: Work and School

List where you have worked or attended school full time or part time during the last five years. Provide information for the complete time period. Include all military, police, and/or intelligence service.

Begin by providing information about your current and most recent employment, studies, or unemployment, if applicable. Provide the locations and dates where you worked, were self-employed, were unemployed, or have studied during the last five years. If you worked for yourself, write "self-employed." If you were unemployed, write "unemployed."

Part 9: Travel Outside of the United States

For the past five years, provide the total number of days (24 hours or longer) you spent outside the United States, the total number of trips, and the trips' destinations and dates (MM/DD/YYYY). Start with the most recent trip and work backwards. Include an additional page if needed.

Part 10: Marital History

Indicate your current marital status and include details about your current spouse, your ex-spouse(s), and your current spouse's ex-spouses.

Part 11: Children

Provide your total number of children. Count all of your children, regardless of whether they are alive, missing, or deceased; born in other countries or in the United States; under 18 years of age or over 18 years of age; married or unmarried; living with you or elsewhere; current stepchildren; legally adopted children; or children born when you were not married. For each child, provide details about their date of birth, country of birth and citizenship, and residence.

N-400 Part 12: Additional Information

For **Item Numbers 1–50,** answer each question by selecting "Yes" or "No," where applicable. If any part of a question applies to you or has ever applied to you, you must answer "Yes." If you answer "Yes" to any of the questions in **Item Numbers 1–44** in this part, include a typed or printed explanation on a separate sheet of paper. You may also provide evidence to support your answers.

If you answer "No" to any question in **Item Numbers 45–50** (Attachment to the Constitution), include a typed or printed explanation on a separate sheet of paper. An example of "No" would be an objection to bearing arms based on religious reasons, and an affidavit from a religious leader would support your exemption. Your answers, whether "Yes" or "No," will not automatically cause your application to be denied. If the exemption is granted, you will take a modified Oath of Allegiance at your Naturalization Oath ceremony.

REMEMBER

During the interview, the USCIS may ask you to define a term. This is not a vocabulary test! The officer is verifying that you understand the actions that you are affirming (for example, paying taxes) or denying (such as voting in a U.S. election).

WARNING

If you do not understand a question or vocabulary word, *do not answer yes or no!* After you understand the question, *then* answer it. Some applicants reflexively answer, "No!" to every question that starts with "Have you ever. . . ." This is a huge mistake! If the officer asks the applicant to explain their answer and they can't, the officer will conclude that the applicant doesn't understand their Form N-400 (with its attendant legal responsibilities and consequences) and will stop the interview. The officer will then note that the applicant cannot speak and understand English and will have to come back for another interview. Please, please, please take the time to review Part 12 vocabulary, be ready to explain the vocabulary terms in English, and possibly give examples.

N-400 Parts 13–18: Signatures

Now you're in the home stretch. It's time to sign the form.

Part 13: Applicant's Signature

Select the appropriate box to indicate whether you read this application yourself or whether you had an interpreter or a preparer assist you. Further, you must sign and date your application. *USCIS will reject your Form N-400 if it is not signed!*

Part 14: Interpreter's Signature

If you use an interpreter to complete your Form N-400, provide their information. The interpreter must sign and date the application.

Part 15: Preparer's Signature (other than the applicant)

If someone else helped you to prepare and complete your Form N-400, provide their information. The preparer must sign and date the application.

If the person who helped you prepare your application is an attorney or accredited representative whose representation extends beyond preparation of the application, they may be obliged to also submit a completed Form G-28, Notice of Entry of Appearance as Attorney or Accredited Representative (www.uscis.gov/g-28), along with your application. USCIS will reject your Form N-400 if it is not signed by the preparer you used to prepare the questions on the application.

Part 16: Signature at Interview

Do not complete this part. The USCIS officer will ask you to complete this part at your interview.

Part 17: Renunciation

Do not complete this part until a USCIS officer instructs you to do so at your interview.

Most people do not have a foreign hereditary title or order of nobility. This part will apply only if you answered "Yes" to **Part 12, Items A and B, in Item Number 4.** If you do have a hereditary title or order of nobility, the law requires you to renounce this title as part of your oath ceremony to become a U.S. citizen. In Part 17 you must affirm you are ready to do so.

Part 18: Oath of Allegiance

Do not complete this part. The USCIS Officer will ask you to complete this part at your interview.

If USCIS approves your application, you must take this Oath of Allegiance to become a U.S. citizen. In limited cases, you can take a modified oath. The oath requirement cannot be waived unless you are unable to understand its meaning because of a physical or developmental disability or mental impairment. For more information, see "A Guide to Naturalization" (M-476). Your signature on this application only indicates that you have no objections to taking the Oath of Allegiance. It does not mean that you have taken the oath or that you are naturalized. If USCIS approves your Form N-400 for naturalization, you must attend an oath ceremony and take the Oath of Allegiance to the United States.

In Chapter 5, we discuss the Oath of Allegiance.

RESEARCHING YOUR HISTORY: FORM G-639

How can you make sure that the information in your immigration files is accurate? By filing a Freedom of Information/Privacy Act Request (Form G-639) (www.uscis.gov/records/request-records-through-the-freedom-of-information-act-or-privacy-act) to access your files. This is where many attorneys start with a new client, especially clients who do not have personal records of prior dealings with the USCIS. By getting copies of previous filings, you can confirm what forms were filed, what information was on the forms, and what the USCIS did with them.

The fee charged for a Freedom of Information/Privacy Act Request may vary. See the instructions on the form itself for further details. You don't need to send any money with your request.

The Freedom of Information Act (FOIA), enacted in 1966, gives the American people the right to access records in the possession of agencies and departments of the executive branch of the United States government. The Privacy Act of 1974 regulates federal

(continued)

(continued)

government agency record-keeping and disclosure practices, allowing most individuals to access federal agency records about themselves. It also restricts the disclosure of personally identifiable information by federal agents and prohibits the government from using information gathered for one purpose from being used for another purpose. The Privacy Act states that personal information in federal agency files must be accurate, complete, relevant, and timely, and gives the subject of a record the right to challenge the accuracy of the information in their own files.

Other Common Forms

Although the forms and documents you need will depend on your individual case, here are some common forms that many naturalization candidates encounter:

» **Application to Preserve Residence for Naturalization Purposes (Form N-470)** (www.uscis.gov/n-470) allows certain lawful permanent residents who need to leave the United States for employment purposes to preserve continuity of status as an immigrant in order to pursue naturalization.

» **Application for Certificate of Citizenship (Form N-600)** (www.uscis.gov/n-600) is filed by those seeking naturalization based on parentage. Depending on the visa, children adopted by U.S. citizens are eligible to file Form N-600 — carefully review the USCIS Adoption website (www.uscis.gov/adoption) for the conditions.

» **Application for Citizenship and Issuance of Certificate Under Section 322 (Form N-600k)** (www.uscis.gov/n-600k) allows children who regularly reside in a foreign country to claim U.S. citizenship based on their parents.

» **Medical Certification for Disability Exceptions (Form N-648)** (www.uscis.gov/n-648) must be completed by a licensed medical doctor or a licensed clinical psychologist and filed along with an application for naturalization (Form N-400) for those who qualify for an exemption from taking the English or civics test portion of the naturalization interview (find out more about this in Chapter 5).

Depending on individual circumstances, many people will encounter these lawful permanent residence forms during the naturalization process:

» **Petition for Alien Worker (Form I-140)** (www.uscis.gov/i-140) is filed by an employer to petition for an alien worker to become a permanent resident in the United States. The filing fee is $700.

- » **Petition for Alien Relative (Form I-130)** (www.uscis.gov/i-130) is filed by a citizen or a lawful permanent resident to establish a relationship to certain alien relatives who want to immigrate to the United States. You must file a separate form for each individual qualifying relative who wants to immigrate. The filing fee is $535.

- » **Affidavit of Support (Form I-864)** (www.uscis.gov/i-864) is a promise made to the U.S. government that a sponsoring relative will be financially responsible for their alien relative. The sponsor is promising that the alien will not become a public charge. Sponsors must file separate forms for each relative they are sponsoring.

- » **Application to Register Permanent Residence or to Adjust Status (Form I-485)** (www.uscis.gov/i-485) is submitted by applicants who want to obtain permanent resident status. You will usually file this form with supporting evidence that you qualify for upgrading your immigration status from temporary to permanent resident, and you may file this form at the same time as other applications or petitions. This form carries a fee of $255 for applicants over 14 years of age and $160 for applicants under 14. Applicants age 14 or older must be fingerprinted at an additional cost of $50 per applicant.

- » **Change of Address (Form AR-11)** (www.uscis.gov/ar-11) is used to report the change of address of an alien in the United States to the USCIS.

  You do not need to mail a paper Form AR-11 if you use the change of address web page unless you are a victim of domestic violence, trafficking, and other crimes, or if you have previously filed a Form I-751 abuse waiver. For more information on these special situations in which you must file a paper Form AR-11, see the How to Change Your Address web page (www.uscis.gov/addresschange). Always make sure the USCIS has your current address.

- » **Application to Replace Permanent Resident Card (Form I-90)** (www.uscis.gov/i-90) is used to obtain a replacement for a lost green card.

SAY CHEESE! TAKING A GOOD PHOTO, USCIS-STYLE

If you neglect to send the USCIS proper photographs with your naturalization application, or with other applications such as an adjustment of status application, they will simply return the application, delaying the entire process. In most cases, you won't have to worry, because the photographer will have experience taking photographs for this purpose. But it doesn't hurt to know what the USCIS wants.

(continued)

(continued)

So what does a good photo mean in USCIS terms? They don't care how glamorous you look or if you were having a good hair day. The USCIS wants to be able to clearly identify that the person in the photograph is you. Likewise, they do have some specific photo requirements and restrictions:

- With your application, include two passport-style (2" x 2") unretouched color (not black-and-white), high-quality photographs with a glossy or matte finish.

- The overall photograph size should be at least 1 $\frac{9}{16}$ inches (40 mm) tall by 1⅜ inches (35 mm) wide.

- The image of your face in the photo should be 1 $\frac{3}{16}$ inches (30 mm) from the hair to the neck just below the chin and 1 inch (26 mm) from the right ear to the left cheek. The image may not exceed 1¼ inches by 1 $\frac{1}{16}$ inches (32 mm x 28 mm).

- Photos should be unmounted and printed on thin paper.

- You should be photographed against a white or off-white background. Contrast between the image of your face and the background is essential. Photos of very light–skinned people should be slightly underexposed, and photos of very dark–skinned people should be slightly overexposed.

- Above all else, your facial features *must* be visible. The photo needs to show a three-fourths profile view of the right side of your face and your right ear.

- Unless your religion requires you to wear a headdress, your head should be bare in the photograph, but either way, your face *must* remain visible.

- The photos need to have been taken within 30 days of the date they are sent to the USCIS.

- Using a pencil, write your name and A-number lightly on the back of your photo.

WHO ARE APPROVED REPRESENTATIVES?

An immigration attorney will be the representative in most immigration cases, but there are other individuals who may be authorized to represent you before the USCIS. Law school graduates and current law students who are supervised by an attorney may represent you so long as you do not pay them. Some nonlawyers are also authorized through a process known as *accreditation,* under which the Department of Justice's Executive Office for Immigration Review (EOIR) grants permission to a representative of a recognized religious, charitable, or social-service organization. The EOIR maintains a list of pro bono (immigration) legal service providers who are approved to help with immigration and naturalization cases (www.justice.gov/eoir/list–pro–bono–legal–service–providers).

Submitting Your Application

In order to ensure the fastest processing of your application, submit it online. In January 2022, USCIS released a very helpful 19-minute video on USCIS YouTube Channel: Apply for Citizenship Online: How to File Your Application for Naturalization Online (`https://youtu.be/s15HbkUAVh4`). This video walks you through the entire online application process: creating your account, checking your eligibility for naturalization, completing the online form (including personal information and skipping sections that are not applicable), uploading evidence, and paying your fee. You can also find this video embedded in the N-400, Application for Naturalization web page (`www.uscis.gov/n-400`) below the File Online section.

The following applies if you are submitting documents by mail. If you are submitting other documents or paperwork with your immigration application, place all the additional documents in a single envelope and clearly write the contents on the outside of the envelope — listing the documents included. You can send family members' applications, payments, and documents together in the same package. Put the Alien Number and name on top of each page of their application, payment, and documents.

WARNING

Scan or make a copy of everything you submit. If the original application is ever lost (and it does happen), you can quickly submit a duplicate. Also, if you need to go over any errors or problems with the USCIS, you can look at the same forms they're looking at while you're on the phone. Of course, if the USCIS ever loses your application, it's a good time to get professional help from an attorney or a qualified immigration service.

If you want to mail your applications, here's the order in which the government likes to see applications assembled, from top to bottom:

>> **Money:** The thing to put at the top is any fees you need to include with the application. Assemble *all* fee payments on the top of each and every case, whether or not the case is filed with one fee payment or multiple fee payments. In other words, if you're submitting several applications or documents, clip the fees for all of them to the top of your application packet. Never, ever send cash.

>> **Form G-28 "Notice of Appearance":** Next in the stack is a Form G-28 "Notice of Appearance" — but only if you're represented by an attorney or other approved representative. (The legal representative will fill out this form for you to include with your N-400 application.) If you are not represented, you don't need to worry about this element.

>> **The actual application:** Next comes the actual application or petition, with photos in a separate envelope attached by a paper clip (if your particular application needs photos).

>> **Any additional evidence:** Now put in the envelope other paperwork and evidence (if applicable).

>> **Supporting documentation:** If you need to include any other documents to help prove your case, add them at the bottom of the pile. Follow the USCIS Document Checklist (www.uscis.gov/sites/default/files/document/guides/M-477.pdf) carefully! Do not send extra documentation such as tax returns or pay stubs. If the USCIS needs to review more evidence, they will send a letter with a detailed list of required documents.

Mail your forms to the address listed on that form's web page. You may submit your forms through USPS, FedEx, DHL, or UPS. See Table 4-1 for the correct address, which depends on where you live. Or check www.uscis.gov/forms/all-forms/direct-filing-addresses-for-form-n-400-application-for-naturalization.

TABLE 4-1

Direct Filing Addresses for Form N-400

If you live in:	Send your N-400 here:
Alabama, Alaska, American Samoa, Arizona, Armed Forces Americas, Armed Forces Europe, Armed Forces Pacific, California, Colorado, Commonwealth of the Northern Mariana Islands, Guam, Hawaii, Idaho, Kansas, Kentucky, Marshall Islands, Micronesia, Minnesota, Mississippi, Montana, Nebraska, Nevada, New Mexico, North Dakota, Oregon, Palau, Puerto Rico, South Dakota, Tennessee, U.S. Virgin Islands, Utah, Washington, Wyoming	**USCIS Phoenix Lockbox** **U.S. Postal Service (USPS):** USCIS Attn: N-400 P.O. Box 21251 Phoenix, AZ 85036-1251 **FedEx, UPS, and DHL deliveries:** USCIS Attn: N-400 (Box 21251) 1820 E. Skyharbor Circle S Suite 100 Phoenix, AZ 85034-4850
Arkansas, Louisiana, Oklahoma, Texas	**USCIS Dallas Lockbox** **U.S. Postal Service (USPS):** USCIS Attn: N-400 P.O. Box 660060 Dallas, TX 75266-0060

If you live in:	Send your N-400 here:
	FedEx, UPS, and DHL deliveries: USCIS Attn: N-400 (Box 660060) 2501 S State Hwy 121 Business Suite 400 Lewisville, TX 75067-8003
Illinois, Indiana, Wisconsin, Iowa, Michigan, Minnesota, Ohio, Missouri, Wisconsin	**USCIS Chicago Lockbox** **U.S. Postal Service (USPS):** USCIS Attn: N-400 P.O. Box 4380 Chicago, IL 60680-4380 **FedEx, UPS, and DHL deliveries:** USCIS Attn: N-400 (Box 4380) 131 S. Dearborn, 3rd Floor Chicago, IL 60603-5517
Connecticut, Delaware, District of Columbia, Florida, Georgia, Maine, Maryland, Massachusetts, New Hampshire, New Jersey, New York, North Carolina, Pennsylvania, Rhode Island, South Carolina, Vermont, Virginia, West Virginia	**USCIS Elgin Lockbox** **U.S. Postal Service (USPS):** USCIS Attn: N-400 P.O. Box 4060 Carol Stream, IL 60197-4060 **FedEx, UPS, and DHL deliveries:** USCIS Attn: N-400 (Box 4060) 2500 Westfield Drive Elgin, IL 60124-7836

WARNING

If you mail your applications, petitions, or requests to the wrong filing location, they may be rejected as improperly filed and returned to you to re-file.

DOCUMENTING IMMIGRATION HELP

If you're using an attorney or other approved representative, they must file another form with your application package — the G-28, Notice of Appearance (www.uscis.gov/g-28). The representative may ask you to sign the G-28; your signature tells USCIS that you grant them permission to communicate directly with your attorney or representative. If multiple applications are submitted for other family members or for different petitioners, make sure that a separate G-28 is submitted for each party being represented. Furthermore, the USCIS requests that you include the contact information of people who helped you complete Form N-400 Part 14 Interpreter and Part 15 Preparer (frequently an immigration legal representative).

If you're using an attorney, they will probably include a cover letter that outlines the immigration benefit you're seeking and the evidence included in the packet that demonstrates your qualifications. **Remember:** When using an attorney, you should read everything the attorney is planning to file with the USCIS (if you have questions, ask them before the forms are filed). Get a copy of the forms for your own files.

TIP

Whenever you send something to the USCIS, make sure that you use a method that ensures proof of delivery — Certified Mail (with a return receipt), Express Mail, or something similar.

Organizing your files

As you may be beginning to realize, you can accumulate a whole lot of paperwork during the course of immigration and naturalization. Maintaining accurate and organized files and always keeping copies of everything are important. If the USCIS ever loses anything important, you'll be able to replace it or prove your case. Keep extra copies of important documents (birth and marriage certificates, for example) in a separate location, so you'll have a backup.

A good way to keep organized files is to get a small file box or an alphabetical accordion file organizer. Organize the papers in a way that makes sense to you — so you will be able to quickly find the paperwork you need at a moment's notice. Get a separate file box for each member of the immigrating family.

Having well-organized paperwork in a single small location will allow you to bring your entire file with you, if you need to.

After you file

After filing your application and paying your fees, you'll receive a receipt number. Don't lose your receipt numbers! You'll need them to use the USCIS case-status service online or to reference your case whenever you contact the USCIS about your case.

2

Doing the Interview, Getting Help, and Following the Rules

Know what to do before, during, and after your U.S. Citizenship interview.

Understand legal changes in recent immigration law.

Determine whether you need immigration legal assistance.

Resolve problems that could affect your case.

Chapter **5**

Acing Your Naturalization Interview

There's no way around it: To become a naturalized citizen of the United States, you have to go through a minimum of two interviews with the USCIS — once to gain lawful permanent resident status (a green card) and a second time to become a naturalized citizen.

In this chapter, we let you know what to expect at your naturalization or citizenship interview. (See Chapter 1 to find out more about the permanent residence interview.)

Who Needs to Interview with the USCIS?

Everyone applying for naturalization has to interview with the U.S. Citizenship and Immigration Services (USCIS), although not all people have to complete *all* parts of the interview. Everyone, except those with certain physical or mental disabilities, must take the Oath of Allegiance.

Age exemptions

REMEMBER

Age has its privileges when it comes to interview exemptions.

>> If you are **over 50 years old** and have lived in the United States **at least 20 years as a lawful permanent resident** at the time of filing your N-400, review Chapter 4 to see if you may be exempt from taking the English test. You may also be allowed to take the civics test in the language of your choice, using an interpreter.

>> If you are **over 55 years old** and have lived in the United States at least **15 years as a lawful permanent resident** at the time of filing your N-400, you may be exempt from taking the English test. You may also be allowed to take the civics test in the language of your choice, using an interpreter.

>> If you are **over 65 years old** and have lived in the United States at least **20 years as a lawful permanent resident** at the time of filing your N-400, you may be exempt from taking the English test. You may study just the 20 questions that have been marked with an asterisk (*) found at the end of each question on the USCIS Civics (History and Government) Questions for the Naturalization Test. These questions are available in multiple languages at the USCIS Citizenship Resource Center (www.uscis.gov/citizenship/find-study-materials-and-resources/study-for-the-test). You may also take the naturalization test in the language of your choice.

TIP

Keep in mind that in order to meet the residency requirements for an age exemption, the time you spent living in the United States as a permanent resident need not have been continuous. Although you cannot count time spent out of the country, you can get credit for the total time you spent here. To see if you qualify:

1. **Add the total number of years you've been a U.S. lawful permanent resident.**

   Note: You may not count time spent living in the United States before you got your green card.

2. **Subtract from this any extended periods (more than six months) you spent outside the United States.**

REMEMBER

In order to qualify for USCIS interview exemptions, you must meet the requirements *as of the time you file your application.* Even though you may be 50 years old by the time you actually interview with the USCIS, if you were 49 when you filed your application, you will still be expected to pass the English test.

Plan to bring an interpreter with you to your interview if you do qualify for an English proficiency waiver (an exemption from having to speak, read, and write English).

Here are a couple of safety-related issues to keep in mind:

>> During the COVID-19 pandemic as of this writing, there are restrictions about people accompanying the interviewee. Before the interview, consult the USCIS Visitor Policy Guidelines (www.uscis.gov/about-us/uscis-visitor-policy) or contact the local field office (www.uscis.gov/about-us/find-a-uscis-office/field-offices).

>> A USCIS interviewing officer can deny permission for an interpreter to participate in the interview because of safety protocol. Before the interview, review Form G-1256, Declaration for Interpreted USCIS Interview (www.uscis.gov/g-1256), which describes the responsibilities of an interpreter. Complete Form G-1256 and bring it with you to the interview, but do not sign it — Form G-1256 must be signed in the presence of the USCIS interviewer.

Disability exemptions

People with disabilities — physical or developmental handicaps or mental impairment — may not have to take the English and civics tests.

REMEMBER

You must file Form N-648 Medical Certification for Disability Exceptions (www.uscis.gov/n-648) with the USCIS if you think you qualify for a disability waiver. Unfortunately, the USCIS requires more than just your word. You'll need to get a licensed medical or osteopathic doctor or licensed clinical psychologist to complete and sign your form. In order to qualify for a disability exception, your condition must be expected to last at least one year and cannot have been caused by illegal drug use.

REMEMBER

Even if you gain a disability waiver, you'll still be required to take the Oath of Allegiance — unless your condition is so severe that you are truly unable to do so.

Passing Your Naturalization Interview

No other part of the immigration process fills as many potential citizens with fear as the interview. They fret and worry about what kind of questions they'll be asked, how they'll be judged, and if they can possibly speak well enough and demonstrate enough knowledge of history, civics, and government to live up to the examiner's standards.

TIP

Relax. Passing the USCIS interview is far easier than you may think. In fact, if you make it through the maze of forms, documents, and paperwork necessary to be in the position to be interviewed for citizenship, you will have made it through the hardest part.

REMEMBER

The USCIS is not looking for brilliance or perfection. They just want to know that you have a basic understanding of how to read, write, and speak English, along with an understanding of U.S. history and how our government functions.

Arriving prepared

You already know that you'll be asked about U.S. history and civics, and that you'll need to demonstrate a working knowledge of the English language. But in order to be completely relaxed and prepared for your interview, be aware that the officer may ask you to talk about any of the following:

>> Your background (where you came from, your family, your moral character, and so on)

>> Evidence and documents that support your case for naturalization (things like your employment records, marriage, and involvement in your community)

>> Where you live and how long you've lived there

>> Your feelings about the United States, its Constitution, and its government

>> Your willingness to take the Oath of Allegiance (you can find more on the Oath of Allegiance later in this chapter)

TIP

Be sure to bring to your interview your Alien Registration Card, your passport, and any reentry permits you obtained. Also, if your appointment letter specifically asks for any additional documentation, be sure to bring it.

WARNING

Lying to the USCIS in writing or during the interview will immediately disqualify you. Even if the USCIS finds out that you lied *after* you have been granted citizenship, your citizenship can be taken away. Being truthful with the USCIS is serious business, but as long as you've been truthful at every step of the process, you should have nothing to worry about. Note that when we talk about the kind of lying that results in disqualification, we're talking about untruths that you *knew* were untrue at the time that you told them. In other words, if you lied about your criminal record, you'll be disqualified; if you've committed an *inadvertent misstatement* — unknowingly providing incorrect information, such as being a digit off on your telephone number or having a new address — you should be fine. However, it's important to notify the USCIS of a change of address within ten days of moving.

You can submit the AR-11 Alien Change of Address card https://www.uscis.gov/ar-11 online or mail in the form. Always keep your whereabouts current with the USCIS so that you can receive your case updates and appointment notices without delay.

Giving yourself the best chance for success

We know that no matter how much we tell you not to be nervous, you're going to be, so try to give yourself a break. By following these easy tips, you'll take off some of the pressure in advance:

>> **Be on time!** Why rush yourself? Find out where to go ahead of time. Some USCIS offices have separate entrances for people with particular appointments. Even with an appointment notice, you may still have to wait as much as an hour at some offices just to get into the building — and then wait again after you get to the office waiting room. Expect lines and you won't be disappointed. Also, everyone entering a federal building must pass through security, which takes time (follow instructions to speed your passage). Talk to people familiar with the process in your area (friends in the community, lawyers, or other service providers); they can help you anticipate how far in advance you should plan to arrive so you'll have time to relax — the day is stressful enough already.

>> **Dress as though you're going to a job interview.** You want to make a good impression on the USCIS officer, and although there are no hard and fast rules for the kind of clothing you should wear, looking nice, neat, and tidy doesn't hurt.

>> **Bring copies of any paperwork you think you may need.** If you've taken our advice and kept accurate, organized files and copies of all your documents, you'll be able to easily bring your entire file with you, so you're always super-prepared.

>> **In addition to USCIS documents, bring documents that will support your case — particularly if there have been life changes since you submitted your Form N-400!** Your naturalization appointment letter will have a list of items to bring. If your eligibility is based on marriage to a U.S. citizen, bring financial statements with your name and your spouse's name and address. If you moved, bring a copy of the lease or utility bill. If you recently changed jobs, bring a payroll stub. If you graduated, bring the diploma. If you took a new trip outside of the United States, bring your passport and copy of the ticket. If you got a divorce, bring the divorce decree. If you had a new child, bring a copy of the birth certificate.

Having these documents at your fingertips will help the USCIS examiner to quickly update your case. But don't go overboard — you do not need to bring copies of your income tax returns unless USCIS specifically requested them. If USCIS needs additional documentation, they will send a letter after the interview. Just get yourself to the interview on time and in one piece!

>> **Tell the truth and don't be nervous.** You'll do fine. The calmer and more relaxed you are, the easier the interview will go. Before you know it, the whole thing will be over and you'll be a giant step closer to becoming a U.S. citizen.

Practicing for the Big Three: Reading, writing, and speaking English

Unless you qualify for an age or disability exemption, you must be able to read, write, and speak English to be eligible for naturalization. The USCIS officer doesn't expect you to have perfect grammar, diction, or accent. They just want to know that you can speak and understand *basic* English — enough to get around and function well within U.S. society.

How does the officer determine your English proficiency? They will probably ask you to read or write some simple sentences in English, as well as ask you a few questions about what the words mean.

TIP

You can find advice and exercises to learn and remember USCIS Form N-400 in Chapter 17. And to prepare for the civics, reading, and writing tests, check out Chapter 18.

>> **Reading:** Although there is no official list of USCIS reading sentences, USCIS does provide a Reading Test Vocabulary List for the Naturalization Test (www. uscis.gov/sites/default/files/document/guides/reading_vocab. pdf). The officer will ask you to read a simple question out loud. Typical questions may be "Who was the second president?" or "What is the largest state?" You must read one out of three sentences correctly to pass the reading test.

>> **Writing:** The officer will then dictate a sentence for you to write. Frequently the sentence is a response to the question that you just read, but don't jump ahead! Listen carefully to the complete sentence — the officer can only repeat it once. Although there is no official list of USCIS writing sentences, USCIS does provide a Writing Test Vocabulary List for the Naturalization Test (www.uscis. gov/sites/default/files/document/guides/writing_vocab.pdf) that complements the Reading List Vocabulary List. Typical sentences may be

"Adams was the second president" or "Alaska is the largest state." You must write one out of three sentences correctly to pass the reading test.

>> **Speaking:** The officer evaluates your ability to speak English by the answers you give throughout the interview, from small talk to explaining vocabulary in Form N-400 Part 12. Keep your answers short and simple. If the officer requires a further explanation, they will ask. If you don't understand what an officer says, ask for clarification before you answer the question. Preparing for the English proficiency part of your USCIS interview is easy for some, difficult for others, and rewarding for all! After all, English surrounds you in the United States. Listen to conversations, have a conversation with someone, read the newspaper or even signs and billboards, watch television, listen to the radio, attend classes — opportunities to improve your English proficiency are everywhere! See Chapter 17 for lots of tips and strategies that will help you communicate in fluent English in no time.

THE READING AND WRITING TESTS GO DIGITAL!

On October 1, 2018, USCIS began using digital tablets to administer the English reading and writing tests during naturalization interviews. Although USCIS applicants already used digital tablets to sign or verify parts of their applications, using tablets for the reading and writing tests expanded tablet usage for the application process. USCIS is able to continue using the paper process on a case-by-case basis.

While the eligibility requirements and the subject material of the naturalization test have not changed, applicants are now using a stylus on a digital tablet instead of a paper application. USCIS officers carefully instruct applicants on how to use the tablets before administering the tests:

- For the reading test, a sentence appears on the tablet and the ISO asks the applicant to read it.

- For the writing test, several lines appear on the tablet, replicating the appearance of a piece of blank paper. The ISO reads a sentence aloud and asks the applicant to write it on the tablet.

Applicants continue to take the civics test verbally, without the tablet.

Getting ready for the interview

Some people focus solely on the civics questions — they can recite all 100 civics questions by heart, but have a difficult time reading or writing, or are not familiar with USCIS Form N-400 questions and vocabulary. Remember that you will only be asked 10 civics questions — when you get 6 civics questions correct, the examiner moves on to the reading and writing tests, followed by the "English Test" — 50 to 75 questions based on the USCIS Form N-400. Plan accordingly! Here are some tips:

>> **Prepare the night before:** Arrange for and confirm child- or elder-care several days before your interview. Gas up your car on the way home or confirm your transportation and print out directions. Prepare your clothing and organize your documents — green card, photo ID, and USCIS appointment letter on top. Sleep well and eat a light breakfast and/or lunch. Go with a clear head and a calm heart.

>> **Heads-up, officer:** If there have been any changes or typos on your document, notify your officer when you arrive in the office and before you are sworn in. The officer will note the changes and will ask for additional info during the appropriate part of the interview.

>> **Listen to the entire sentence or command:** Even though you may be anxious, do not anticipate or interrupt the officer. Let them finish giving the entire command or asking the entire question; *then* respond.

>> **Keep it short and sweet:** Speak up. Do not give long answers; keep them short. A simple yes or no response is appropriate. If the officer asks for further information, answer as simply and clearly as you can.

>> **Listen for key words:** Listen for the *key words* — the words that unlock the correct answer to a question.

>> **Clarify before you answer:** Don't guess — clarify! If you missed the key word or do not understand the question, ask the USCIS officer to clarify the question *before* you answer yes or no. For example, you can confirm the word that the officer used (for example, "Did you say 'terrorism' or 'totalitarian'?"); ask the officer to explain unknown vocabulary ("Can you explain 'totalitarian,' please?"); or request that a question be asked in a different way ("Can you ask the question a different way, please?").

>> **I don't remember:** If you do not remember an answer, tell the officer any part of the answer that you do remember. The officer will appreciate your effort and maybe you will remember the answer!

>> **Please repeat:** You can ask the officer to repeat a question, ask the question more slowly, or speak louder. Listen to the full question, and again, pay attention to key words.

>> **More time:** Sometimes you know the answer but need a moment or two to remember and respond. Don't just stare at the officer. You can say, "Let me think," and repeat the key words of the questions to jog your memory.

>> **Reading:** You must read aloud one out of three sentences correctly. Take your time and "sound out" the words before you actually read the sentence aloud for the officer. Remember there is no official list of reading and writing sentences, but we do have a list of 35 practice sentences in Chapter 18.

>> **Dictation:** You must write one out of three dictated sentences correctly. The officer will say the dictated question only two times. When the officer dictates the question the first time, write as many words or letters as you can. If you miss a word, draw a line to remind yourself to listen especially for that word. When the officer reads the sentence again, confirm that you have the correct words and try to fill in the missing word. After the officer finishes the sentence, you then have a moment to fix your sentence and correct your spelling. Focus on the words from the USCIS Writing list — if you spell these words correctly, you will pass the writing test.

A typical citizenship interview

A naturalization interview begins when the officer calls your name. As you walk to the office, the officer will engage you in some "small talk" about the weather, sports, your commute, your family, and so on. "Small talk" has a two-fold purpose: to calm down the applicant and allow the officer to quickly assess your English ability and adjust the language and pace of the interview accordingly.

After you enter the office and are directed to your seat, the officer "swears you in." You must raise your right hand and affirm that you will tell the truth. The officer will then ask you to be seated. The officer will ask if you have any questions or concerns. If you have any updates to your N-400, such as a new trip or a correction such as your middle name, simply say that you have a change or correction. The officer will note this and will ask you further about the change or correction when the appropriate section of the Form N-400 comes up.

The officer will then ask to see your ID, and then will administer the civics, reading, and writing tests. If you successfully complete these tests, you will move on to the Form N-400 section of the interview. If you fail one of these tests but otherwise demonstrate that you can speak and understand English, the officer will move on to the Form N-400 portion of the interview and tell you to come back only on the test that you failed. If a person simply shuts down or responds poorly, the officer will stop the interview and will note that the applicant failed the English portion of the interview, as well as the other tests that they did not pass. Each applicant is given one opportunity for another interview.

Although a USCIS can ask you every single question on your Form N-400, they usually don't because they have thoroughly reviewed your case and will not ask questions that are not applicable to your situation. To be thorough and fair, they will closely follow the sequence of Form N-400.

The officer may ask you to explain one or two terms to verify that you understand what you are affirming or denying. For example, you may be asked: "Have you ever voted in the United States?" Most applicants will say, "No." The officer may follow up with "Why?" An appropriate response would be, "Because I am not a U.S. citizen yet." This demonstrates to the officer that you understand the rights and responsibilities of U.S. citizenship.

There are also several questions about violence. These questions were added in 2014 as a result of changes in national security laws. Although the vocabulary is difficult, the concept is simple: You support human rights and follow the rule of law. You are affirming that you support the democratic principles that are the foundation of the U.S. Constitution. You are confirming that you will be a good U.S. citizen.

Here is an example of a typical interview. Remember, the USCIS officer can ask more questions as required to prove that you are an eligible candidate for naturalization.

1. How are you eligible to become a U.S. citizen?

2. Who sponsored you to become a lawful permanent resident?

3. What is your legal name?

4. Is your legal name different than the name on your green card?

5. What is your date of birth?

6. What date did you become a lawful permanent resident?

7. What is your country of birth?

8. What is your country of nationality?

9. Are you requesting an accommodation because of a physical disability?

10. What is your current home address?

11. How long have you been living in your current home address?

12. Do you have a previous home address?

13. Was your mother or father a U.S. citizen before you were 18 years old?

14. How do you financially support yourself?

15. How many total days were you outside of the United States?

16. How many total trips have you taken outside of the United States?

17. Tell me about your last trip: When did you leave and return to the United States?

18. What is your marital status?

19. Is your spouse a U.S. citizen?

20. Do you have any children?

21. Are any of your children U.S. citizens?

22. Have you ever claimed to be a U.S. citizen?

23. Have you ever voted in any U.S. elections?

24. Do you pay your taxes every year?

25. Do you belong to any groups or organizations?

26. Have you ever been a member of the Communist party?

27. Have you ever been a terrorist?

28. Have you ever badly hurt or killed a person on purpose?

29. Have you ever participated in a rebel group, militia, or army?

30. Have you ever worked in a place like a prison or labor camp?

31. Have you ever been a member of a gang?

32. Have you ever sold or given weapons to another person?

33. Have you ever received military or weapons training?

34. Have you ever forced a child (under 15) to become a soldier?

35. Have you ever committed a crime?

36. Have you ever been arrested?

37. Have you ever been a habitual drunkard?

38. Have you ever sold or smuggled illegal drugs?

39. Have you ever married someone to get a green card?

40. Have you ever lied to the U.S. government to get public benefits (for example, welfare)?

41. Have you ever been deported?

42. Have you ever served in the U.S. armed forces?

43. Do you support the Constitution and the form of government of the United States?

44. Do you understand the full Oath of Allegiance to the United States?

45. Are you willing to take the full Oath of Allegiance to the U.S. government?

46. If the law requires it, are you willing to bear arms in the U.S. Army?

47. What does "bear arms" mean?

48. Are you willing to perform non-combatant services in the U.S. Army?

49. Are you willing to help the government during a national emergency?

50. Do you promise that everything that you said is true?

Studying for the civics test

During your interview, you'll also be required to show that you know about U.S. history and government. You don't need to be an expert and know every important historical date and event that ever happened in the United States. The USCIS just wants to make sure you understand and appreciate what it means to be an American. Find out the important principles that make up our government's foundation and show a basic understanding of the history and events that made our Founding Fathers structure our government the way they did, and you're sure to pass.

REMEMBER

It may seem like a lot to absorb, but if you stay aware, you can't help but pick up new knowledge every day — even by simply watching television! We cover what you need to know, in detail, in Parts 4, 5, and 6 of this book.

Helping your family prepare for their interview

A key component of USCIS immigration policy is family reunification. As soon as many noncitizens gain lawful permanent residence status, they can immediately petition for immediate family members: spouses, minor children, and parents to immigrate to the United States (www.uscis.gov/family). As permanent residents gain citizenship, they can petition for more relatives to immigrate, thereby strengthening family bonds and contributing to the common good.

REMEMBER

Just as your family encouraged you to study hard for a better life, now it is your turn to encourage them to do the same. Just as your father refused to let you quit school early to get a job, insist that he go to his English classes. Just as your mother sat with you to make sure you did your homework, now it is your time to sit with her and practice for the citizenship interview. Remember how your grandparents' stories taught you the whole truths that history books cannot contain.

Remember how your brother's old books and your sister's flash cards gave you an edge over other students. Your family's commitment to you made you a successful person.

>> **Enroll in an English Second Language (ESL) course.** Because the citizenship interview is conducted in English, the best way to prepare is to learn basic English. Check local adult-education centers, community colleges, libraries, and community organizations for classes. Learning is a social activity, and the students learn more from each other than their teachers. Learning English will also help the new immigrant to regain a sense of independence and confidence that they had in their home country.

>> **Speak English at home.** Encourage the new immigrant to practice speaking English at home. Take a couple of minutes every day and review one worksheet or lesson from their ESL class and adapt it to a family situation.

>> **Teach your native language to your children.** Teach your children not only to speak and understand but also read and write in your native language. Native language practice closes the generation gap and encourages fluency, literacy, self-confidence, and cultural identity.

>> **Try USALearns Access America.** USALearns.com has free online self-paced ESL and Citizenship courses. The new course, Access America, is an updated, online version of the old USCIS publication: Welcome to the United States: A Guide for New Immigrant, and is available to download in 14 languages (www.uscis.gov/citizenship/civic-integration/settling-in-the-us). This online course compliments the standard Adult Education ESL civics curriculum focused on American life skills and language acquisition. You can supplement this course with level-appropriate ESL course and then move on to USALearns Citizenship course. Part 2, N-400, is particularly helpful to prepare for the interview.

>> **USCIS Lesson Plans and more.** USCIS Citizenship Resource Center (www.uscis.gov/citizenship) has lesson plans and resources for beginning and intermediate language learners. Extend these lessons by watching videos from Preparing for the Oath (https://americanhistory.si.edu/citizenship), which is a collaboration between the USCIS and the Smithsonian National Museum of American History. Use these resources to create a rich context for the student to understand American civics and history and gain English fluency.

>> **Start small to go big.** Currently applicants have to wait 12 to 18 months from the time they submit their application until the citizenship interview. However, USCIS is committed to reducing the wait time to six months. Start by practicing N-400 questions and civics questions *immediately.*

In the first week, ask five simplified N-400 questions: name, date of birth, country of birth, marital status, and support of the U.S. Constitution plus two civics questions about elected official names. Slightly vary the wording of the questions through the week. Next week, add two more N-400 questions from different parts of the N-400 such as home address and work, plus two more civics questions. Every week, add more two or three N-400 questions, gradually including questions from each part of the N-400 Part 1-12, then start pulling two questions from each section. Add civics questions from printed material (ex: USCIS lesson plans — just a page or two a day). What you are trying to do is implicitly teach your family member the scope and sequence of the N-400 and citizenship interview. You can vary the questions by asking why a question is asked and/or vocabulary definitions. Keep these practice sessions short, about ten or fifteen minutes, which is the approximate length of an actual USCIS interview. Try to practice the citizenship interview the same time every day and get other family members involved. Short, frequent practice slowly and surely builds fluency and civic knowledge.

>> **Get out and about with the family.** Because the citizenship interview occurs outside of the home and classroom, it is important to practice in public by exploring the community and America. Notice street signs related to civics answers (Washington Ave., Adams Dr.). Go to library story times and have fun in the park. Visit local historical sites and discuss how they are connected to American history. Make an extra effort to attend community celebration of federal holidays such as Independence and Juneteenth parades and picnics. Enjoy America!

Communicating with the USCIS

Be sure to notify the USCIS each and every time you move. Your accurate address is the only way they have to stay in touch with you. If your interview appointment notification gets sent to the wrong address, you can miss your opportunity for naturalization simply because you didn't know about it. Don't take chances with your immigration proceedings by being careless about communications.

What should you do if you have to miss your USCIS interview appointment? Unless you have absolutely no other choice, do everything in your power *not* to miss your scheduled interview. Yes, you can reschedule, but be aware that rescheduling is likely to add several months to the naturalization process. If you must miss your interview, call the National Customer Service Center (NCSC) at 800-375-5283 to request rescheduling. The NCSC will record the information and pass it on to the local office, which will make the final decision regarding whether to reschedule your appointment. To be on the safe side, also send a request by certified mail (with return receipt) to the USCIS office where your interview is scheduled and ask to have it rescheduled as soon as possible — the earlier the better!

WARNING

If you miss your scheduled appointment without notifying the USCIS, they will close your case. If you let this happen, there may still be hope as long as not more than one year has passed since your case was closed. Contact the USCIS and ask for your interview to be rescheduled. If you knew about the interview and have let more than one year go by since your case was closed, the game is over — your request and application will be denied, and the only way to get it started again is to file a new application.

Following Up: What Happens After the Interview

After your interview, the officer will give you a Form N-652, which simply tells you whether your application was granted, denied, or continued. It will also note which portion of the interview you will be re-tested on. If your application was granted, congratulations! The letter will tell you where and when to go to attend your swearing-in ceremony.

If your application was *continued* (put on hold) or even denied, don't panic. The game is not over yet. If your case is continued, you probably just need to provide more documents (as detailed in an N-14 letter) or retake the English or civics portion of the test. If your application was denied, you still have an appeal process that may result in the denial being overturned. Chapter 1 gives more detail about both scenarios.

WARNING

Keep in mind, you only have 30 days after receiving your denial letter to file for an appeal hearing. After 30 days, the USCIS will close your case.

Taking the Oath of Allegiance

Assuming your interview and tests went well, you'll probably be scheduled to come back for a swearing-in ceremony where you'll take the Oath of Allegiance. Taking the oath, also known as Attachment to the Constitution, demonstrates your loyalty and allegiance to the United States of America. At some USCIS offices, you can choose to take the oath the same day as your interview rather than come back for a group ceremony. If you choose this option, you will usually be asked to come back later that same day. The USCIS officer will then give you the oath on the spot. Most new citizens, however, come back at a later date for a group ceremony at the USCIS office or in a court. In either case, you officially become a naturalized citizen as soon as you take the Oath of Allegiance to the United States.

Just before you become naturalized, be ready to surrender your green card. Don't worry, you won't need it anymore.

When you take the Oath of Allegiance at your naturalization ceremony, you make several important promises of loyalty to the United States. Loyalty means showing consistent support to something or someone. At your naturalization ceremony, you will raise your right hand and say the oath. After the oath, you become a U.S. citizen. As a new citizen, you have new responsibilities and duties that you promised in the oath. We talk more about the Oath of Allegiance's meaning and vocabulary in Chapter 17.

Here are the key principles of the Oath of Allegiance:

>> I promise not to follow or obey the leader of the country which I came from.

>> I promise to follow the laws of the United States.

>> I promise to be loyal to the United States.

>> I promise to use a weapon to protect the United States if needed.

>> I promise to work in the U.S. armed forces without using a weapon if needed.

>> I promise to do important work for the safety and security of the United States.

>> I promise to fulfill all of the responsibilities of U.S. citizenship.

This is the actual oath that you recite:

"I hereby declare, on oath, that I absolutely and entirely renounce and abjure all allegiance and fidelity to any foreign prince, potentate, state, or sovereignty, of whom or which I have heretofore been a subject or citizen;

. . . that I will support and defend the Constitution and laws of the United States of America against all enemies, foreign and domestic;

. . . that I will bear true faith and allegiance to the same;

. . . that I will bear arms on behalf of the United States when required by the law;

. . . that I will perform noncombatant service in the Armed Forces of the United States when required by the law;

. . . that I will perform work of national importance under civilian direction when required by the law; and

. . . that I take this obligation freely, without any mental reservation or purpose of evasion; so help me God."

After you take the oath, you have all the rights and benefits given to United States citizens who were born here. Well, almost — you won't be eligible to become president or vice president, but other than that, the sky's the limit!

Taking care of a few more important tasks

Apply for a passport as soon as you receive your Certificate for Naturalization. A passport also serves as proof of your citizenship and it's much easier to carry than the certificate itself (not to mention the fact that getting a replacement certificate, if you ever lose your original, can take up to a year). Pick up a passport application at your swearing-in ceremony or at your local post office — or online at www.travel.state.gov.

If it is not already in your seat at the ceremony, people from your county Registrar of Voters will hand you a voters registration card on your way out. Don't wait another minute — register to vote and exercise your right to participate in democracy!

You should also update your record with the Social Security Administration by applying for a new Social Security card (www.ssa.gov/forms/ss-5.pdf). Proudly check the "U.S. Citizen" box on Line 5, Citizenship.

If you have a U.S. driver's license or state-issued identification card (ID), take this opportunity to update your record with the agency that issues driver's licenses in your state. You may update your ID information and photo or apply for a REAL ID.

TIP

Now that you are a citizen, share this gift with others. Volunteer at your local adult school or community center and help people prepare for their citizenship interview. Find volunteer opportunities at www.volunteer.gov/s/ht.

Chapter **6**

Keeping on Top of Changes in Immigration Law

mmigration laws change constantly. In the past 20+ years, there have been two major revisions of the entire body of immigration law, and two major updates to the USCIS Form N-400 application for naturalization, as well as a variety of measures that have enhanced security and provided additional benefits to would-be immigrants. And it's not just the laws that change — just this year the entire United States immigration authority was restructured.

This chapter not only fills you in on the newest and most significant changes in immigration law, but it also shows you how to stay up-to-date with any new changes that may take place long after this book is published.

Understanding the Post-9/11 Changes to the Immigration System

The terrorist acts of September 11, 2001 (USCIS 100:86), which were perpetrated by non-U.S. citizens, prompted policymakers to examine how the U.S. polices its borders and administers immigration.

Balancing the prevailing notion that immigration is good for the United States (and part of our heritage) with border-security concerns, Washington decided against maintaining a unified immigration authority. Instead, lawmakers separated the primary functions of deciding eligibility for benefits and enforcing restrictions on immigration, taking them out of the Department of Justice and placing them under the authority of a new government agency — the Department of Homeland Security (DHS). Three separate divisions now handle these functions:

>> **U.S. Customs and Border Protection (CBP):** Controls U.S. borders and enforces immigration and customs regulations

>> **U.S. Immigration and Customs Enforcement (ICE):** Enforces immigration law

>> **U.S. Citizenship and Immigration Services (USCIS):** Administers the naturalization and immigration system

TECHNICAL STUFF

As of March 1, 2003, the Immigration and Naturalization Service (INS) technically ceased to exist and the USCIS took over the immigration benefits portion of the INS's former duties. Designed to enhance the service of the tens of thousands of people who interacted with the INS in the past, as well as new immigration cases, the bureau now serves the following functions:

>> *Adjudication,* or judgment, over family- and employment-based immigration petitions

>> Issuance of employment authorization and travel documents

>> Asylum and refugee processing

>> Naturalization and implementation of special status programs such as Temporary Protected Status

Overhauling Immigration Laws in 1990

The Immigration Act of November 29, 1990 (IMMACT90) significantly over-hauled and changed the system. In some ways the laws broadened opportunities for people wanting to immigrate to the United States, but in other ways it made immigrating a lot tougher. Important points of the 1990 changes include the following:

>> It increased the total number of immigrants allowed to legally live and work in the country.

>> It revised the grounds for exclusion and deportation, especially on the grounds of politics or ideology. For instance, the act repealed the bar against the admission of communists as nonimmigrants.

>> It gave the attorney general the power to grant temporary protected status to undocumented alien nationals of designated countries subject to armed conflict or natural disasters.

>> It revised certain existing nonimmigrant visa categories as well as established new ones.

>> It established the Diversity Visa (DV) Lottery Program.

>> It substantially altered existing permanent resident categories by establishing new employment categories and redefining who constitutes an "immediate relative" in case of family-based immigration.

>> It broadened the authority to naturalize aliens to allow administration of the oath by the attorney general, as well as by federal district and certain state courts.

>> It changed some requirements for naturalization, including reducing residency requirements.

>> It broadened the definition of *aggravated felony* and imposed new legal restrictions on aliens convicted of such crimes.

>> It revised criminal and deportation provisions.

>> It restructured the 32 grounds for exclusion into nine categories, including revising and repealing some of the grounds (especially some health grounds).

After the 1990 restructuring, changes continued to be made in immigration law, but they were either smaller changes or laws that affected only certain small groups of immigrants. However, by the time 1996 rolled around, U.S. immigration law underwent another round of major changes.

Understanding the Significance of the 1996 Immigration Law Changes

The immigration law changes of 1996 (known as the Illegal Immigration Reform and Immigrant Responsibility Act, or IIRAIRA) made things considerably tougher for many immigrants. Spurred by terrorist activities abroad, a growing domestic crime problem, as well as financial worries, the laws got tougher on crime, reduced government benefits to immigrants (both legal and illegal immigrants), and sought to better protect the U.S. borders.

Getting tougher on crime

The 1996 immigration laws took the issue of crime very seriously, expanding criteria for removal, including allowing deportation of nonviolent offenders prior to completion of their sentence of imprisonment. In addition, those with criminal records had a harder time immigrating, because the law also

>> Established a criminal alien identification system

>> Provided access to certain confidential immigration and naturalization files through court order

>> Granted the government authority to conduct alien smuggling investigations

>> Expedited the process of removing criminal aliens from the United States

>> Established deportation procedures for certain nonimmigrant criminal aliens

Updates to USCIS Form N-400, Application for Naturalization

In 2014, USCIS updated USCIS Form N-400, Application for Naturalization, adding questions about war crimes, participation in violent groups, weapons training, and child soldiers (Part 12:14-22) to conform to a provision in the Intelligence Reform and Terrorism Prevention Act (IRTPA) of 2004 and Child Soldier Prevention Act of 2007. The additional information was important for USCIS to make a complete and informed determination of an applicant's eligibility for U.S. citizenship. The questions relate not only to concerns associated with good moral character but also to issues relating to the security of the United States. Also, a bar code was added to the bottom of the form in order to track an individual application more easily. The N-400 expanded from 10 to 21 pages!

In 2016, a slightly reformatted Form N-400 was introduced with a double-bar code, which encoded your information into the bar code as it was filled out as a PDF. In late 2017, USCIS release the My USCIS online account, which allows applicants to compete the N-400 and submit evidence and payment online. Since then, USCIS has also introduced a growing set of case management tools. To support accessibility, USCIS is currently working on an audio component to the online Form N-400 for the visually impaired. USCIS is committed to improving customer service by transitioning from a paper-based to a digital environment.

TECHNICAL STUFF

Technically, deportation proceedings don't exist anymore — thanks to IIRAIRA. In the past, there were two kinds of proceedings in immigration court:

>> **Exclusion:** For folks stopped while trying to come into the country

>> **Deportation:** For folks already here whom INS wanted to ship out

Now there is just one form of proceeding: removal. However, you can get involved in removal proceedings in one of two ways:

>> Through being denied admission to the United States (which is based on exclusion grounds)

>> Through being required to leave the United States after being admitted (which is based on deportation grounds)

These two bases for removal are similar to the prior deportation procedures.

THE IMMIGRATION AND NATIONALITY ACT OF 1952

The Immigration and Nationality Act (INA) — the basic body of immigration law in the United States — collected and restructured the many immigration-related laws of the time. Over the years, the Immigration and Nationality Act has been *amended,* or changed, many times. Amendments allow Congress to change or modify one or more parts of a law without having to rewrite the entire statute. Sometimes the changes or amendments cover entire sections of the act; other times the changes are as subtle as a word or two that provides further clarification of an issue.

Proving you won't be a burden to the system

Meeting financial obligations and requirements also got tougher for immigrants in 1996. The Personal Responsibility and Work Opportunity Reconciliation Act severely limited access to public benefits for non–U.S. citizens — whether in a legal immigration status or not — in the following ways:

>> It barred non-U.S. citizens (with certain exceptions) from obtaining food stamps and Supplemental Security Income (SSI) and most other federal public-assistance programs as well as established screening procedures for current and future recipients of these programs. Of course, the law also prohibits illegal aliens from receiving most federal, state, and local public benefits.

>> It provided states with flexibility in setting public benefit eligibility rules for legal immigrants, allowing them to bar legal immigrants from both major federal programs and state programs.

>> It increased responsibilities for those sponsoring family members, including instituting a new, legally enforceable affidavit of support. (You can find out more about the affidavit of support in Chapter 3.)

>> It required immigration status to be verified in order for eligible aliens to receive most federal public benefits.

All the preceding applies to both legal and illegal aliens as well as nonimmigrants.

Protecting America's borders

The Illegal Immigration Reform and Immigrant Responsibility Act of 1996 increased border personnel, equipment, and technology at ports of entry, increasing penalties for illegal entry, passport and visa fraud, and failure to depart. The law also sought to enforce laws and protect the United States by

>> Increasing penalties for alien smuggling

>> Speeding deportation proceedings

>> Instituting temporary bars to admissibility for aliens seeking to reenter the country after having been unlawfully present in the United States

>> Prohibiting those individuals who renounced their U.S. citizenship in order to avoid U.S. tax obligations from reentering the country

Recognizing Helpful Immigration Law Changes

Not all new immigration laws are designed to make things tougher for people trying to immigrate. Through the years a variety of laws have been passed to help victims — victims of violence, victims of war, victims of oppressive regimes, and so on. For more information, see the USCIS Humanitarian website (`www.uscis.gov/humanitarian`). Some of the most important new laws of this type include the following:

>> **The Victims of Trafficking and Violence Protection Act, 2000:** An expansion of the Violence Against Women Act (VAWA) of 1994, the newer act helps victims of domestic violence (both men and women) escape the cycle of violence. These laws allow abused spouses and children of sponsor citizens or legal permanent residents (LPRs) to self-petition for immigration benefits. It is important to note that even though this is known as the Violence Against *Women* Act, it is not for women only. Abused husbands can also seek relief through this avenue.

>> **The Legal Immigration and Family Equity (LIFE) Act, 2000:** The LIFE Act provides for the following:

- Expansion of the Nicaraguan Adjustment and Central American Relief Act (NACARA) of 1997 to provide eligibility for adjustment to certain Nicaraguans, Cubans, Guatemalans, Salvadorans, and nationals of the former Soviet bloc.

- Expansion of the Haitian Refugee and Immigration Fairness Act (HRIFA) of 1998 to provide eligibility for adjustment to certain Haitians.

- Expansion of the eligibility for certain benefits to all applications filed by April 30, 2001, provided the beneficiary was in the United States on December 21, 2000 (the date the LIFE Act was signed). It also created new nonimmigrant visas to allow spouses and dependents of lawful permanent residents and citizens to come to the United States when processing of their permanent resident petitions is delayed.

» **The Child Status Protection Act (CSPA), 2002:** This act allows child/dependent-beneficiaries of citizens to maintain their eligibility even after they *age out* (turn 21) as long as the original petition was filed before the child turned 21. However, if the sponsor is an LPR, different rules apply, based on the priority date.

» **The Cuban Family Reunification Parole (CFRP) Program, 2007:** This program allows U.S. citizens and LPRs to apply for parole for their family members in Cuba. If granted parole, these family members may immigrate to the United States without waiting for their immigrant visas to become available.

» **The DREAM Act, 2010, and the Deferred Action for Childhood Arrivals (executive action), 2012:** On June 15, 2012, the Secretary of Homeland Security announced that certain people who came to the United States as children and meet several guidelines may request consideration of deferred action for a period of two years, subject to renewal. They are also eligible for work authorization. Deferred action is a use of prosecutorial discretion to defer removal action against an individual for a certain period of time and does not provide lawful status.

» **The Central American Minors (CAM) Refugee and Parole Program, 2014:** This program allows certain qualified children who are nationals of El Salvador, Guatemala, and Honduras to apply for refugee status and possible resettlement in the United States.

» **The Haitian Family Reunification Parole (HFRP) Program, 2014:** This program allows U.S. citizens and lawful permanent residents to apply for parole for their family members in Haiti. If granted parole, these family members may come to the United States before their immigrant visa priority dates became current. Once in the United States, these noncitizens can apply for temporary work permits while they wait for adjustment of status.

» **Filipino World War II Veterans Parole (FWVP), 2016:** This program allows certain Filipino World War II veterans and their U.S. citizen and lawful permanent resident spouses to apply for parole for certain family members. If approved for parole, family members may immigrate to the United States before their immigrant visas become available.

- **Afghan SIV Program, 2014 and 2021:** The Emergency Security Supplemental Appropriations Act, 2021, as enacted on July 30, 2021, authorized 8,000 additional Special Immigrant Visas (SIVs) for Afghan principal applicants, for a total of 34,500 visas allocated since December 19, 2014. The Department of State's authority to issue SIVs to Afghan nationals under section 602(b) of the Afghan Allies Protection Act of 2009, as amended, will continue until all visa numbers allocated under the act are issued.

  For the latest update about the Afghan SIV program, see `https://travel.state.gov/content/travel/en/us-visas/immigrate/special-immg-visa-afghans-employed-us-gov.html`.

  For further information about Afghan immigration petitions, see `www.uscis.gov/humanitarian/information-for-afghans`.

- **Deferred Enforced Departure (DED):** A temporary order issued by the president to the DHS prevents the removal of DED individuals from the United States for a specified period of time. The DED also allows these individuals to get a work permit. As of January 2022, people from Liberia, Hong Kong, and Venezuela are protected by DED. For more information, see the DED section of the USCIS Humanitarian website (`www.uscis.gov/humanitarian`).

- **Temporary Protected Status:** The United States may extend temporary protected status (TPS) to noncitizens from countries under severe threat of danger due to war, environmental disasters, or political instability. Under TPS, noncitizens cannot be deported, can work, and can travel outside the United States. It is difficult, but not impossible, to adjust one's status from TPS to permanent residence as long the applicant is vigilant in maintaining legal status. As of March 2022, TPS countries include Afghanistan, Burma (Myanmar), El Salvador, Haiti, Honduras, Nepal, Nicaragua, Somalia, South Sudan, Sudan, Syria, Ukraine, Venezuela, and Yemen. For more information, see the TPS section of the USCIS Humanitarian website (`www.uscis.gov/humanitarian`).

Staying Abreast of Changes in Immigration Law

With immigration laws changing so frequently, how can you keep up with what's going on? The USCIS Humanitarian website (`www.uscis.gov/humanitarian`) should keep you up to date with the latest changes in immigration law. Reading newspapers or listening to or watching comprehensive television or radio news should also keep you up-to-date with major changes (although some smaller ones may not get coverage). *The Immigration Law Daily* (www.ilw.com), an internet-based immigration publication, is also a good source of news.

Another great source for immigration law changes is the nonprofit National Immigration Law Center (www.nilc.org). Specializing in immigration law and the employment and public benefits rights of immigrants, the center protects and promotes the rights and opportunities of low-income immigrants and their family members.

One final source is the dark blue news alert banner near the top of the USCIS.gov home page that features critical immigration policy alerts. You can read all of USCIS news releases by selecting the Newsroom tab at the top of the page. While you are in the Newsroom, click the Social Media Directory and follow USCIS on Twitter, Facebook, Instagram, LinkedIn, and YouTube for news alerts. If you need some inspiration, search on the hashtag #newUScitizens to see photos and stories of new citizens and their proud families basking in the afterglow of their natural-ization ceremonies.

TIP

Are you ready to petition for a family member to join you in the United States? For information about visa wait times, you can see current and past issues of the monthly *Visa Bulletin* at the State Department website at https://travel.state.gov/content/travel/en/legal/visa-law0/visa-bulletin.html.

REMEMBER

Rumors of amnesty and other provisions often spread through immigrant communities. If you hear of something that you think may benefit you, the best thing to do is to check with a qualified immigration attorney or legal service provider. You can find out more about hiring a reputable attorney in Chapter 7.

Chapter **7**

Getting Help When You Need It

The immigration process can be complex. Sometimes even seemingly simple cases can get bogged down in endless rounds of documentation and complicated forms and paperwork. Often, the best thing you can do is get professional help. But how do you find ethical, reliable help? Not all attorneys or immigration services are worth the money. Some may not be what they seem or may make false promises. In this chapter, we show you how to find attorneys and organizations that can help you in your quest for citizenship, and we help you avoid those that can waste your time or money.

Recognizing When You Need Professional Help

In almost all cases, potential immigrants and/or citizens can benefit from consulting with a qualified immigration attorney or legal service provider, especially if their case involves any unusual circumstances such as a criminal record, long-term absences from the United States, or being out of legal immigration status.

An *immigration attorney* is licensed to practice law by at least one state or the District of Columbia and should have some level of expertise in immigration matters.

Your attorney may or may not have studied the subject of immigration in law school, but they should have some foundation in the subject and continually work to keep up with changes in the law.

You can also find lots of non-attorney legal-service providers, which provide legal-service programs for immigrants. These programs are usually staffed primarily with non-attorneys — sometimes called *counselors.* Counselors do much the same work that attorneys do, and some have been doing it much longer than most attorneys you'll meet. Legal services provided by a reputable organization — whether an attorney or a counselor — should be satisfactory. You should feel confident that any work done by a counselor in a reputable organization is reviewed by an attorney. Generally, counselors are not authorized to represent you before the U.S. Citizenship and Immigration Services (USCIS) or in court — unless they become accredited immigration representatives.

Not quite attorneys, *accredited immigration representatives* are like super-counselors, specially trained in immigration law. In order for a representative to be accredited, the U.S. government must officially recognize the organization that counselor works for. In order to qualify for recognition, the organization must agree to keep any fees for their services low.

REMEMBER

These organizations exist to help people who can't otherwise afford the services of a qualified immigration attorney.

TECHNICAL
STUFF

The designation of accredited representatives is given by the Executive Office for Immigration Review (EOIR), part of the Department of Justice (DOJ). Technically, an agency must first apply to be recognized by the EOIR and then apply to have its non-attorney staff accredited. For a monthly updated list of low-fee organizations accredited by the DOJ EOIR to help you with your naturalization or represent you in immigration court, see the DOJ EOIR's list of pro bono legal service providers at www.justice.gov/eoir/list-pro-bono-legal-service-providers.

You may also want to make sure that your attorney is *not* on the DOJ EOIR's list of attorneys and representatives who are currently ineligible to practice immigration law at www.justice.gov/eoir/list-of-currently-disciplined-practitioners.

Of course, free or low-cost legal services don't necessarily have to be provided by a recognized agency or an agency with accredited representatives. For instance, an agency that relies solely on lawyers for representation does not need to be recognized or have accredited representatives.

An attorney or accredited representative can advise you on what to expect from the immigration process, as well as warn you of the risks. They can help you obtain legal status from the USCIS or represent you in immigration court.

WARNING

You'll find lots of websites that will offer you the privilege of downloading or filling out forms online for a fee. Don't pay it. Not only can you download forms for free at the USCIS website (www.uscis.gov/humanitarian), but also, the forms at for pay websites are often not even current. By going directly to the source — namely the USCIS — you'll always be guaranteed that you're getting the most recent forms.

Seeking Professional Help

With all the questionable services and attorneys out there, how do you go about finding ethical, reliable help? If you don't know any qualified attorneys personally, stay away from quick internet searches — not because there aren't any good attorneys on the web (there are plenty), but because distinguishing a reputable immigration service or lawyer from a less-than-qualified one simply by looking at an online ad is difficult if not impossible.

A good place to start is with friends or family members who have already successfully gained lawful immigrant status. Ask for recommendations from people you already trust.

TIP

Another good way to find a qualified reputable attorney is to search the American Immigration Lawyers Association (AILA; www.ailalawyer.com), a national association made up of over 15,000 attorneys and law professors who practice and teach immigration law. Nonprofit and *nonpartisan* (meaning they have no political affiliation), AILA provides its members with information, legal services, and continuing legal education that keeps them current with immigration law changes. AILA's members represent tens of thousands of people throughout the United States seeking lawful permanent residence, often representing foreign students, entertainers, athletes, and asylum seekers on a *pro bono* (free-of-charge) basis. AILA can help you find an attorney in your area who is currently a member in good standing of the state *bar association*. (In this case the word *bar* refers to a legal organization — it has nothing to do with cocktails, or steel beams . . . yet another example of how English can be a confusing language to master. Not to worry, you can find tips for improving your English in Chapter 17.)

Knowing the warning signs to watch out for

WARNING

Recognizing the warning signs that indicate that you may be dealing with an unethical attorney or immigration service is critical. Keep in mind the following, and if any of these items apply to your situation, take it as a sign to investigate further and make sure you're getting the qualified help you need from a reputable representative and at a reasonable price:

>> **Beware of any services that can't or won't give you an honest estimate, in advance, of the cost of their services.** Ideally, you should be asked to sign a written agreement (called a *retainer*) that specifies the service the attorney or representative will provide, how much it costs, how payment is to be made, and how to terminate the agreement.

>> **Never give money to anyone who asks for money to influence, or *bribe*, an immigration official, even if that person claims to know someone who can help you in this way.** It is never a good idea to take bribes. The world can be a cruel place, and there have been operators who will take your money and then leave it to you to sort it out with the USCIS.

>> **If something sounds too good to be true, it usually is.** According to AILA, you should beware of notaries, consultants, service bureaus, travel agents, or anyone else who promises a quick, easy solution to your immigration problems. One of the key words here is *promises.* Anyone who absolutely *guarantees* to get you a visa, green card, or other immigration benefit after you pay them a designated fee should seriously raise your suspicions.

>> **Most citizenship applicants *don't* need a lawyer, but. . . .** Although most people can fill out USCIS forms without legal assistance (especially if you submit your N-400 application online via `https://my.uscis.gov`), you may want to consult an immigration legal services organization *if* you have any "red flags" — problems that may affect your naturalization case such as deportation, visa irregularities, arrests, tax problems, marriage problems, medical issues, and so on.

>> **Beware when dealing with lawyers from other countries who don't know U.S. laws and are not licensed to practice in the U.S.** They can't provide the help you really need, cannot represent you, and cannot help you resolve any legal issues in a U.S. court.

TIP

If you aren't sure whether the person offering you immigration services is a lawyer or an accredited representative, ask to see the accreditation letters or state bar admission certificate. If you're still not sure, call the state bar association. You can usually find the contact information for your state's association through a quick internet search. Entering "state bar associations" will bring up lots of sites with links to the various state bar associations — look for the ".gov" domain.

REMEMBER

In the United States, practicing law without a license is illegal.

Consulting an immigration attorney

Because United States immigration law is so complex, with countless exceptions to every rule, a good attorney can really help your chances by thoroughly analyzing your unique case and circumstances and recommending the best way for you to obtain legal immigration status. A good immigration attorney is worth their weight in gold, because they stay current with the latest changes in immigration law — something very difficult for a layperson without legal training to do. A good attorney also has the experience to work every possible angle and advantage to help you gain legal permanent immigration status. Other ways an attorney can help your case include the following:

» Determining the best way to pursue your immigration goals

» Explaining all the immigration benefits for which you may be eligible

» Properly completing and submitting your immigration forms and documents

» Representing you in court or in discussions with the USCIS

» Filing appeals if necessary

Don't be afraid to shop around for an immigration attorney, asking many questions in the process. Try to visit or talk with an attorney personally before making a final decision to hire them. If you decide to go to an attorney, provide honest information and the correct documents so that the attorney can give you accurate information, resolve irregularities, and present your case in the best light.

TIP

Before you make an appointment to talk with a lawyer, always ask whether there's an initial consultation fee. Although charging an initial consultation fee is a common practice, you want to be sure you know in advance what you'll have to pay.

Try to get an idea of how knowledgeable your potential attorney is about current immigration law. Get their opinion on your particular case, including its strengths and weaknesses. Your lawyer should be able to tell you how much their services cost, giving you an honest estimate of how much it will cost to represent your case. The attorney should also agree to keep you informed of any additional costs that come up during the immigration process.

If for any reason you're not satisfied with the attorney, or with their qualifications or answers to your questions, keep looking. In immigration, as in love, you have to shop around!

Reaching for a helping hand: Nonprofit immigration organizations

Local nonprofit immigration assistance services are very low cost or even free, as long as you're able to meet the particular organization's low-income eligibility requirements.

Before working with an immigration organization, meet with them and ask for references to make sure that they have a good reputation. Find out whether an attorney, a counselor, or an accredited representative will handle your case. Be aware that many accredited representatives offer only limited types of assistance, so make sure you feel comfortable that the agency has the skills to help in your unique circumstances.

The Executive Office for Immigration Review (EOIR) provides listings of competent free immigration help throughout the country. The agency created the *pro bono program* in April 2000 to help improve access to legal advice and counseling for low-income aliens. The program also gives many people who may not otherwise have it access to legal representation in immigration court and during appeals. To find listings of agencies in your geographical area, visit the EOIR website at www.justice.gov/eoir/list-pro-bono-legal-service-providers. Click your state and download a list organized by county. This list includes contact information and languages spoken by their representatives. Start by contacting the organization closest to you and call for an appointment. Many organizations host weekly free drop-in clinics, which is a good introduction to the team that will support you during the naturalization process.

TIP

SEEKING OUT LOW- OR NO-COST IMMIGRATION ASSISTANCE

Many churches and religious organizations offer low- or no-cost immigrant assistance, so asking your clergyperson to see if any programs may be available to help you is always a good idea.

Be sure to check at any nearby law schools as well because they often offer immigration clinics where supervised students hone their immigration law skills while helping low-income aliens realize their immigration dreams.

Three of the largest immigration legal-services networks are

- Catholic Legal Immigration Network, Inc. | CLINIC Affiliate Directory: cliniclegal. org/find-legal-help/affiliates/directory

- International Rescue Committee | IRC: www.rescue.org/where-we-work

- New Americans Campaign Partners & Affiliates: www.newamericanscampaign. org/finding-assistance

Taking advantage of free immigration help from the government

Although the government won't provide someone to represent you in immigration proceedings, it does offer a lot of free information to help you in your quest for citizenship.

As we discuss in earlier chapters, the internet is the best way to get the latest and most up-to-date information and forms. Start at the USCIS website (www.uscis.gov).

REMEMBER

You can download all USCIS forms from www.uscis.gov/forms. Emma, the USCIS virtual assistant, pops up when you visit USCIS.gov — she can answer many questions and guide you to the correct info. Visit the USCIS Tools page www.uscis.gov/tools to check your case status, processing times, fees, and other vital info. If you still need to contact USCIS, go to the USCIS contact page at www.uscis.gov/about-us/contact-us or call the USCIS toll-free in the United States at 800-375-5283, 24 hours a day. If you call Monday through Friday from 8 a.m. to 8 p.m. Eastern, except on federal holidays, you can even ask questions of a real live person.

TIP

The old USCIS booklet *A Guide to Naturalization* (M-476) is now a webpage (www.uscis.gov/citizenship/learn-about-citizenship/citizenship-and-naturalization/a-guide-to-naturalization), which features clearer language and informative graphics about immigration and naturalization. Also, the entire USCIS website is accessible in Spanish at www.uscis.gov/es and the USCIS Multilingual Resource Center www.uscis.gov/tools/multilingual-resource-center offers information in many languages including American Sign Language, braille, and large print.

Taking citizenship test-prep classes

Some people opt to take classes to help them prepare to take the citizenship English and civics tests. Although taking a class isn't necessary or required (you may study on your own), many people find that the classroom environment helps them stay focused on the subject at hand and accomplish their goals in a reasonable time period. Another advantage of attending citizenship preparation classes is that the class forces you to interact with others, which in turn will improve your communication skills.

Check adult-education centers and libraries in your area to find low- or no-cost citizenship test-prep classes. These classes are often held after hours at high schools, community colleges, community centers, or churches. Look for flyers or ask questions at any of these locations to find classes near you.

REMEMBER

Taking a General Educational Development (GED) test-prep class will not only help you prepare to take your citizenship test, but it will also earn you the equivalent of a U.S. high school diploma — a minimum educational requirement for many jobs. Look for GED prep classes in the same places you look for citizenship classes.

AVOID SCAMS

You worked hard to get to America, and you probably work even harder to stay here. Unfortunately, there are people who are ready to take advantage of you and separate you from your hard-earned money. USCIS has joined together with the Federal Trade Commission in developing anti-scam resources to protect the integrity of the immigration system and the immigrant community.

Report scams to your state consumer protection office. If you lost money or other possessions in a scam, report it to your local police, too. Find your state agency at www.uscis.gov/scams-fraud-and-misconduct/avoid-scams/report-immigration-scams.

You can also report fraud, scams, and bad business practices to the federal government's website: https://reportfraud.ftc.gov.

Scams can range from government imposters, fake job importunities, identity theft, or paying money to "jump the line." For a quick list of common immigration scams and how to avoid them, visit www.uscis.gov/scams-fraud-and-misconduct/avoid-scams/common-scams.

You can use this form is for reporting suspected immigration benefit fraud and abuse to USCIS: www.uscis.gov/report-fraud/uscis-tip-form.

Forward suspicious fraudulent immigrant services-based social media accounts and phishing emails to the USCIS Webmaster USCIS: webmaster@uscis.dhs.gov.

Recent refugees and immigrants (multiple languages) can find information at https://consumer.ftc.gov/features/avoiding-scams-information-recent-refugees-immigrants.

Stories based on complaints can help detect and stop common scams. Of particular interest are the fotonovelas (graphic novels) about notario scams and government imposters. These fotonovelas are available for free download or bulk purchase:

English: https://consumer.ftc.gov/features/fotonovelas

Spanish: https://consumidor.ftc.gov/destacado/destacado-s0031-fotonovelas

Chapter **8**

Troubleshooting Immigration Glitches

Like dealing with any government agency, dealing with the USCIS involves *bureaucracy* — a complex set of procedures that you must follow exactly in order to successfully complete the immigration process. As frustrating as it may be, following rules and protocol — even when dealing with the worst-case immigration scenarios like denials, rejections, or even removal from the country — is important.

Communicating with the USCIS

By accessing the USCIS Tools and Resources website at `www.uscis.gov/tools/uscis-tools-and-resources/uscis-tools-and-resources`, you can check your case status, see case processing times, submit a case inquiry, download forms, check fees, and much, much more. Ask Emma, the USCIS digital assistant, a question and it can immediately guide you to the correct page. USCIS Tools and Resources are available 24 hours a day, 7 days a week, from a cellphone, tablet, or computer.

If you need to talk to a representative for another reason and you're in the United States or a U.S. territory, call the USCIS Contact Center at 800-375-5283 (TTY 800-767-1833) or outside the United States at 212-620-3418. Representatives are available Monday through Friday from 8 a.m. to 8 p.m. Eastern time, except on federal holidays.

You may have to wait to speak to a representative by phone. Please try the USCIS online tools first. If you want to speak to someone and your issue can't be resolved right away, your request will be sent to an Immigration Services Officer. USCIS will send you an email to confirm your request and give an estimate as to when a USCIS representative will contact you. You will also receive a text message and/or email one to two business days before USCIS contacts you. The USCIS representatives cannot give you legal advice about your case, but they can give you information about naturalization and immigration forms and rescheduling appointments.

Call the Contact Center at 800-375-5283 to request proof of your immigration status for work or travel, pending expiration of a temporary visitor's lawful stay (and the need to show "satisfactory departure"), or emergency travel documents. The USCIS representative can make an appointment for you at a local USCIS field office to resolve your issue.

USCIS makes two attempts to contact customers by phone. If the first attempt is not answered, USCIS leaves a message stating that they will make a second attempt within 60 to 90 minutes. If USCIS is unable to reach the individual after the second attempt, the Contact Center will send an email stating that the agency tried to reach them and instruct them to call back or use other tools.

For more information about the USCIS Contact Center, go to www.uscis.gov/contactcenter.

WARNING

Before you call the Contact Center, please have your green card, all USCIS correspondence, and a fully charged phone. The USCIS officer will quickly ask you about your N-400 Application Receipt Number, Alien Number, and date of correspondence. Also have your contact info such as your phone number and email address (an account which you check frequently). If you are not fluent in English, it is helpful to have someone with you who can interpret for you. However, before the person can interpret for you, the USCIS officer will ask your personal identification question in English (such as, "What is your full name and date of birth?"), and you must be able to answer these questions in English, as well as give permission to let the person speak for you.

REMEMBER

Filling out immigration forms incorrectly can cause them to be sent back for further clarification, or worse, to be denied. If you have any questions about how to properly complete forms, getting help *before* sending them in is best.

WHAT IF YOU LOSE YOUR CERTIFICATE OF NATURALIZATION?

Use the form N-565, Application for Replacement Naturalization/Citizenship Document, to apply for a replacement Declaration of Intention, Naturalization Certificate, Certificate of Citizenship, or Repatriation Certificate, or to apply for a special certificate of naturalization as a U.S. citizen to be recognized by a foreign country. You can submit this application online or by mail. See www.uscis.gov/n-565.

Be aware that getting a new Certificate of Naturalization can take up to year or more. That's why we always suggest you get a U.S. passport as soon as you receive your Certificate of Naturalization at your Naturalization Oath Ceremony — a passport also serves as evidence of citizenship.

Many USCIS naturalization ceremonies have representatives onsite ready to assist new citizens in applying for passports and registering to vote. You can also download passport applications from the State Department at https://travel.state.gov/content/travel/en/passports/how-apply/forms.html and schedule an appointment to submit the forms and fees at a designated Passport Acceptance site at https://iafdb.travel.state.gov/office. Please check the comments section of each facility for the link to schedule the appointment.

Because of higher call volumes on Monday, the best times to call the NCSC for personal assistance are Tuesday through Friday. A phone with an automatic-redial function will help you to get through with less frustration.

If you live outside any of the preceding locations, contact the nearest U.S. embassy or consulate for immigration-related customer service. See the State Department's list of Embassies and Consulates at https://travel.state.gov/content/travel/en/us-visas/visa-information-resources/list-of-posts.html.

Registering changes

When it comes to your immigration goals, neglecting the simplest tasks can have serious consequences. Be sure to tell the USCIS each and every time you change your address. If the USCIS doesn't have your current address, you can easily miss important correspondence. Without this information, you may miss crucial appointments that will put an end to your immigration dreams. The USCIS must always know how to get in touch with you. Not keeping them informed of your current whereabouts is a misdemeanor and a removable offense.

If your naturalization application is currently *pending,* or being processed, you must submit a change of address form, AR-11, to the USCIS. You can file online or mail the form. Filing Form AR-11 online will update your address on all pending applications, petitions, or requests that you include on the form. See the USCIS AR-11 web page at www.uscis.gov/ar-11 for details.

TIP

Changing your address with the U.S. Postal Service (USPS) will not change your address with USCIS or with the Executive Office for Immigration Review (EOIR) if you have an active or pending court case. Please update your address with both USCIS and USPS at https://moversguide.usps.com and with EOIR-33 at www.justice.gov/eoir/form-eoir-33-eoir-immigration-court-listing if you are in immigration proceedings.

Changing appointments

WARNING

The USCIS takes its appointment schedule very seriously. Unless it is a dire emergency, do not miss your appointments for interviews, fingerprinting, or any other immigration processing. Missing appointments can get you disqualified from the immigration benefits you're seeking.

If an emergency arises and you absolutely cannot make your appointment, be sure to contact the USCIS Contact Center at 800-375-5283 to request to have your appointment rescheduled — and do it as soon as you know about your conflict. The Contact Center will pass along the information to the local USCIS field office, which makes the final decision. Our experience suggests you should also send a letter directly to the local field office, clearly indicating on the envelope that you're writing to request a rescheduled interview (and send it certified mail, return receipt). Be aware there is no guarantee you'll get another chance.

Filing a complaint

What if you think you've been treated unfairly by a USCIS employee? You do have recourse, and filing a complaint will not affect your eligibility for naturalization.

The first step is to try to speak with the offending employee's direct supervisor. If the supervisor doesn't handle the complaint to your satisfaction (or if for some reason you're never able to speak with the supervisor), the next step is to write a letter to the director of your Field Office or Application Support Center at https://egov.uscis.gov/office-locator/#/.

If you still don't get satisfaction, you can report corruption, abuse, or misconduct by submitting a DHS OIG Hotline Complaint Form online at https://hotline.oig.dhs.gov/ or calling 800-323-8603 (TTY 844-889-4357).

If you have a legitimate complaint, be sure to file it in a timely fashion. Many people, knowing that filing a complaint may slow the immigration process, neglect to file one in the hopes that their case will be looked upon favorably. If you wait an undue length of time before raising your concerns in an official matter, the government may want to know why you didn't raise the complaint sooner.

Dealing with Rejection and Appealing USCIS Decisions

What if the USCIS denies your application for lawful permanent residence or naturalization? Don't panic. It's not over yet. You can appeal your case, and in many instances, you may reapply. If USCIS makes an unfavorable decision on a benefit request, the office that issued the decision will send a letter to the petitioner or applicant that explains the reason for the unfavorable decision and, if applicable, how to file a motion or appeal. Most appeals must be filed on Form I-290B, Notice of Appeal or Motion, with a fee and within 30 calendar days after personal service of the decision, or 33 calendar days if the decision was mailed. Some immigration categories have different appeal requirements, so please carefully review the denial letter and the USCIS website for specific and current instructions. In immigration proceedings, two separate government agencies share the appellate review authority:

>> **The Administrative Appeals Office (AAO),** which is part of the Bureau of Citizenship and Immigration Services (USCIS), a division of the Department of Homeland Security (DHS). See www.uscis.gov/about-us/organization/directorates-and-program-offices/the-administrative-appeals-office-aao.

>> **The Board of Immigration Appeals (BIA),** which is under the jurisdiction of the Executive Office of Immigration Review (EOIR), which is part of the United States Department of Justice (DOJ). See www.justice.gov/eoir/board-of-immigration-appeals.

Naturalization rejections

If you are denied naturalization, you can go through an administrative review process. Your denial letter will explain how to request a hearing with an immigration officer and will include the form you need to file the appeal — a Request for Hearing on a Decision in Naturalization Proceedings (Form N-336). You can file the N-336 and submit evidence online at www.uscis.gov/n-336.

WORKING AND TRAVELING DURING THE CITIZENSHIP APPLICATION PROCESS

Of course, because you must be a lawful permanent resident in order to apply for citizenship, working during the naturalization process is okay. Travel should not be a problem either, as long as it doesn't interfere with your continuous residency requirements. If you leave the United States for more than six months, you will, in most cases, disrupt your continuous residence. Consult with your attorney before leaving the country for any extended periods of time before gaining citizenship.

Of course, if you are applying for lawful permanent residence, you aren't allowed to work unless you have an employment authorization document, which you can apply for as soon as a visa is available for your classification and you file your Form I-485 (Application to Register Permanent Residence or to Adjust Status). See www.uscis.gov/i-485.

The denial letter will also tell you the date on which you may reapply for citizenship. If your application was denied because you failed the English or civics test, you may reapply for naturalization as soon as you want.

Reapplying for naturalization is just like starting the entire naturalization process all over again. You must do the following:

>> Complete and submit a new Application for Naturalization (Form N-400)

>> Pay the required fee for applying again (check the USCIS Fee Calculator tool at www.uscis.gov/feecalculator)

IMMIGRANT VISA REJECTIONS

If you get a denial notice, read it carefully — it contains information about your right to appeal the decision and how to go about doing so.

You, or most likely your immigration attorney, will file a *brief*, or explanation, that supports the reasons for your appeal. After reviewing your case, the appellate authority for your particular case — either the AAO or the BIA — will decide to change the original decision, uphold the rejection, or send the case back to your local immigration office for further action.

In some cases, you may also file a *motion to reopen* or a *motion to reconsider* your case. This means that you're asking the office to reconsider their decision. In order to file either of these motions, you must have compelling reasons to do so:

- In order to successfully file a *motion to reopen,* you must provide affidavits and documents that prove new facts in your case that didn't come into play during your original hearing.

- In order for an immigration office to *reconsider* its decision, you must prove that the decision was based on an incorrect application of the law or USCIS policy.

Needless to say, we can't recommend strongly enough that you get the help of a qualified immigration attorney in these cases, because you're dealing with highly complex issues.

The right to appeal immigration decisions comes with strict time deadlines. Read your denial notice carefully and make sure that you file your appeal before the deadline or you will *forfeit,* or lose, the right to appeal. Make sure you also include the proper fees or, again, you may lose your chance. In most cases

- You have 30 days to appeal the denial of a petition or application. Increase that to 33 days after the date of the decision if you received the notice by mail.

- If you're appealing a revocation of an approved immigrant petition, you must file the appeal within 15 days of the date of the decision or within 18 days of the date of the decision if the decision was delivered by mail.

If an attorney or other representative is filing the appeal, they should include a Form G-28 — or if it is an appeal to the BIA, an EOIR-27.

The person who submitted the original visa application or petition is the only one who may file an appeal. The beneficiary of a visa petition may *not* appeal a decision unless the beneficiary is also the petitioner. For instance, if you live abroad and your potential U.S. employer filed an immigrant visa petition on your behalf, your employer must file the appeal (you cannot do so yourself).

Demonstrating Good Moral Character

As we discuss in previous chapters, to become a naturalized U.S. citizen (and in some cases even to become a lawful permanent resident), you must demonstrate that you possess good moral character.

Aggravated felonies committed on or after November 29, 1990, and murder represent permanent bars to naturalization. Other crimes constitute *temporary bars*, meaning you must wait a designated period of time before applying for citizenship.

Your Application for Naturalization form will ask you about crimes. Reporting all crimes on your record — even crimes that have been *expunged* or removed from your record — is important. If you neglect to inform the USCIS about a crime and they find out about it later, they can use it as grounds to deny your naturalization application — even if the crime itself was not serious enough to originally deny your case. Worse, some crimes can not only jeopardize your eligibility to naturalize, but they can also cause revocation of permanent resident status and removal from the United States.

After you file your naturalization application, the information in it is fair game for the USCIS (and the Immigration and Customs Enforcement, or ICE), even if you ask to withdraw your application (a request that the USCIS can deny).

TIP

If you have any crimes in your record, consult an immigration attorney for help with your case — preferably *before* you file. (Chapter 7 shows you how to find a reliable attorney.)

WARNING

So what other things may result in a USCIS denial on grounds of lack of good moral character? If, within the five- or three-year period of permanent residence prior to naturalization, any of the following apply to you, you may have something to worry about:

>> You've committed any crime against a person with intent to harm.

>> You've committed any crime against property that involves fraud or evil intent.

>> You've committed two or more crimes for which the combined sentence was five years or more.

>> You've violated any controlled-substance law of the United States, any state, or any foreign country.

>> You've been confined in jail, prison, or a similar institution for which the total confinement was 180 days or more during the past five years (or three years if you're applying based upon your marriage to a U.S. citizen).

>> You've lied to gain immigration benefits.

>> You've participated in prostitution (either working as a prostitute or hiring one).

>> You've been involved in illegal alien smuggling into the United States.

>> You've engaged in *polygamy* (marriage to more than one person at a time).

- >> You've earned your income principally from illegal gambling or were convicted for two or more gambling offenses.

- >> You have been a habitual drunkard.

- >> You've failed to make court-ordered child support or alimony payments.

- >> You had an extramarital affair that destroyed an existing marriage.

- >> You participated in group violence or war crimes.

- >> You were affiliated with totalitarian or terrorist organizations.

- >> You committed unlawful acts not mentioned in this list, but which otherwise adversely affect your good moral character.

REMEMBER

If you've recently been ordered deported or removed, you aren't eligible for citizenship. If you're currently in removal proceedings, you may not apply for citizenship until the proceedings are complete and you've been allowed to remain in the country as a lawful permanent resident.

Avoiding Removal

Even if you have been legally admitted to the United States on a temporary or permanent basis, under certain circumstances you can still be *removed*, or forced to leave the country. Granted, this is the worst-case scenario, and we hope you will never have to deal with this situation, but nonetheless, you should be aware of the reasons for removal and what you can do if you ever find yourself facing it.

REMEMBER

After you become a naturalized citizen, you will no longer need to worry about removal, because you'll have the same rights as a natural-born United States citizen. Your citizenship can only be revoked under extreme circumstances, such as a treason conviction.

TECHNICAL
STUFF

Prior to the immigration law changes of 1996 (IIRAIRA), the process of removing an alien already in the country was known as *deportation.*

Understanding the reasons for removal

The reasons for removal are many, but most people who face forced exile from the United States fall into one of these categories:

- >> Entering the country illegally
- >> Violating the terms of admission

- » Working in the United States without permission

- » Having criminal convictions

- » Being a member of certain prohibited organizations (such as a terrorist organization)

- » Becoming a public charge within five years of entering the United States

Appealing removal decisions

Removal is a serious and complicated subject. After you're forced to leave the country, chances are good you won't be allowed back in for at least five years — unless you get a waiver, which is not easy.

WARNING

Do not attempt to contest removal on your own — whether before the immigration court or on appeal. Seek out the services of a qualified attorney or immigration organization. (Chapter 7 shows you how to find a good lawyer or other representation — even if you have little or no money.)

WARNING

Beware of additional sanctions for failing to depart the United States following a final order of removal. You continue to accrue unlawful presence, which can result in additional bars to reentry and ineligibility for future immigration benefits. You also run the risk of facing a permanent bar to entering the United States.

3

Exploring U.S. History, Government, and Culture

IN THIS CHAPTER

» Looking at the years prior to the formation of the United States

» Becoming a new country

» Growing as a country

» Engaging in the Civil War

» Entering the Industrial Revolution

Chapter **9**

U.S. History in a Nutshell, Part I: Pre-U.S. to World War I

Your journey through the fascinating history of the United States of America begins here, starting before there ever was a United States. Hold on tight — we cover a lot of territory in a very small amount of space in this and the following chapter. But don't worry; you'll find out more than you need to pass your citizenship test — you only have to show a *basic* understanding of U.S. history.

TIP

Information that refers directly to the USCIS history and civics questions will be noted with USCIS:100 and the appropriate question number.

Before We Were the United States

Long before we were a country, the land that is now the United States was considered *undiscovered* by the more civilized nations of Europe and Asia; however, indigenous peoples lived in various parts of the land — tribes as different from each other as the terrain of the land that they called home.

Native Americans

Native Americans, also known as American Indians and other terms, were the first people living in America (USCIS 100:59).

The ancestors of living Native Americans arrived in what is now the United States at least 15,000 years ago, possibly much earlier, from Asia via the Bering Straits archipelago. Through migration and adaptation to different habitats, tribes formed different social systems based on trade, hunting, fishing, and agriculture. Native American tribes spoke different languages, followed different customs, and practiced unique belief systems. The diversity of native cultures is preserved in early-contact narratives, as shown in these examples:

>> In 1492, the *Arawak* (Taino) encountered by Columbus lived in open thatched buildings, grew cassava, and traveled extensively throughout the Caribbean in dugout canoes.

>> In the Southwest during the 1560s, the Spanish met the *Pueblo* and *Hopi* tribes, who lived in multi-story adobe villages and used dry farming techniques to cultivate corn, beans, and squash.

>> In the 1700s, the *Iroquois Great Law of Peace* which bound six tribes together for mutual protection, common resource management, and government through consensus-building, evolved from extended-family long houses of upstate New York. The *Iroquois Confederacy* influenced isolated self-governing American colonies to unite as interdependent states with a loose federal government (USCIS 100:88).

Migrating to the New World

As soon as news of Columbus's discovery spread, explorers from around the world, including England, France, Holland, Italy, and Spain, couldn't wait to set sail for the New World. Throughout each of their journeys, the early explorers created maps and kept detailed journals of their voyages, which in turn helped other explorers who came later.

An Italian explorer by the name of Amerigo Vespucci was the first to declare the New World a continent in its own right. The land was named *America* in Vespucci's honor. The British and French claimed most (but not all) of North America, and the Spanish dominated Central and South America.

Slowly at first, European settlers soon began to populate America. Simply put, people came seeking freedom. In many countries at that time, the monarch was the political and religious leader of the country. In some situations, political or religious dissent led to death. People were compelled to leave their own countries and come to America where they could exercise their political liberty and religious freedom. Here they could engage in self-government and practice their religion or not practice a religion according to the dictates of their conscience. Then, as now, people came to America to escape persecution of all kinds. Others came for the economic opportunities the land offered — like most people, they wanted a better life for their families (USCIS 100:58).

However, in pursuing freedom, European colonists displaced Native Americans from their ancestral homelands. Some sought to increase their economic advantage by buying people brought from Africa that were sold as slaves (USCIS 100:59). These two fundamental sins would lead to the Trail of Tears, the Civil War, countless Indian Wars, racial discrimination, the Civil Rights movement, and ongoing reparations to the Native Peoples. Generation after generation of Americans have worked tirelessly to bend the arc of the moral universe toward justice!

Founded in 1565, the Spanish settlement at St. Augustine, Florida, holds the honor of being the oldest permanent settlement in North America. In 1610, Spanish settlers went on to found Santa Fe, New Mexico. In 1607, the British established their first colony at Jamestown, Virginia. In 1624, the Dutch founded the future New York City and occupied the Hudson River Valley. In 1638, the Swedes settled along the Delaware River (USCIS 100:64).

Finding out about the American colonies

Before they united into a nation of states, there were 13 British colonies. But the philosophy and ideals that would inspire the yet-to-be-born nation of the United States of America were already firmly in place.

Some colonies were settled by groups with specific interests in mind, such as the Pilgrims (see the nearby sidebar, "Seeking religious freedom: The Pilgrims") and the Puritans. Others, known as *proprietary colonies*, formed when the king bestowed large pieces of land to certain members of the nobility. These colony "owners" made money by renting and/or selling their land. Still other colonies were born when residents of one colony traveled in search of better land and economic opportunity.

Generally speaking, democracy thrived in the New World. In the charters that established the colonies, the King of England gave the colonists most of the same rights citizens living in England enjoyed. Some colonies employed *representative assemblies* — elected officials who determined the laws for the colonies — to govern their citizens. Others believed in a more direct form of democracy where voters would gather at town meetings, vote on the laws of their town, and elect representatives to the colonial assemblies. Today, most of our government depends on representatives, although some examples of *direct democracy* still exist at the local level in a few tiny towns. Although rare in today's modern world, the laws of some small U.S. towns are still determined through votes taken at local town meetings.

Still, the colonies could not be considered completely democratic. Their laws exercised significant restrictions on who was allowed to vote or hold a representative office — namely male landowners. In some instances, voters were also compelled to meet certain religious qualifications. In addition, the King of England and his representatives still maintained a lot of control. With the exception of Connecticut and Rhode Island, king-appointed governors retained the power to *veto*, or override, any laws passed by the continental assemblies. The governor also had the power, or *jurisdiction*, to appoint certain government officials.

SEEKING RELIGIOUS FREEDOM: THE PILGRIMS

The Pilgrims, who came to America in 1620, were the first group of settlers seeking religious freedom.

Even before their ship, the *Mayflower*, landed at Plymouth Rock in what is now Massachusetts, the Pilgrims outlined the kind of government they wanted in a document called the Mayflower Compact. The Pilgrims wanted to form a democracy where the people voted on the laws they lived by and the government that regulated them. The Mayflower Compact (a *constitution*) established the basis of written laws and legal forms of government in the new land.

The Pilgrims were ill prepared for their first winter in the new land, and only about half of them survived. With help from friendly Native Americans, the remaining Pilgrims learned how to hunt, fish, and farm in order to survive in the harsh new environment.

In addition to setting forth principles of government that were later incorporated into the United States Constitution, the Pilgrims gained fame for starting the holiday of Thanksgiving, which is celebrated every year on the fourth Thursday of November. On this day, Americans celebrate with a great feast and give thanks for their blessings. (See Chapter 14 for more on Thanksgiving.)

Recognizing the "lucky thirteen"

The 13 British colonies united for greater good, and freedom forms the foundation of our nation. In respect and honor, our flag has 13 stripes — the stripes represent the original colonies, and there were 13 original colonies (listed here in order of their admission to the United States) (USCIS 100:64, 96):

>> Delaware

>> Pennsylvania

>> New Jersey

>> Georgia

>> Connecticut

>> Massachusetts

>> Maryland

>> South Carolina

>> New Hampshire

>> Virginia

>> New York

>> North Carolina

>> Rhode Island

Forming a New Country

During much of the time between 1689 and 1763, the English found themselves at war with the French over differences in the ways the two countries settled and colonized the new land. The American colonists became accustomed to a lot of freedom because England's monarchs were too preoccupied with matters of war to give much thought to them. The colonists enjoyed a relatively democratic self-government and more or less free trade with Europe. However, all that was about to change.

Understanding the events leading to the Revolutionary War

At the time, the French occupied most of the land that is now Canada, while England controlled most of what is now the United States. However, both countries claimed rights to the land that is now Virginia, and war broke out over the disputed land. Because the French allied themselves with many of the Native American people who were already living there, the war became known as the French and Indian War. It lasted from 1754 to 1763.

George Washington, who would later become the first president of the United States, heroically fought for the British during the French and Indian War.

Although France and its allies dominated most of the war's earlier battles, England took stock, reorganized, and sent additional troops. The war ended with the 1763 Treaty of Paris, in which France lost her colonies and England took control of most of North America.

After the French and Indian War, England's King George III turned his attention back toward the American colonies. Burdened with a large financial debt, he intended to take full advantage of England's colonial properties by

>> Severely restricting the sale of American raw goods (timber, fur, fish, and so on) to British merchants and then selling goods made in England with American raw materials back to the American colonists at inflated prices

>> Prohibiting colonists from settling on land protected by treaties with Native American tribes

>> Requiring colonists to *quarter,* or house, British soldiers in private homes, as well as provide them with food and basic supplies *(board)* (USCIS 100:61b)

>> Appointing colonial governors loyal to the king and repressing self-government by colonial legislative assemblies (USCIS 100:61c)

As bad as all these laws were, what most angered the colonists was taxation without representation (USCIS 100:61a). While Britain forced the colonists to pay high taxes, the colonies were not allowed to send representatives to the English government to vote on those taxes and represent the colonists' interests.

Resisting tyranny: The colonists unite and fight

The colonists, a feisty bunch, did not just sit back and let England walk all over them. They rebelled by no longer buying British goods. They found homemade or homegrown substitutions wherever possible and smuggled other necessary goods into colonial harbors. In a 1774 show of unity, the colonists gathered together in Philadelphia at the first meeting of the Continental Congress. Every colony except Georgia sent representatives to this historic first meeting.

At the time, only a few of the more radical colonists were even considering breaking away from England. The main purpose of the first Continental Congress was to express colonists' grievances against British policy. The colonists accomplished this by writing a Declaration of Rights that included a request for the king to repeal the restrictions. Not content to simply sit and wait for an answer, the colonists resolved to prepare *militias,* or citizen armies, should the need to fight for their rights arise. The colonies also agreed to boycott British manufactured goods by giving local committees the power to fine or arrest those who did not honor the boycott.

Britain ignored the colonists' requests and instead sent troops to Massachusetts to seize military supplies and find the men instigating the rebellion. On April 18, 1775, in the small Massachusetts village of Lexington, the British caught colonists by surprise, killing eight minutemen (members of the Massachusetts militia) and wounding others. When the British soldiers pushed on to Concord, the colonists opened fire in the "shot heard 'round the world" and started the Revolutionary War.

At the start of the war, whether the colonists were actually fighting for independence from England or merely for their rights as British subjects remained unclear. Many factors influenced the colonists' ultimate decision to break away from England, although some remained loyal to England throughout the war.

The British brought in *mercenary* (paid) soldiers known as the Hessians from Germany to help fight their battle. This greatly angered the colonists, and they looked to France for help. The French refused to help, however, unless the colonists declared independence from England.

TECHNICAL STUFF

George Washington served as commander in chief of the colonial military. He was an experienced military man — he also fought in the French and Indian War — but General Washington's troops lacked the training, ammunition, and supplies of their British counterparts. Nonetheless, they could shoot more accurately, knew the land better, and had the strength of their beliefs to help them through the tough battles ahead.

Declaring independence from England

After a lot of fighting, hardship, and loss of life, the colonists were forced to conclude that England was never going to treat them any better — in fact, it seemed that stricter and harsher punishments lay ahead.

TECHNICAL STUFF

At the request of the Second Continental Congress, Thomas Jefferson wrote the original Declaration of Independence (USCIS 100:62) with help from fellow committee members Benjamin Franklin and John Adams. The first part of the Declaration declares the break with England and the reasons for the break.

The second part of the document lists the colonists' complaints against England's King George III in order to illustrate that England had ignored the colonists' complaints. The final draft of the Declaration of Independence was adopted on July 4, 1776. (USCIS 100:63) (For more detailed information about the Declaration of Independence — one of the most important documents in the United States — see Chapter 11.)

October 19, 1781, marked the final battle of the Revolutionary War. While marching from Virginia to New York, British commander Lord Cornwallis became trapped in Yorktown on the Chesapeake Bay. While his troops waited for reinforcements, the French navy blocked their escape. After a series of battles, the British surrendered to the Continental Army, essentially ending the Revolutionary War.

Benjamin Franklin, John Adams, and John Jay traveled to Paris to write the treaty that officially ended the conflict. Signed in 1781, the Treaty of Paris defined the boundaries of the United States as

>> The Atlantic Ocean to the east

>> The Mississippi River to the west

>> The Great Lakes to the north

>> Florida to the south (Florida itself was controlled by Spain at the time, so the southern border of the United States was actually the northern border of Florida.)

Establishing the new nation

Suddenly the 13 original colonies became a new nation, complete with all the debts, responsibilities, and challenges that went along with winning independence from England. Although the Declaration of Independence had established a foundation for government, each of the original 13 states operated under its own individual laws. New Americans found themselves having to make tough choices in defining their government structure and powers.

After fighting so hard to break from the oppression of British rule, many colonists naturally feared a strong central government. Yet practical concerns like the need to establish trade and foreign policy necessitated some form of centralized government.

In 1781, Congress *ratified* (adopted) the Articles of Confederation — the first national constitutional agreement of the 13 new United States. Under the Articles, the federal government retained little power, delegating most authority to the individual states. Although many early Americans liked the agreement because it prevented the federal government from growing strong enough to overthrow the will of the people, as well as opened up the West to peaceful settlement, the Articles of Confederation neglected to address many of the problems that the new country encountered, such as regulating trade, dealing with foreign governments, and matters of defense.

REMEMBER

Under the Articles, Congress lacked the authority to enforce laws. The federal government wasn't even able to collect taxes to pay basic legislative and defense expenses, not to mention the debt the colonies had accumulated during the Revolutionary War. Congress also lacked the authority to recruit troops, despite the fact that the federal government was expected to provide defense for the new country.

To make matters worse, many states began printing their own money, which undermined the value of the money produced by the federal government.

Because the Articles of Confederation required at least 9 of the 13 states to meet and agree on issues, and all 13 needed to agree on any *amendments* (changes) to the Articles, the young country soon found itself on the verge of bankruptcy. Debates erupted about whether the states should be independent entities that operated like separate countries or 13 mutually dependent states, operating as one united country.

These problems led to the calling of a meeting to replace the Articles of Confederation. The Constitutional Convention took place in Philadelphia from May 25 to September 17, 1787; during this convention, the Founding Fathers wrote the United States Constitution (USCIS 100:65, 66), the supreme law of the land and our most important historical document.

For more details about the United States Constitution, see Chapter 11. For now, know that the Constitution makes these important points:

>> No other laws may contradict any of the principles set forth in the Constitution.

>> No person is exempt from following the laws set forth in the Constitution, nor is the government itself.

>> The Constitution guarantees the essential "self-evident" rights Thomas Jefferson set forth in the Declaration of Independence — rights and freedoms guaranteed to *all* people living in the United States, whether they are United States citizens or not.

ANSWERING THE SLAVERY QUESTION

To the delegates of the first Constitutional Convention, slavery — which had existed in the colonies since 1619 — was not a moral issue but rather a matter of debate about the economy. Generally speaking, most Southern states approved of slavery because the practice provided low-cost labor for their plantations. Most Northern states didn't practice slavery or were undertaking measures to outlaw it. Still, there was little talk of actually outlawing slavery at the first Constitutional Convention. The Northern states' only real issue concerned how to count the slave population. The South thought each slave should count toward the number of representatives the state was allowed to send to Congress. However, it did not want to count slaves when it came to matters of taxation. Of course, the North held the opposite view. The states finally agreed to the *three-fifths compromise,* in which every five slaves would be counted as three people for purposes of determining a state's number of representatives and the amount of taxes owed. As part of the compromise, the Constitution also guaranteed the South's slave trade for at least 20 years.

After the delegates of the Constitutional Convention agreed upon the Constitution, it was sent to the state assemblies to be ratified. Between October 1787 and August 1788, 85 essays supporting the passage of the U.S. Constitution appeared in newspapers. This series, known as the "Federalist Papers," was published under collective name "Publius" (Alexander Hamilton, James Madison, and John Jay) (USCIS 100:67) and explained the new form of government. Large states with large populations favored a system of government where population determined representation in government. Smaller states believed each state should be delegated the same designated number of representatives. The great compromise, ratified by nine states in 1788, created the legislative branch of government, consisting of two senators from each state (regardless of size of area or population) (USCIS 100:24) and a number of congressional representatives determined by the state's population (USCIS 100:25). The first assembly of the new U.S. government met in the country's temporary capital, New York City, in 1789.

Growing a nation

After the U.S. Constitution was ratified, George Washington was elected as the first U.S. president and served from April 30, 1789, to March 4, 1797. He believed in the importance of uniting the 13 states to work as a strong, single nation. During his two four-year terms in office, he influenced all the presidents who later held the office by

>> Establishing the practice of consulting a presidential Cabinet of advisors (which is covered in more detail in Chapter 12)

>> Setting the precedent for presidents serving no more than two terms in office, thereby preventing any single person in the government from gaining too much power

>> Establishing a practice of staying neutral in foreign politics, a practice that would remain in force for more than 100 years

Soon after the seating of the new government, political factions arose (which would later solidify into political parties). Washington and other Federalists, including Alexander Hamilton, believed a national bank was necessary to stabilize the young country's economy. The Federalists favored a loose interpretation of the U.S. Constitution, preferring a broadening of the federal government's financial power. The Anti-Federalists (later to become the Democratic-Republican party, only later to split into two separate parties) feared that a national bank would give too much power to the federal government. Furthermore, the Anti-Federalists lobbied to add a Bill of Rights to the U.S. Constitution to guarantee personal freedom and set clear limitations on the government. Through debate and compromise, the First Nation Bank was created in early 1791, to support the U.S. financial system. Later in 1791, the Bill of Rights was ratified as the first ten amendments to the U.S. Constitution (USCIS 100:4, 5).

Democratic-Republican Thomas Jefferson and Federalist John Adams battled it out in the election to become the second president. In the election of 1796, Adams defeated his rival by only three electoral votes. Despite the fact that the two maintained a difficult and antagonistic relationship and only spoke to each other during debates, as outlined in the Constitution, the man with the second-highest number of votes — in this case, Thomas Jefferson — became the vice president.

REMEMBER

The Twelfth Amendment gave the president and vice president separate ballots in the Electoral College system. Before the amendment's adoption, the candidate with the most electoral votes became the president and the candidate with the second-highest number of votes became the vice president, resulting in some strained and counterproductive political pairings like that of John Adams and Thomas Jefferson.

John Adams had a lot of factors working against him:

>> The immensely popular George Washington was a tough act for anyone to follow.

>> Although the public believed in Adams's experience and qualifications, he was not well liked — the public perceived him as a snob.

>> His political archrival and vice president, Thomas Jefferson, continually undermined his credibility and efforts.

TECHNICAL STUFF

Adams also lost popularity when he approved the Alien and Sedition Acts, as outlined in the following list. Designed to counter the growth of Jefferson's Democratic-Republican Party (heir of the Anti-Federalist faction) and never strictly enforced, the Alien Act expired in 1800 when Thomas Jefferson was finally elected President.

>> **The Naturalization Act of 1798** increased the amount of time (from three to five years) an immigrant had to reside in the United States before becoming a citizen. This act was the first to maintain government immigration records (such as country of origin and date of arrival) for white immigrant aliens to qualify for citizenship.

>> **The Alien Enemy Act** empowered the president to imprison or deport immigrants of countries at war with the United States or those the president believed to be dangerous to the country.

>> **The Sedition Act** made it illegal to publish negative or defamatory statements about the federal government or its officials.

THE IMPORTANCE OF THE CENSUS

Following America's independence from England, there was an almost immediate need for a *census,* or population count, of our new nation. Article I of the U.S. Constitution requires a census to be taken every ten years. The first census, conducted in 1790, counted the population at 3.9 million people. By comparison, the 2020 census counts that number at over 331 million.

Census 2020 was the first census that households could complete online or by phone. Nonresponding households received paper forms and/or follow-up visits from census takers. Uncle Sam wants to know how many people live in each house as well as their ages, sex, and race. It's not that the government is nosy — the sole purpose of census surveys is to secure general information. The government takes the confidentiality of census replies seriously. By law, no census taker or any other Census Bureau employee can reveal identifiable information about any person, household, or business, and schedules and questionnaires from any census cannot be released for 72 years. Even then, only the heirs or legal representative of the named individuals are allowed access to the records.

The information provided by the census guides the government's planning for U.S. needs now, just as it did back in the 1700s. Through the years, the census questions evolved with the country's growth and progress. The broad profile of the people who make up this nation helps the federal government determine how to best meet the needs of its people. For instance, a town with a growing population of children will probably need more schools, but a town with a growing population of senior citizens would better benefit from reliable public transportation and senior services.

After the first apportionment occurred based on the 1790 census, each member of the House represented roughly 34,000 people. Now, the average population size of each House district based on the 2020 census will be 761,169 people. Based on the 2020 census, six states will gain seats, seven will lose seats, and the remainder will have no change. Representatives from remapped districts will be seated as the 118th United States Congress in 2023.

The census also plays an important role in upholding democracy, because the number of representatives a state sends to the House of Representatives in Congress is based on the state's population. For an accurate count of the state's population, the government consults — you guessed it — the census results.

You can easily see why filling out census forms is such an important citizen responsibility — if you neglect to complete your census forms, you may be helping to cheat your local community of the representation it deserves and the public services it needs.

The Census Bureau's website (www.census.gov) offers a fun place to surf and check out facts about your state or region or the United States in general. You'll also find a wealth of statistical information about the United States as well as census information in Spanish and a fun Census for Kids educational website.

Warring after the Revolution

Like Washington before him, Presidents John Adams and Thomas Jefferson worked hard to keep the United States neutral in matters of foreign politics. They knew the new nation lacked the strength and resources to win a battle against any of the European nations. But Adams and Jefferson were really put to the test when the British and French violated the United States' neutral status by seizing merchant ships. Instead of going to war, Adams negotiated a treaty with the British, which angered the French. Jefferson kept the country out of war by prohibiting U.S. exports to other countries, hoping that the need for U.S. exports would force the warring nations of Britain and France to change their politics. Eventually, the United States offered to resume trading with whichever nation first changed its neutral trading restrictions. France changed its policies, and trade between the United States and France resumed.

By 1812, our fourth President, James Madison, and the Congress reluctantly declared war on Great Britain, our largest trading partner, over the following issues:

>> Britain's renewed seizure of ships and impressment of U.S. sailors into British military service

>> Britain's aid to the Native Americans attacking white American settlers on the Western frontier

>> America's desire to annex British Northwest Territories and possibly even Canada, as well as to acquire Florida from Britain's ally, Spain

During the War of 1812, the British managed to invade and burn most of Washington, D.C., including the U.S. Capitol Building and the White House. Then the British fleet moved up the coast to bomb Fort McHenry at the entrance of the Baltimore harbor. The sight of the American flag, which still flew over the fort, inspired a poem that was later set to music as "The Star-Spangled Banner," our national anthem (USCIS 100:98).

Although the Treaty of Ghent restored peace, it did not address the conflicts that led to the War of 1812 in the first place. But because the European nations were no longer at war, some of the issues, such as free trade conflicts, simply disappeared. Still, the War of 1812 ushered in a new era in U.S. history, characterized by the following:

>> A desire to settle the Western territories

>> An increased emphasis on manufacturing and industry

>> The end of the Federalist political party

Expanding the Country's Borders

Several land acts in the early 1800s lowered the price of land, making it easier for prospective settlers to acquire it and encouraging people to move west. The vast territories of open land and rich natural resources led Americans to believe it was the destiny of the American people to grow rich and prosper. This belief in *Manifest Destiny* led American politicians and settlers to push west, acquire new lands, and extend the American way of life far beyond its earlier boundaries. With this newfound strength, stability, and sense of purpose, the United States began acquiring new territories and adding new states to the Union:

>> **The Louisiana Purchase:** As a result of a European war, France gained control of the area around the Mississippi River and the port of New Orleans in 1802; President Thomas Jefferson bought the Louisiana Territory from France in 1803 (USCIS 100:71) for only $15 million. Overnight, the size of the country doubled, expanding the borders to what are now Santa Fe, New Mexico, and Pikes Peak, Colorado, in the west, and to the current

U.S.-Canadian border in the north. Jefferson immediately dispatched the Corps of Discovery to map one of America's longest rivers, the Missouri, to its source. Co-led by U.S. Army officers Lewis and Clark; guided by a Shoshone woman, Sacajawea (and her baby!); and attended by an African-American slave, York, the 45-member expedition of the corps was to make contact with the local Native Americans, take a scientific survey of the plants and animals, and hopefully find an all-water route to the Pacific Ocean on the West Coast (USCIS 100:89).

» **The Florida Purchase:** After losing part of Florida to the United States in the War of 1812, Spain decided to sell the rest rather than risk losing the entire territory in another war. The United States paid $5 million for Florida in 1819, completing its occupation of the East Coast of the United States and free access to the Atlantic Ocean (USCIS 100:90).

» **Annexation of Texas:** The Florida Purchase recognized that Spain still held the land rights to Texas. However, soon after the purchase, the Mexicans revolted, winning their independence from Spain and gaining control of Texas. The Mexicans, eager to settle the land, welcomed U.S. settlers with the understanding that they would become Mexican citizens. The American Texans, however, didn't completely agree with this arrangement, and skirmishes started. The Mexican government tried to prevent further immigration into Texas, but the Texans rebelled and declared their independence from Mexico in 1836. The Battle of the Alamo, in which the Texans were defeated by Mexican General Santa Anna, so angered the Texans that Sam Houston, commander in chief of the Texas territory, led his troops to defeat Santa Anna and form the Lone Star Republic. Houston then asked the U.S. to *annex* Texas, or add it as a new state to the Union. The United States didn't immediately agree, however, due to political differences having to do with slavery. The Texans then began to look toward France or England for help. Because having France or England so close to the U.S. was unacceptable to our government, Congress agreed to annex Texas as a state in 1845, leading to the Mexican-American War (1846–1848) (USCIS 100:72).

» **The Mexican Cession:** Even after the annexation of Texas, U.S.-Mexican relations remained strained. Losing Texas angered the Mexicans, and a war over the territories west of Texas to the Pacific Ocean took place from 1846 to 1848. Americans living in what is now California established the California Bear Flag Republic. The United States' goal was to add territory to the country, not necessarily to defeat the Mexicans. The Treaty of Guadalupe-Hildago in 1848 ended the war with Mexico. For a purchase price of $15 million, Mexico officially gave up disputed areas of Texas as well as all the territory west of the Louisiana Purchase to the Pacific Ocean. The states of California, Arizona, New Mexico, Texas, and parts of Utah, Nevada, and Colorado were formed from this purchase.

>> **Oregon Country:** The United States and Great Britain had both claimed rights to the land in the northwestern part of the country, known as the Oregon Country. During the War with Mexico, President James Polk agreed to an offer with England to divide the territory — the northern part in what is now Canada would belong to England, while the southern part would remain the property of the United States. This territory purchase completed the border between the contiguous United States and Canada. The states of Maine, New Hampshire, Vermont, New York, Pennsylvania, Ohio, Michigan, Minnesota, North Dakota, Montana, Idaho, and Washington border Canada. A later purchase of Alaska completed the list of states that border Canada. (USCIS 100:92).

>> **Gadsden Purchase:** In 1853, the $10 million Gadsden Purchase completed what is now the continental United States by adding a small piece of property in Southern California. Although the property may seem expensive compared to land areas like the Louisiana Purchase, it did provide a convenient railroad into what is now the state of California. This territory purchase established the U.S.-Mexico border. The states of California, Arizona, New Mexico, and Texas border Mexico (USCIS 100:93).

>> **Alaska:** In 1867, the territory that is now our largest state, Alaska, was thought of as a barren wasteland, populated only by a few Native American tribes. When then Secretary of State William Seward offered to pay the Russians $7.2 million for the land, people thought he was crazy, sarcastically referring to the purchase as "Seward's Folly" or "Seward's Icebox." Those thoughts quickly vanished in 1896 when gold was discovered in Alaska. Today, the state is one of the country's richest stores of natural resources, including fish, timber, oil, and gold. Alaska added a second northwestern U.S.-Canada border (USCIS 100:94).

>> **Island Territories:** In February 1898, an explosion from a mine in the Bay of Havana crippled the United States' warship *Maine*. The incident sparked the Spanish-American War (1898) (USCIS 100:72) that the U.S. easily won by April of the same year. A peace treaty was signed in which the United States received Puerto Rico, Guam, and the Philippine Islands (now an independent country). As a result of the same treaty, Cuba received its independence. Currently, Guam and Puerto Rico are U.S. territories along with American Samoa (1899), the Virgin Islands (Denmark, 1917), and the Northern Mariana Islands (Japan, 1945) (USCIS 100:91).

>> **Hawaii:** Although Queen Liliuokalani of Hawaii had previously given the United States naval rights to Pearl Harbor in 1887, Hawaiian settlers over-threw her regime in 1893 and asked the United States to annex Hawaii as a state. Hawaii officially joined the United States in 1898 and became a territory in 1900, but it would take until 1959 before the islands became our 50th state.

Engaging in Civil War

At no time in our history was our Union more threatened than during the Civil War (1861–1865), also known as the War Between the States (USCIS 100:72, 73), the war in which United States citizens of the North (the Union) and South (the Confederacy) took up arms against one another. In some instances, family members on opposite sides of the conflict (and opposite sides of the *Mason-Dixon line,* which divides the North from the South) actually fought each other in the war's bloody battles.

Many people believe slavery (USCIS 100:74) to be the issue that prompted the Civil War, but in reality, a combination of factors caused the division that almost destroyed the United States:

>> **Economic reasons:** Different economic strengths and weaknesses led the two territories to argue over the protective tariff and the issue of slavery. The *protective tariff* placed a tax on imported goods in order to give U.S. manufacturers a market advantage. The industrial North needed the tariff to compete with otherwise lower-priced foreign goods. The agricultural South, which purchased a large amount of those goods, resented paying higher prices for the U.S.-made versions. Likewise, the South argued it needed inexpensive slave labor to compete in the international market. The North resented slavery on both moral and economic grounds (USCIS 100:74).

>> **States' rights:** Different beliefs about the type of union the country should be and struggle for control of the central government greatly contributed to the Civil War. The North viewed the nation as a union of the people that could not, under any circumstances, be divided. The South, on the other hand, interpreted the Union as an agreement among the states that could be broken if a state disagreed with federal law — allowing that state to *secede,* or withdraw, from the Union (USCIS 100:74).

Before the Civil War: Contributing factors and compromises

In the 1820s, *nationalism* (the belief in a strong, united country) gave way to feelings of *sectionalism* (loyalty to a particular state or region). The United States unofficially divided itself into three main sections, each with its own thoughts and beliefs on how the country should be run:

>> **The Northeast,** which was dependent on industry and factory workers for its economy

>> **The South,** which was dependent on agriculture produced by plantation owners and slave labor for its economy

>> **The West,** which was dependent on agriculture produced by independent farmers and ranchers for its economy

TECHNICAL STUFF

The Indian Removal Act of 1830 forced the Chickasaw, Choctaw, Muscogee-Creek, Seminole, and Cherokee of the southeast United States to be forcibly uprooted from their ancestral lands and marched to federal territory west of the Mississippi River. This catastrophic migration became known as the Trail of Tears. The removal of the Native Americans allowed settlers moving south and west to buy large tracts of land for the cultivation of cotton and strengthen the spread of an economy based on slavery.

Slavery quickly became the most emotional issue of the war. Although the North generally objected to slavery because of the unfair economic advantage it gave Southern plantation owners, a growing number of *abolitionists* (people who believed slavery should be outlawed because it was morally wrong) were starting to make their voices heard.

As more states joined the Union, the slavery issue grew more heated and divisive — the North believed that new states admitted to the Union should be slave-free, while the South still fought for the right to own slaves. Federal politicians tried to avoid a civil war by creating compromises to the controversial and explosive issue. In the end, none of these ideas pleased either side enough to stop the conflict from growing into a full-fledged war between the states. But before the states began actually fighting with one another, they first tried the following:

>> **The Missouri Compromise (1820):** Admitted Missouri to the Union as a slave state, while at the same time admitting Maine as a free state. The Missouri Compromise, which kept the country's balance between free and slave states equal, declared that all territories north of the 36°30″ latitude would become free states, and all territory south of that latitude would become slave states.

>> **The Compromise of 1850:** Admitted California to the Union as a free state but left the remaining Mexican territories to decide the issue by the vote of the people living there, an act known as *popular sovereignty.* Still, California's admission to the Union permanently upset the even balance between free and slave states in the United States. The Compromise of 1850 also ended the slave trade, although not the practice of slavery itself, in the District of Columbia. Because this was a *compromise* (a give and take of issues on both sides) another part of the law enacted a strict *fugitive slave law,* which made it easier for slave owners to recapture runaway slaves and took away the runaways' rights to testify or to be tried by a jury for the crime of running away.

>> **The Kansas Nebraska Act of 1854:** Established the rule of popular sovereignty in the Kansas and Nebraska territories. People in Kansas and Nebraska could vote regarding whether they should be a free or slave state. Abolitionists and slave owners alike rushed to settle the territories, and as you may guess, their conflicts turned violent. The act led to the forming of the new Republican political party, made up of groups that opposed slavery. After only two years of existence, the Republicans dominated the House of Representatives.

The number of representatives a state can send to Congress is based upon that state's population. Because more people lived in the North, this gave the antislavery Republicans the chance to gain power quickly.

Any attempts at compromise ended when the Dred Scott case reached the Supreme Court. Dred Scott, a slave who lived with his master in a free territory for five years, sued for his freedom when he was returned to his slave-state home. The Supreme Court ruled against Scott, stating that slaves were private property and not citizens, and therefore did not have the right to sue in court. The decision pleased the South and enraged the North. Republicans declared the decision could not be legally binding, and tensions between the North and the South increased.

The strengths of the North and South

The seeds of the Civil War were planted long before the conflict ever came to battle. As far back as the drafting of the Constitution, the North and South disagreed on the issues of slavery and *tariffs* (taxes) on imports and exports. The agricultural South wanted protection against export taxes that would make goods like tobacco, rice, and indigo too expensive on the world market. The industrial North demanded protection against lower-priced imports cutting into their business.

ABOLITIONISTS

The white abolitionist movement in the North was led by social reformers, especially William Lloyd Garrison, founder of the American Anti-Slavery Society; activists Sarah and Angelina Grimké; and writers such as John Greenleaf Whittier and Harriet Beecher Stowe. Black activists included former slaves such as Frederick Douglass and Sojourner Truth; Black educator Frances E. W. Harper; and free Blacks such as the brothers Charles Henry Langston and John Mercer Langston, who helped found the Ohio Anti-Slavery Society. After the abolition of slavery, many abolitionists worked for other progressive movements such as universal male *suffrage* (voting rights), women's suffrage, and *temperance* (prohibition of alcohol).

Throughout the Civil War, the North and the South had differing strengths and weaknesses, which led to a long, bloody war that caused enormous loss of money, property, and human lives.

The South's strengths included the following:

>> Large land areas, including long areas of coastline

>> Ownership of most of the existing military equipment and supplies

>> Ongoing income from cotton exports

>> The defensive position, which meant they only needed to keep the Northerners out of their states in order to win the war

But the North had its own strengths, too, some of which eventually overpowered some of the South's advantages:

>> A bigger population — almost double that of the South — and, therefore, more troops

>> A stronger navy

>> Better transportation (railroads!)

>> Enormous financial reserves, as well as the industrial capability to create their own munitions and supplies

The war between the states

In 1860, Abraham Lincoln was elected the 16th president of the United States. His primary purpose was to preserve the Union (USCIS 100:75) of all 34 states of the United States. After the election of Lincoln, South Carolina, followed by ten other states, *seceded* (withdrew) from the Union and formed the Confederate States of America. The Confederacy demanded that all federal property in the state be surrendered to state authorities. Fort Sumpter, one of only two forts in the South still under Union control, refused. On April 12, 1861, the Confederate Army attacked Fort Sumpter, which surrendered two days later. Congress officially declared war on the Confederacy the very next day.

At the beginning of the war, the South dominated. The Battle of Antietam marked the turning point, when the North began to take control. Soon after the battle, on September 22, 1862, President Abraham Lincoln's Emancipation Proclamation freed slaves in the Confederacy (USCIS 100:75, 76). Although Lincoln had little power to actually enforce the law in the South, the proclamation provided the basis for freeing all slaves after the war (13th Amendment, 1865).

THE BIRTH OF THE RED CROSS

Clara Barton, Superintendent of Nurses for the Union Army during the Civil War, treated the wounded of both sides of the conflict on the battlefields. She founded the American Red Cross in 1881.

The American Red Cross still operates today, working closely with government agencies during times of major crises. In 1905, Congress granted a charter to the American Red Cross that required it to act "in accord with the military authorities as a medium of communication between the people of the United States and their armed forces."

Today, the American Red Cross provides humanitarian services to members of the U.S. military and their families around the world. Living and working in the same difficult and dangerous environment as our troops, the Red Cross gives comfort to soldiers and provides emergency-message services (about deaths and births, for example), comfort kits, and cards for the troops to send home to loved ones.

Although the Union had always dominated the West, the North's most important victory in the East came with the three-day-long Battle of Gettysburg. President Lincoln's Gettysburg Address, a speech made to dedicate the cemetery on the battlefield, inspired Americans then (as it does now) to make sure that a government "of the people, by the people, and for the people, shall not perish from this earth."

The Civil War's final battle raged between General Robert E. Lee for the South and General Ulysses S. Grant for the North. Equally powerful and skilled military men, Grant had the advantage of more supplies and more troops, which allowed him to capture the Confederate capital of Richmond, Virginia, before trapping Lee and his men at Appomattox Court House (also in Virginia). Lee surrendered on April 9, 1865, and the war was over. North and South once again came together as the United States of America. Six days later, Lincoln — who had freed the slaves (through the Emancipation Proclamation), saved the Union, and led the United States during the Civil War (USCIS 100:75) — was assassinated.

Reconstruction after the Civil War

Although arguments between the North and South still continued for years after the Civil War, nationalism won out over sectionalism. The country united and set about rebuilding its strength during a period called *Reconstruction*, which lasted from 1865 to 1877.

After the war, the Reconstruction Acts of 1867 set up five military districts, each headed by a general with absolute power, in the South. States could not be readmitted to the Union until they ratified the 14th Amendment, which defined the qualifications of U.S. citizenship, extending citizenship to former African-American slaves previously denied their rightful legal status, and guaranteed suffrage (the right to vote) for African-American men, later codified as male citizens of any race (can vote) in the 15th Amendment (1870) (USCIS 100:48).

Entering the Industrial Revolution

The Civil War also had a significant impact on the United States' growing industry. After the Southern states left the Union, the Northern Congress was able to pass bills on banking, homesteading, and the building of the transcontinental railroad. Republican legislation during the Civil War opened the path to America's Industrial Revolution — a period of massive and rapid growth in manufacturing and industry, not to mention the discovery of gold in California.

At the same time, many adventurous Americans traveled west to settle the frontier, escape crowded Eastern cities and factory jobs, and seek their fortunes. True, the settlers had to endure many hardships, and survival could be difficult, but the rewards were also great. People had to work together, which made the West a place of greater equality and social democracy than other parts of the country. In fact, the American West gave rise to the Populist political party. Although short lived, the Populists had a great impact on U.S. government, including the concept of *graduated income tax,* by which the amount of tax a person pays increases as their income increases (16th Amendment, USCIS 100:56), the *direct election of senators* (17th Amendment, USCIS 100:19,24), and *women suffrage* (19th Amendment, USCIS 100:48). Most important, the Populist movement showed politicians that poor people could have political power and influence, further cementing the notion of a government by and for the people.

The importance of immigrants to a growing nation

U.S. demand for workers during the Industrial Revolution exceeded birth rates, and immigration was encouraged to fill factory jobs, build railroads, and settle the Western lands. Government policy at this time encouraged immigration, and immigrants helped the country to grow strong and rich. Between 1880 and 1930, over 27 million people entered the United States. Families often immigrated together, although men frequently came first, found work, and later sent for their families.

By the 1880s, steam power significantly shortened the time it took to travel to the United States, and immigrants poured in from around the world. Although they came seeking opportunity, life for new immigrants during the American Industrial Revolution was not easy. Immigrant workers often lived in crowded slums in industrial cities. Low wages meant wives and even children had to work to help the family survive.

In addition to jobs in factories and mines, thousands of immigrants found work on the transcontinental railroad, settling in towns along the way west. News of the California Gold Rush quickly spread throughout the world, drawing even more immigrants from both Asia and Europe.

TECHNICAL
STUFF

U.S. government policy toward immigrants generally stayed friendly until the time of World War I (see Chapter 10), with the exception of the Chinese Exclusion Act of 1882. Fears and prejudice in the Old West led to some Americans blaming Chinese immigrants for economic hardships and loss of jobs, despite the enormous positive impact Chinese immigrants had in helping to build the transcontinental railroad and working the mines in the West. The act was repealed in 1943 as a result of our wartime alliance with China, allowing legal Chinese immigration for the first time in 60 years, although until 1965, the quota of Chinese immigrants allowed to enter the country remained lower than that of Europeans.

IMPORTANT AMERICAN INVENTIONS OF THE INDUSTRIAL REVOLUTION

Although the influence of people, especially immigrants, was integral to the growth of the Industrial Revolution, several important inventions also contributed to the rapid industrialization of the United States:

- Eli Whitney was instrumental in the success of America's cotton mills with his invention of the *cotton gin,* which separated cotton fiber from seeds 50 times faster than by hand. Whitney also developed a manufacturing system using standardized identical and, thus, interchangeable parts. Before this important industrial contribution, each part of a given machine was designed only for that single purpose, making replacement parts nearly impossible to obtain. Standardized parts made ordering replacement parts from manufacturers easier, making repairs simple and inexpensive. Whitney first used the system to make muskets for the U.S. government.

- Elias Howe's invention of the sewing machine further advanced the clothing industry.

(continued)

(continued)

- Robert Fulton designed and built America's first steamboat, the *Clermont,* as well as the first practical submarine, the *Nautilus.*

- The Boston Associates, a group of Boston businessmen, built the first power loom. The power loom was able to make cloth so cheaply that American women began to buy it rather than make it by hand.

- One of the U.S.'s most important inventors, Thomas Edison, gave us the light bulb, electric battery, phonograph, mimeograph, and moving pictures.

- Samuel F. B. Morse constructed the first electromagnetic system in 1844, when he built a line from Baltimore to Washington, D.C. Within ten years after the first telegraph line opened, 23,000 miles of wire crisscrossed the country, making railroad travel safer and allowing businessmen to conduct their operations more efficiently and profitably.

- With his invention of the telephone in 1876, Alexander Graham Bell took communications to an even higher level.

- Christopher Sholes revolutionized written communication with his invention of the typewriter.

- George Washington Carver, a Black chemist, invented many new uses for a variety of agricultural crops such as peanuts, soybeans, and sweet potatoes. Carver came up with 325 products from peanuts alone, including food products, household items, shampoos, cosmetics, dyes, paints and stains, and many more. These products offered Southern farmers alternatives to growing cotton and contributed to rural economic development.

- John A. Roebling pioneered the development of suspension bridges and designed the Brooklyn Bridge, although he unfortunately died before his masterpiece was completed.

- Louis Sullivan designed the first steel-skeleton skyscraper.

- Joseph Glidden solved the problem of how to fence in cattle on the Great Plains, where lumber was scarce, with his invention of barbed wire.

The rise of labor unions

After the Civil War, factories were rapidly replacing cottage industries and hand-crafted merchandise in supplying the U.S.'s consumer needs. The growth of industry created endless opportunities for immigrants, but it also created conditions where factory owners and employers could take advantage of their workers, forcing them to work long hours in unsafe conditions for low wages.

Individually, the workers didn't have enough power to change their lot in life — if one worker complained, the employer would simply replace that person. But by uniting as a group, workers gained enough clout to influence their employers and create better working conditions. After all, if a factory owner lost all their employees, production halted.

Labor unions used many tactics to fight for their causes, including *strikes* (in which workers would stop working until their conditions were met) and *boycotts* (in which consumers, frequently in cooperation with unions, refused to buy goods until their demands were met).

Although labor unions were feared at first, they have become a respected part of the American political process, fighting for fair wages, improved working conditions, and job security for their workers. In some cases, union membership is even required in order to hold certain jobs.

The following labor unions had a great impact on creating fair working conditions for American laborers:

>> **The Knights of Labor (1869):** One of the first successful labor unions, the Knights of Labor fought for the rights of both skilled and unskilled laborers. The union worked to reduce the workday to 8 hours at a time when the average workday lasted 12 hours; it also fought to abolish child labor. Although it enjoyed some early successes, the Knights of Labor failed by the late 1880s due to a lack of common interests between skilled and unskilled workers and the huge pool of unskilled laborers willing to replace those who fought for their rights.

>> **The American Railway Union (1893):** The American Railway Union fought for the rights of railroad workers. In 1894, the ARU led the Pulman Strike, shutting down most of the railroads in the Midwest. In response, federal troops used violence to break up the strikes. In an effort to reconcile with organized labor after the strike, Congress designated Labor Day as a federal holiday.

>> **The American Federation of Labor (AFL, 1886):** The AFL, founded in 1881, also fought for better wages and working conditions, but it only admitted skilled laborers. Because skilled workers proved harder to replace, the union enjoyed greater success than the Knights of Labor had been able to achieve.

>> **The Congress of Industrial Organizations (CIO, 1935):** The CIO organized workers according to the industry they worked in rather than their level of skill. CIO strikes proved successful because they effectively shut down the entire industry involved.

   The AFL and CIO merged in 1955 to create one of the most powerful labor unions in our nation's history, the AFL-CIO.

>> **International Ladies' Garment Workers' Union (ILGWU, 1901):** THE IWGWU was one of the first U.S. unions to have a primarily female membership and

leadership. The union also became more involved in electoral politics, in part as a result of the Triangle Shirtwaist Factory fire on March 25, 1911, in which 146 garment workers (most of them young immigrant women) died. Many of these workers were unable to escape because the doors on their floors had been locked to prevent them from unauthorized breaks. The union fought for safe working conditions and fair wages.

» **Service Employees International Union (SEIU, 1921):** SEIU is a labor union focused on three areas: healthcare (hospitals, home care), public services (government employees, law enforcement), and property services (janitors, food service workers).

» **United Mine Workers of America (UMW or UMWA, 1890):** UMWA is a labor union best known for representing coal miners. The Union has since expanded to represent health care workers, truck drivers, manufacturing workers, and public employees loosely associated with the mining and energy industries.

» **Company unions:** In addition, many small unions called *company unions* formed when the employees of a particular company united to fight for better wages, working conditions, and hours. There is renewed interest in forming company unions in response to the short-fall of the 2010s "gig economy," intensified by the COVID-19 pandemic.

TRACING YOUR ROOTS THROUGH ELLIS ISLAND

Ellis Island in New York served as the gateway for more than half of the immigrants entering the United States between 1892 and 1924. During the height of the immigration influx, as many as 10,000 people would file through Ellis Island in a single 24-hour period. It's estimated that more than 40 percent of all current U.S. citizens can trace their ancestry back to an immigrant who entered the country through the Ellis Island processing center.

If you have ancestors that came to the United States through Ellis Island, the Statue of Liberty–Ellis Island Foundation has made tracing your roots online easy by cataloging Ellis Island immigration records. A simple internet search of your family's names can instantly bring up their immigration records. Trace your family's history by visiting www.statueofliberty.org/ellis-island/family-history-center/.

Although not every immigrant came through Ellis Island, the dream remains the same: a better life in a free land. Currently, Ellis Island sponsors The American Immigrant Wall of Honor where you can add the name of a family member — or even your own name — to celebrate your heritage and journey. Go to www.statueofliberty.org/support/wall-of-honor for more information.

Chapter **10**

U.S. History in a Nutshell, Part II: World War I to the Present

After surviving the hardships of the Civil War (see Chapter 9), industry was thriving in the United States, attracting thousands of immigrants seeking better opportunities and more freedom.

But although things were good here, trouble was brewing in Europe. Wars between European nations began to break out. True to the Constitution, the United States tried to remain neutral in the battles raging among many European countries. Most Americans believed that the complicated political alliances between the various battling nations caused the war. A period of neutrality, known as *isolationism,* continued for over 100 years — from the end of the War of 1812 until the United States declared war against Germany in 1917.

President Woodrow Wilson issued an official Proclamation of Neutrality in 1914 stating that the United States would not favor one side over another. This neutral stance allowed the United States to continue trading with all sides. However, all that was about to change.

The World War I Years

The circumstances that led to World War I (1914–1918) had been building for quite some time due to various European nations making enemies of some countries while forming *alliances,* or friendships, with others. National rivalries and conflicts over control of colonies, along with economic competition and an arms race, all contributed to the world going to war.

The causes behind World War I (The Great War)

Conflicts and territory disputes had been raging in Europe for years. In central Europe, the dual monarchy (a government ruled by a king or queen, and in this case one for each country) of Austria-Hungary controlled a large, fractious empire, populated by people of many nationalities: Austrians, Hungarians, Croats, Czechs, Hungarians, Romanians, Serbs, Slovaks, and Slovenians. Despite its ethnic diversity, only Austrians and Hungarians had the right to rule. Of course, the other groups desired political independence from such an unfair rule.

The area of Serbia particularly gave the monarchy trouble because it served as the heart of an independence movement. The Austrian-Hungarian empire believed if it could gain control over the Balkans, and thereby Serbia, its political control problems would be over.

On June 28, 1914, while on a visit to Sarajevo, Bosnia, the Black Hand, a Serbian political group, assassinated Archduke Ferdinand, an heir to the Austria-Hungary throne. This single incident set the wheels of World War I in motion. The resulting chain of events forever changed the course of history.

Austria-Hungary carefully considered its reaction to the killing. Looking for an excuse to go to war and squash the rebellious Serbs, the Austrian-Hungarians decided, three weeks later, to issue an official Ultimatum to Serbia. The document blamed the Serbian government itself for the assassination and accused them of trying to undermine the Austrian-Hungarian government. The Ultimatum to Serbia challenged Serbia's *sovereignty,* or governmental authority.

Austria-Hungary expected Serbia to reject the Ultimatum's harsh terms, thereby giving them a reason to launch a war against the small country. Although Austria-Hungary was aware of Serbia's alliance with Russia, they never expected the larger country to get involved in so small a conflict. They were wrong. By enforcing the Ultimatum, Austria-Hungary began the unlikely chain of events that ended with the entire world being at war.

Dissatisfied with Serbia's response to the Ultimatum, Austria-Hungary declared war on Serbia on July 28, 1914. A month later, Russia sent troops to help her ally, Serbia.

Germany saw the Russian involvement as an act of war against its ally Austria-Hungary. It declared war on Russia on August 1, 1914. France responded by declaring war against Germany and, therefore, against Austria-Hungary. Germany, looking for the quickest route to France's capital city, Paris, invaded neutral Belgium. On the same day, Britain, in order to uphold an old treaty to defend Belgium, and to aid its ally France, declared war on Germany. Of course, Britain's colonies, including Australia, Canada, India, New Zealand, and the Union of South Africa also offered financial and military support to the cause. Although Italy was technically allied with Germany and Austria-Hungary, Italy initially declared its neutrality, then allied with France, England, and Russia.

President Woodrow Wilson officially declared the United States neutral in the conflicts in Europe, and the U.S. continued trade with all sides. The United States finally entered the war on April 6, 1917, as a result of Germany's submarine warfare, which threatened America's commercial shipping industry. Before long, countries the world over from Asia to South America were involved in the conflict.

U.S. participation in the Great War

The United States managed to stay neutral in the European war from 1914 until 1917, but remaining neutral eventually became impossible. Germany's use of its new submarines to attack both military and merchant-marine ships angered Americans. Although the United States didn't necessarily want to enter a war, they would if they felt it could help the greater good of the world.

Most Americans already sympathized with the Allies — England, France, Italy, and Russia. Germany's aggressive acts of unrestricted warfare on nonmilitary ships were the final straw — the United States felt they had a moral obligation to help.

Prior to the United States entering the war, Germany had the upper hand. State-of-the-art war machinery like rockets, tanks, airplanes, and submarines created a new way of fighting, and the Allies were losing the long, hard struggle. U.S. involvement brought fresh troops and more supplies — enough to turn things around and for the Allies to triumph.

After they entered the war, Americans did so with commitment and enthusiasm. Congress authorized the Selective Service Act of 1917 to begin drafting young men for battle (USCIS 100:57). People bought savings bonds in order to raise funds for the war effort, and industry changed its focus from producing items for consumers to making items needed for war — weapons, ammunition, uniforms, and military supplies. Ordinary citizens pitched in by conserving resources such as oil and gasoline and by giving up items they normally enjoyed. For instance, each week had a "meatless" day. On this day, people were asked to give up meat so more food could be sent to the troops.

The combined military and civilian efforts paid off. Germany signed an *armistice* (a treaty to stop fighting) on November 11, 1918. This day is now celebrated as Veterans Day (USCIS 100:100h).

The Treaty of Versailles

President Woodrow Wilson had a 14-Point Plan for peace that he outlined in a speech given to Congress on January 8, 1918. Wilson believed enacting his 14 points would form the foundation for lasting peace. After the war, Wilson and leaders of England, France, and Italy tried to negotiate a peace treaty based upon these important political ideals:

>> No secret treaties or alliances

>> Freedom of the seas

>> Freedom of international trade

>> Reduction of armaments

>> Fair settlement of colonial claims

>> *Self-determination* (the right of the people of a country to determine what type of government they want)

>> The establishment of a League of Nations (see the nearby sidebar)

Although the allies did not agree with all of Wilson's ideas, some were incorporated into the Peace Treaty of Versailles, signed on June 18, 1919. However, the treaty was much harsher and more restrictive than Wilson ever intended. Germany was expected to formally accept *all* the blame for the war, cede territory, and pay war reparations. In addition to limiting German power and redistributing territories and boundaries, the treaty created new countries, including Czechoslovakia, Estonia, Finland, Hungary, Latvia, Lithuania, Poland, and Yugoslavia. The Ottoman Empire was dissolved from which emerged the countries of Iraq, Iran, Lebanon, Syria, and Turkey.

Between 1920 and 1939, a total of 63 countries became member states of the League of Nations. The Covenant forming the League of Nations was included in the Treaty of Versailles (1920) and was dissolved in 1946 when it was superseded by the United Nations.

World War 1 combatants and original League of Nations members:

- » Belgium
- » British Empire (UK, AU, CA, IN, NZ, SA)
- » France
- » Greece
- » Italy (withdrew 1937)
- » Romania (withdrew 1940)

World War I combatants who joined the League of Nations later:

- » Austria (joined 1920; annexed by Germany 1938)
- » Bulgaria (joined 1920)
- » Hungary (joined 1922; withdrew 1939)
- » Germany (joined 1926; withdrew 1933)
- » Soviet Union (joined 1934; expelled 1939 for invading Finland)

World War I non-combatants and League of Nations original members:

- » China
- » Japan (withdrew 1933)

THE LEAGUE OF NATIONS

The forming of the League of Nations, a precursor to today's United Nations, was one of the most important points of the Treaty of Versailles. Those countries that ratified the treaty became members of the League, agreeing to settle any disagreements through negotiations. Supporting diplomacy, economic cooperation, and peaceful solutions to international disputes, the League optimistically sought to eliminate the need for war.

But the United States never actually *ratified* (officially accepted) the Treaty of Versailles. Many senators longed to go back to the U.S. foreign policy of isolationism. Ironically, even though it was part of President Woodrow Wilson's 14-Point Plan, the U.S. Senate refused to ratify the treaty (USCIS 100:41d) because it would mean joining the League of Nations. The senate favored going back to a neutral position in foreign matters, as outlined by President George Washington.

World War I combatants who did not join the League of Nations:

>> United States

Unresolved issue from World War I were not resolved by membership in the League of Nations. Eventually old grievances re-emerged, leading to further hostilities in World War II and the Cold War.

TECHNICAL STUFF

The Treaty of Versailles remains controversial to this day. Many people then, as now, thought the terms far too harsh. After all, how could Germany be expected to accept *all* the responsibility? Furthermore, the money demanded in reparations proved an unreasonable amount. Many historians blame the treaty for establishing the groundwork that led to World War II (more on that later in this chapter).

World War I started the dismantling of European empires and the rise of independence movements in Central Europe, the Middle East, Asia, and Africa. Before the end of the war, depravations caused the Bolsheviks and other anti-monarchal factions to rise up and violently overthrow the Russian imperial family. Under Lenin's leadership, Russia adopted a communist form of government and exported its revolutionary policies to other countries, most notably China.

Surviving the Great Depression

After World War I, Americans wanted life to get back to normal — peaceful times and an American policy of isolation and neutrality in foreign affairs. On the other hand, it was a time of extreme political and social change. The 1800s social reform movements of temperance (no alcohol), women's suffrage, and abolition (no slavery) were revitalized by the Great Plains' populism, Western egalitarianism, and social justice movements. Women led the campaigns for the passage of the 18th Amendment (prohibition of alcohol) and the 19th Amendment (women's suffrage). They also cut their hair, worked in factories, and shopped from newly fashioned catalogues and department stores. African Americans, a generation or two removed from slavery, left regressive "Jim Crow" laws in the South, and migrated to the Northwest to serve in the U.S. armed forces, work in factories, and develop independent Black communities.

The capitalist economy (USCIS 100:11) that had thrived during the war and in the period immediately following, was known as the *Roaring '20s* or the *Jazz Age*. But by the end of the 1920s, the economy was on a downslide. The efficiency of American industrialization was largely responsible:

>> The U.S. produced more goods than it could sell.

>> Due to high tariffs, sales of American goods to foreign countries were down.

>> Because of low working wages, Americans were unable to purchase many of the goods they were producing.

>> Many Americans lost jobs due to new machinery that automated a lot of the tasks that used to be done by hand.

>> The high investment returns of the Industrial Revolution led many people to speculate and overinvest in the stock market.

Tough economic times caused people to panic and quickly sell their stocks, which in turn caused the stock market crash that occurred on October 29, 1929, known as Black Tuesday. Businesses, including over 5,000 banks, failed. Factories shut their doors. By 1932, over a quarter of the U.S. workforce was out of work, and many of those who were employed were forced to accept reduced wages for their labor.

In 1932, as a result of the economic hardships of the Great Depression, the United States saw a significant change in the way its government functioned. Franklin D. Roosevelt became our 32nd president (USIS 100:80) with the promise to help the "forgotten man" (the common working man). Before his presidency, as the governor of the state of New York, Roosevelt had spent government money to give aid to those hurt by the Depression. His presidential campaign had three key points, collectively known as the *New Deal:*

>> **Relief:** Relief efforts provided government jobs or other financial assistance to the unemployed, as well as mortgage loans designed to prevent home- and landowners from losing their property.

>> **Recovery:** Designed to help put people back to work, recovery efforts gave aid to farmers and business owners (in other words, the employers).

>> **Reform:** Reform efforts sought to increase people's confidence in the economy and to prevent another Depression from ever happening. They protected bank deposits and other investments and regulated businesses and banks.

Roosevelt's policies represented a significant expanding of the government's role, which some saw as a movement against the principles of the Constitution. Nonetheless, people were worried about money. They believed in Roosevelt's policies and his optimism about the United States. He won the presidential election by a landslide.

ECONOMIC DEPRESSIONS IN EUROPE

World War I left Europe burdened with overwhelming debt. Not only did the European governments need to repay bills accumulated during the war, but they were often left with the task of having to rebuild areas left ruined by the war's destruction. The United States' wartime allies France and Great Britain owed money to privately owned American companies as well as to the U.S. government. To make matters worse, trade and industry failed to thrive after the war, creating mass unemployment.

Instead of working together, the difficult conditions caused many European countries to place high tariffs on imported goods in order to protect domestic trade. Political instability followed. In addition, new countries were constantly threatened by the growing strength of communist Russia. Italian citizens overthrew their government, and Germany hoped for a revision of the Treaty of Versailles. The aftereffects of the war weakened even France and England, the two countries that truly favored the Treaty of Versailles.

Despite the controversy, Roosevelt's measures helped the economy, at least in the short term, and people's confidence began to rise. Soon, the government employed over 5 million people to build highways, public buildings, dams, and parks. The United States slowly climbed out of the Depression, and by 1939, over ten years after it had begun, the Great Depression was finally over.

The World War II Years

Conditions in Europe in the early 1930s set the stage for World War II (1939–1945):

>> Economic depressions increased fear and distrust, allowing extreme political groups and dictators to gain power.

>> The countries that were part of the Treaty of Versailles had such a desire for peace that they neglected to properly prepare for military defense.

As soon as he gained power, Adolf Hitler began working on his dream of Germany dominating Europe by planning to conquer more territory. In October 1933, Germany withdrew from the League of Nations, claiming that the Treaty of Versailles had left them militarily weak. Over the next few months, the German army grew three times as large as it had been under the conditions imposed by the treaty.

World War II officially began when Hitler's troops invaded Poland, without a Declaration of War, on September 1, 1939. Using new military techniques like mechanized and air warfare, the Germans quickly crushed the unprepared Polish defenses.

The attack prompted Poland's allies, Great Britain and France, to declare war on Germany. Other League of Nations members soon followed suit.

Choosing sides: The Axis and the Allies

Germany banded together with Italy and Japan to create the most important *Axis powers* (USCIS 100:81). The countries the United States eventually went to war against had several things in common:

HITLER'S RISE IN GERMANY

Many Germans did not agree with the politicians who signed the *armistice* (peace agreement) that had brought World War I to an end on November 11, 1918. General unrest about the conditions of the Treaty of Versailles also prevailed. For one thing, the financial reparations required were unrealistic and, in fact, the German government gave up trying to pay them after only one year. The hatred felt for the Treaty of Versailles created a perfect environment for extremist political parties to thrive, including the German Workers' Party and the National Socialist, or Nazi, Party.

As the leader of the Nazi Party, Adolf Hitler possessed the skills of inspiring and mobilizing his followers. Hitler was appointed Reich Chancellor of Germany in 1933 and, after the 1934 death of the German president, he also assumed the title of *Führer* (leader).

In Hitler's Germany, individuals had no freedom of protest. Politics were completely under the control of the Nazis, and elections, both local and national, were abolished. It was under Hitler's leadership that Germany started World War II and under his orders that the atrocities of the Holocaust — including the murder of an estimated 6 million Jews and about 5 million other civilians — were committed.

Despite early dominance in World War II, by 1943 it became clear to many German officers and government officials that Germany was destined to lose the war. Statesmen, government officials, and allies suggested Germany negotiate a peace agreement with England and the United States, but Hitler firmly rejected the idea.

When Soviet troops entered Germany near the end of the war, Adolf Hitler opted to commit suicide rather than risk capture by his enemies.

>> All eventually adopted some form of dictatorship government that gave the state supreme authority.

>> All were ambitious, fighting for expansion of territory at the expense of neighboring countries.

>> All used an intolerance of communism as a way to gain support for their early actions from conservative groups.

The Allied countries — France and England at first, then later the Soviet Union, the United States, and many other smaller countries — opposed the Axis countries.

At first, the United States did not want to get involved in Europe's problems. Congress passed several Neutrality Acts before the war started. The acts stated that if a war in Europe began, the United States would not sell war goods or make loans to any country involved in the conflict. Regardless of public policy, most Americans sympathized with the Allied forces.

When war actually did break out in 1939, Congress passed yet another Neutrality Act. This one allowed the United States to sell war goods to countries involved in the conflict, providing those countries paid cash and picked up the goods them-selves. Congress knew that the only countries who were in the position to take advantage of the arrangement were France and England. The Neutrality Act allowed the United States to unofficially help the Allies, while technically remaining neutral.

As the war went on, American sympathy for the Allies grew, and by 1940 most people in the United States favored some sort of intervention. Congress passed the Selective Service Act of 1940, which allowed the government to start drafting men to enter the military (USCIS 100:57). The United States also suspended trade with Japan, making it clear to the world that Americans clearly sided with the Allies, even though they had not officially entered the war.

The United States under attack: Pearl Harbor

On Sunday, December 7, 1941, a day that President Roosevelt said would "live in infamy," the Japanese unexpectedly attacked the United States military base at Pearl Harbor in Hawaii.

The United States declared war on Japan the next day. Within a few days, Germany and Italy declared war on the United States (USCIS 100:81). The Allies had gained another powerful partner and the Axis countries a formidable enemy. General

Dwight D. Eisenhower commanded American forces in North Africa and was promoted to the Supreme Allied Commander for the invasion and liberation of Europe (USCIS 100:82).

At first, the Axis countries prevailed in the war in the Pacific, with Japan conquering the Philippines, Burma, the Netherlands East Indies, and many other Pacific islands. The United States lacked significant military forces in the area, although Australia and China helped.

TECHNICAL STUFF

The first Allied naval successes against Japan were scored in the battles of the Coral Sea and Midway. U.S. bombers forced Japan into retreat, eliminating a big part of Japan's carrier fleet in the process.

"Relocating" citizens: Japanese internment in World War II

Compelled by a Congress caught in the grips of anti-Japanese hysteria, President Franklin Roosevelt signed Executive Order 9066, effectively suspending the civil liberties of both American citizens of Japanese ancestry and legal resident aliens from Japan. Japanese Americans found themselves, on the government's orders, being rounded up and sent to internment camps, officially called *relocation camps.*

In the name of national defense, Roosevelt's order permitted the military to bypass constitutional safeguards guaranteed to American citizens (USCIS 100:02c).

MUSSOLINI'S RISE IN ITALY

After the chaos of World War I, Benito Mussolini founded the Italian fascist party, a political movement with a harsh centralized government led by a dictator with absolute power. In 1921, he was elected by the Italian fascist party and quickly gained power through manipulation and alliances. Within a year of taking office, he dissolved all political parties except his own and turned Italy into a police state. However, Mussolini was so skillful at *propaganda* (manipulation of the press to further his own causes) that he had little opposition. Under his dictatorship, laws were rewritten and Italy's parliamentary system of government was destroyed.

Mussolini supported the fascists in the Spanish Civil War and pursued wars of aggression in North Africa, the Balkan Peninsula, and Greece where his troops were defeated. In 1945, with the end of the war near and Allied troops approaching, Mussolini tried to escape to Switzerland, but he was captured and executed by Italian patriots.

KOREMATSU V. UNITED STATES

Fred Korematsu, a 23-year-old Japanese-American man, refused to go to his assigned internment camp and instead challenged the order on the grounds that it violated the Fifth Amendment Due Process Clause: "No person shall . . . be deprived of life, liberty, or property, without due process of law." In the case of *Korematsu v. United States,* (1944), six Supreme Court justices upheld Executive Order 9066, citing wartime security concerns. Three Supreme Court justices vehemently dissented, saying that the exclusion order fell "into the ugly abyss of racism" and contradicted democratic principles. The decision was widely criticized by scholars and civil rights activists and was formally repudiated as part of a Supreme Court decision, *Trump v. Hawaii* (2018), which sought to exclude travelers from specific Muslim-majority countries.

Executive Order 9066 never specifically mentioned people of Japanese ancestry. Instead, its broad wording could also be taken to include those of German or Italian descent. In reality, though, only a few thousand "enemy aliens" of German or Italian descent were ever arrested, most immediately after the bombing of Pearl Harbor. And although no German or Italian citizens were rounded up and herded into internment camps, over 100,000 people of Japanese ancestry were.

The camps were overcrowded and provided poor living conditions. People lived in simple barracks–style buildings, without heat, plumbing, and cooking facilities. Because food was short during the war, it was strictly rationed in the camps. Fortunately, families were generally kept together.

Eventually, the government agreed to allow internees to leave the camps if they enlisted in the U.S. military. Not surprisingly, the offer wasn't met with much enthusiasm, and only about 1,000 internees enlisted.

Two and a half years after signing Executive Order 9066, Roosevelt rescinded the order during his second term in office. The last internment camp was closed by the end of 1945.

Today, the sad history of the Japanese internment camps reminds us that no citizen should ever be denied the basic rights guaranteed by the Constitution, regardless of how unusual the circumstances.

Fighting Germany and Japan

France, although fighting valiantly, was quickly overpowered by Germany and signed an *armistice*, or peace agreement, with Germany in June 1940. Under the leadership of Winston Churchill, Britain resisted, despite constant German bombing attacks that left many of England's important cities devastated.

When Germany had the bad sense to invade the Soviet Union in June 1941, England gained a powerful ally. The 1943 German defeat at Stalingrad allowed the allied Soviet army to advance from the east. Germany remained on the retreat for the remainder of the war, and Italy unconditionally surrendered in September 1943.

By 1944, the Allies had developed their air warfare skills, destroying many German cities and undermining industry and transportation throughout the German-controlled portions of Europe. The efforts of the Air Force also allowed allied ground forces to regain control of most of France and Belgium. The famous D-Day invasion of Normandy, France, in June 1944, began a massive effort to regain German-occupied territory of Europe and led to the ultimate defeat of Adolf Hitler. Germany surrendered by May 1945.

Despite substantial Allied military victories in the Pacific, the Japanese refused to unconditionally surrender. Harry S Truman, who succeeded to the presidency after the death of Franklin Roosevelt, made the difficult decision to use the new atomic bomb. On August 6, 1945, the United States dropped the first atomic bomb on Hiroshima, Japan. An estimated 70,000 people were killed, but still the Japanese would not surrender. The United States dropped a second bomb on Nagasaki on August 9, 1945. Unable to sustain further losses, Japan surrendered on August 10, 1945, on the condition that Emperor Hirohito retain at least nominal power. World War II was officially over.

OFFICIALLY ENDING INTERNMENT

Interestingly enough, Order 9066 was never officially removed from the books until 1976, when President Gerald Ford, in a show of bicentennial-celebration goodwill, officially repealed it on February 19, 1976.

Then in 1988, almost 50 years after the camps closed, Congress passed the Civil Liberties Act of 1988 (also known as the Japanese American Redress Bill), admitting that "a grave injustice was done" and mandating payment of $20,000 in reparations to each victim of internment. Reparations were sent with a signed apology from the president on behalf of the American people.

The effects of World War II

The scope of World War II, being even greater than World War I, left many after-effects. Europe and Japan had to deal with bombed-out cities that were formerly populous centers of industry. The Axis countries of Germany, Italy, and Japan suffered nearly complete devastation. Even England and France lost large parts of their former empires.

The losses motivated countries to work together to overcome their hardships. The idea of an international organization again gained favor. In fact, Allied forces were working to set up the United Nations (UN) even before the war was over. Still in existence today, the UN works to promote peace by providing a forum where countries can come together to discuss peaceful solutions to problems and conflicts. It also provides educational and economic aid to countries in need.

The Allies also recognized the importance of free trade in order to avoid a depression like the one that followed World War I. They made tariff agreements that kept the flow of goods open between international communities.

The Cold War Years

With countries like England, France, Germany, and China sustaining devastating losses of people, property, and progress after World War II, the world was left with two main superpowers:

>> The United States of America which had a democratic government and capitalist economy (USCIS 100:11).

>> The Soviet Union which had a communist government and state-planned economy (USCIS 100:83)

Dominance in the arms race (by the 1950s, both superpower countries had nuclear bombs) and economic struggle for world power created these two superpowers.

TECHNICAL
STUFF

The Soviet Union emerged a superpower after World War II despite sustaining the highest losses of any country involved in the war — 7.5 million military personnel and 15 million civilians.

The United States and the Soviet Union both believed their system of government worked best. Despite unifying efforts in Europe and the work of the United Nations, the world began to take sides. The United States *allied*, or joined forces with, Western Europe, while the Soviet Union maintained control over much of Eastern Europe.

Fighting communism: The Cold War between the world's superpowers

The Cold War (1947–1991) between the United States and the Soviet Union was not actually a war in the traditional sense. No guns or ammunition were used, and no actual battles were fought. Instead, money and trade were the weapons the two sides used to win their victories.

These years represent the United States' further distancing from neutral foreign policy — a change that exists to this day. The 1947 Truman Doctrine declared that the United States would support any nation threatened by communism. In addition, under the Marshall Plan, the United States provided massive economic aid to Europe to help revitalize the failing European economies and to help prevent the spread of communism. The United States also helped to found and fund the International Monetary Fund and the World Bank — both of which lend money to developing nations in order to help them avoid communist influence.

In 1949, the alliance between the United States and Western Europe became formal with the forming of the North Atlantic Treaty Organization (NATO). NATO's policy was to limit, or *contain*, the Soviet Union to the areas where it already had influence. Members in the organization also vowed to defend each other if ever attacked.

To counter NATO, the Soviets enacted the Warsaw Pact, which formed a military organization with the nations of Eastern Europe. The Warsaw Pact sought to promote a peaceful coexistence of the world's powers, but also to defend member nations if necessary. The Warsaw Pact was dissolved in 1991 with the reunification of Germany and NATO membership of several formerly Soviet countries, most notably Poland and the Baltic and Balkan countries. As of this writing, Russia is invading Ukraine over potential NATO membership. Russian aggression has inspired neutral countries Finland and Sweden to explore the possibilities of NATO membership. Bosnia and Herzegovina, Georgia, Ireland, Moldova, and Serbia are also considering NATO membership.

Battling communism in Asia: The Korean War

After World War II, Korea was divided into a northern zone governed by the Soviet Union and a southern zone helped by the United States. Eventually, the Soviets withdrew, leaving a communist government in the North. In June 1950, North Korea attacked its Southern neighbor without warning, inciting the Korean War (USCIS 100:83c).

At a meeting not attended by the Soviets, the United Nations voted to send troops to help South Korea defeat the intruders — the first use of UN military forces to enforce international peace. Initially, the UN troops — comprised of mostly South Koreans and Americans — were smaller and less prepared than the North Koreans, who were supported by the Chinese. Eventually, other countries sent reinforcements, and the North Koreans and Chinese retreated. Korea remained divided at the end of the Korean War, and it remains divided to this day.

The Vietnam War

During the time of President Eisenhower, the United States began to provide economic and military aid to the tiny country of South Vietnam.

In the mid-19th century, the French had established tentative control over the southernmost provinces of Vietnam. When the French expanded to central and northern Vietnam, they were met with an aggressive resistance movement. But the large French military defeated the insurgents and began to exploit Vietnam's resources:

>> Huge tracts of land in southern Vietnam were turned over to French settlers and Vietnamese collaborators.

>> Vietnamese contract workers in mines and rubber plantations could be fined or even jailed if they tried to leave their jobs.

>> Educational opportunities generally declined under French rule.

>> Political rights and participation by the Vietnamese remained strictly under French control.

>> The French used force to squash any protests, driving many Vietnamese into exile.

One of the most prominent Vietnamese rebels was Ho Chi Minh, known for organizing the League for Vietnamese Independence (abbreviated in Vietnamese as *Viet Minh*) in 1941. During World War II, the French lost their hold over Vietnam when they surrendered to Germany, and Japan assumed control of the country. The Viet Minh worked behind Japanese lines to supply information on Japanese troop movements to America's Office of Strategic Services (OSS). In return, they received some arms and supplies from the OSS and began building a small guerrilla force. When Japan surrendered to the United States, the Viet Minh were the most powerful political force in Vietnam.

On September 2, 1945, hoping his wartime allies would help restrain the French from trying to dominate Vietnam again, Ho Chi Minh proclaimed Vietnam a free and independent country.

Although the United States didn't necessarily approve of French tactics, a growing concern over Communist power in Asia led them to support the French war effort. Vietnam was soon under French control again, and the Viet Minh resumed their fight for independence.

The 1945 Geneva Conference brought a temporary end to fighting by dividing Vietnam at the 17th parallel.

Eisenhower believed the United States should support any country that was threatened by communism. Vietnam was a country divided:

>> The northern part of Vietnam, led by Ho Chi Minh, was communist.

>> The southern part of Vietnam, led by Ngo Dunh Diem, who became prime minister of South Vietnam as the defeated French forces left, was fervently anticommunist.

When Kennedy succeeded Eisenhower as president, aid to South Vietnam increased. In 1964, when the North Vietnamese allegedly attacked two American destroyers, Congress passed the Gulf of Tonkin Resolution that gave then President Lyndon Johnson the authority to do whatever he thought was militarily necessary to protect our country. Suddenly, the United States was at war with the tiny country of North Vietnam, a war that would last from 1964 until 1973 (USCIS 100:78d).

In discussions of the Vietnam War, you'll often hear the term *Viet Cong*. This was the name given to guerilla fighters on the Communist side. The North Vietnamese Army (NVA), on the other hand, were regular troops.

Many Americans did not think the United States should be involved in this war. Bitter antiwar protests broke out throughout the country. President Richard Nixon campaigned on the promise to withdraw from Vietnam honorably. After his election, Nixon continued peace talks, which had been going on throughout the war, but with little result.

The war finally ended with the 1973 Paris Peace Agreement. Everyone involved compromised, and Vietnam returned to being a divided country.

Despite the Paris Peace Agreement, fighting between the South Vietnamese and the communists continued. In early 1975, North Vietnam launched an attack on its southern neighbor. This time the U.S. Congress denied South Vietnam's requests for aid. On April 30, 1975, North Vietnamese troops marched into Saigon, and the

South Vietnamese resistance collapsed. Vietnam was formally reunified in July 1976, and Saigon was renamed Ho Chi Minh City, after the leader of North Vietnam.

TECHNICAL STUFF

U.S. casualties in Vietnam during the era of direct U.S. involvement (1961–1972) were more than 50,000 dead. The war divided the United States along political lines as well — those who opposed the war and those who believed the U.S. should fight. It made people again examine the Founding Fathers' beliefs in American neutrality in foreign conflicts, although we have never again been able to return to those earlier ideals.

The Civil Rights Movement

The fight against communism abroad wasn't the only problem the United States had to deal with after World War II. Domestic unrest that started during the Civil War and raged during the Vietnam War years continued.

REMEMBER

President Lincoln's Emancipation Proclamation freed the slaves during the Civil War (for more on the Civil War, turn to Chapter 9).

Nonetheless, African Americans in 1950s America, especially in the South, still suffered from *discrimination,* or unfair treatment based upon their race (USCIS 100:84). Some states limited the rights of African Americans to vote. Schools, buses, trains, and public businesses like theaters and restaurants were often *segregated,* or separated into facilities for blacks and whites.

The civil rights movement actually began during World War II when President Roosevelt established the Fair Employment Practices Committee, which prohibited discrimination practices on the basis of race, creed, color, or national origin, by the United States defense industry. His successor, President Harry S. Truman, furthered the cause by issuing Executive Order 9981 which abolished discrimination "on the basis of race, color, religion or national origin" in the United States Armed Forces and led to the re-integration of the services during the Korean War. Furthermore, Truman founded the Committee on Civil Rights, which stated that discrimination based on race or religion prevents the American ideal of democracy.

The Supreme Court chimed in on the fight in 1954 in a landmark ruling that stated, "Separate educational facilities are inherently unequal" (Brown v. Board of Education of Topeka, Kansas). This historic decision meant that segregation in schools was declared unconstitutional or against the supreme law of the land. The court ordered the schools to be desegregated.

African Americans finally had official government support in their fight for equality, but it was a constant struggle, especially against prominent Southern government officials who continually blocked civil rights legislation. Even the court's order to desegregate schools was tested. In 1957, President Eisenhower had to send U.S. Army units to Arkansas to safely escort Black children to a previously all-white school.

Reverend Martin Luther King, Jr., the most famous civil rights leader, believed Blacks could change society through nonviolent means (see Chapter 21 for more information on King) (USCIS 100:85). African Americans began to organize. Peaceful demonstrations and boycotts led to the desegregation of buses, restaurants, restrooms, and other public places. In 1963, about 250,000 participants, Blacks and whites — the largest gathering of people to that date — marched on Washington, D.C., to demand civil rights. To guarantee equality for Blacks, the federal government passed Civil Rights Acts in 1957, 1960, 1964, and 1968.

The 24th Amendment, which outlawed taxing voters at presidential or congressional elections, passed in 1964 as another way to remove barriers to Black voters (USCIS 100:48b). But evidence of continuing interference with attempts by African-American citizens to exercise their right to vote prompted Congress to pass the Voting Rights Act in 1965, with amendments added in 1970, 1975, and 1982 (USCIS 100:48). The Voting Rights Act is considered to be the single most effective legislation Congress ever passed. Black voter registration saw a marked increase soon after its passing. In order to battle unfair voting processes, the acts

>> Ended the use of literacy requirements for voting in six Southern states and in many counties of North Carolina

>> Prevented changes in voting procedures from being legally enforceable in those jurisdictions until they were approved by either a three-judge court in the District of Columbia or by the Attorney General of the United States

>> Gave the U.S. Attorney General authority to appoint federal voting examiners to ensure that legally qualified persons were free to register for federal, state, and local elections, and to assign federal observers to oversee elections

Despite these advances made during the 1960s, there are ongoing attempts to subvert the electoral process. Americans must be ever-vigilant to safeguard voting rights!

Understanding the U.S. Today

Although popular interpretations of the Constitution have changed over the years, Americans still look to their most important document when creating laws and deciding the best way to run the country. Changes in public sentiment along with complicated international politics have forever changed the U.S. policy of neutrality in foreign affairs. Nonetheless, our government's system of checks and balances (UCIS 100:14) still ensures against any one person or group gaining so much power that they can overthrow the will of the people. Over the last few decades, the United States has had to grow and adapt to new challenges, especially in the area of international relations.

Important recent historical events from the late 1960s to the 1990s

Several important historical events have taken place from the Vietnam War through the 1990s:

>> **The fight for women's rights (1966):** The National Organization for Women (NOW) was founded to "to take action" to bring about equality for all women, including equal rights with men, equal employment opportunities, equal pay for equal work, divorce-law changes, and legalized abortion.

>> **The U.S. wins the moon race (1969):** Neil Armstrong became the first man to walk on the moon on July 20, 1969.

>> **Delano Grape Strike (1965–1970):** Mexican- and Filipino-American farm workers led by Cesar Chavez, Dolores Huerta, and Larry Itliong joined together to form the United Farm Workers of America. Their demand for safer working conditions led to a series of consumer boycotts and changed agricultural labor practices. This strike inspired Chicano Pride and subsequent Hispanic and minority identity movements.

>> **Occupation of Alcatraz (1969–1971):** A group of Native Americans occupied Alcatraz Island, the site of a former prison, under an 1868 treaty between the U.S. government and the Sioux and Lakota tribes (USCIS 100:88) that out-of-use federal land must be returned to the Native Americans who once occupied it. The group protested against the federal Native American termination policy, which sought to assimilate Native Americans, disband their tribes, and occupy their lands. This occupation inspired the "Red Power" movement and increased indigenous activism.

>> **The Watergate Scandal (1972):** Five men were arrested for breaking into the Democratic National Committee's executive quarters in the Watergate Hotel on June 17, 1972. Further investigation showed that President Nixon himself might

be involved. Although he withheld them at first, the Supreme Court ordered Richard Nixon to turn over tape recordings of the plans for the cover-up of the scandal. Senate hearings began in 1973, and Nixon finally admitted his involvement. When his *impeachment trial* began — a trial that could remove him from office if he were found guilty — he decided to resign instead.

>> **Title IX (1972):** Introduced by Senator Patsy Mink of Hawaii, Title IX of the Education Amendments of 1972 addressed sex-based discrimination in any school that receives funding from the federal government. Increased funding led to the rise of women's collegiate teams and professional sports leagues.

>> **Panama Canal Treaty (1978):** Passed by President Jimmy Carter, the treaty called for the gradual return of the Panama Canal to the people and government of Panama by 1999.

>> **Iran hostage crisis (1979):** The overthrow of the Shah of Iran by Islamic rebels led to a steady decline in U.S.-Iran relations. In protest of the United States admitting the exiled Shah to America for medical treatment, a crowd of Iranians seized the U.S. embassy and took hostages. Ironically, the hostage crisis was finally resolved the day Carter left office and Ronald Reagan was inaugurated.

>> **Fall of the Berlin Wall (1989):** "Mr. Gorbachev, tear down this wall!" The destruction of the Berlin Wall by Germans massed on both sides marked the symbolic end to the Cold War and the start of the transition from communist to republican forms of government and market economies in former Soviet-bloc countries. German Unification took place the following year, and the realignment of Central and Eastern European alliances is still evolving.

>> **Economic growth and the digital revolution (1990s):** The 1990s in the United States saw a time of great economic growth and birth of the digital revolution. Just as the Industrial Revolution fueled a period of economic growth, so did the birth of the internet and digital revolution in America in the 1990s. Like the Industrial Revolution, it also led to wild speculation, overinvesting in the stock market, and an economic recession that followed (although not nearly as bad as the Great Depression).

THE ONLY PRESIDENT NEVER TO BE ELECTED

Gerald R. Ford holds the unusual honor of being the only United States president to never have been elected. How is this possible? When Richard Nixon's vice president, Spiro Agnew, resigned, Nixon selected Gerald Ford for the vice president spot. When Nixon resigned, after the Watergate scandal, Ford became the nation's new president.

Trouble in the Middle East: The Gulf War

Iraq's invasion of Kuwait on August 2, 1990, began a conflict that included the United States, England, Egypt, France, and Saudi Arabia, along with a coalition of 27 other nations. Iraqi President Saddam Hussein defended the attack by claiming that overproduction of oil in Kuwait had cost the Iraqi economy millions of dollars. He also accused the Kuwaitis of illegally pumping oil from Iraq's Rumaila oil field.

The United Nations placed a trade embargo on Iraq, setting a deadline of January 15, 1992, for a peaceful withdrawal of Iraqi troops from Kuwait. Saddam Hussein stood his ground and refused to leave. In response, the U.S.-led coalition of nations launched Operation Desert Storm, a massive air war that destroyed much of Iraq's military *infrastructure,* or foundation. The main coalition ground forces invaded Kuwait and Iraq on February 24 and in only four days defeated the Iraqis, freeing the people of Kuwait. Despite victory, both sides sustained enormous losses.

Worst of all, Saddam Hussein, a brutal dictator, retained power in Iraq. Although he agreed to coalition peace terms on paper, in reality he took great efforts not to comply with the terms, especially on the issue of UN weapons inspections. Continued resistance to weapons inspections led to the coalition resuming bombing raids against Iraq.

In March 2003, a military coalition was led by the United States to remove Saddam Hussein and the Ba'ath Party from power. The quick takeover turned into a long occupation as the coalition forces fought against insurgents. U.S. troops and coalition forces withdrew in 2011, only to return again in 2014 to fight against Islamic State of Iraq and Syria (ISIS) terrorists. Despite the many setbacks, the Iraqi people continue to build a modern Islamic republic with a strong federal government composed of the executive, legislative, and judicial branches, as well as independent commissions.

Historical events of the 21st Century

On September 11, 2001, terrorists attacked the United States (USCIS 100:86), the worst attack since the Japanese attack on Pearl Harbor in World War II. New York's World Trade Center and the Pentagon building in Washington were hit by commercial airliners, hijacked by Middle Eastern terrorists.

This center of world commerce, along with the headquarters of United States military operations, provided prominent political targets for the terrorists. Thousands of lives were lost; calculating the loss to the U.S. society is impossible because the results are still being felt.

For the first time, the United States found itself in a war against not a country, but against terrorists who know no borders.

Significant happenings of the 21st century include the following:

>> **Patriot Act (2001) and Homeland Security Act (2020):** Enacted after the September 11 attacks, both acts focus on the strengthening of U.S. national security. The Patriot Act includes provisions for expanded surveillance abilities of law enforcement, increased data sharing between federal agencies, and an expanded list of activities that qualify for terrorism charges. The Homeland Security Act led to the creation of a new cabinet-level department under the Secretary of Homeland Security, which assumed a large number of services, offices, and other organizations previously conducted in other departments, such as the U.S Citizenship and Immigration Services (USCIS), U.S. Immigration and Customs Enforcement (ICE), U.S. Customs and Border Protection (CBP), and Transportation Security Administration (TSA).

>> **Afghanistan War (October 2001–August 2021):** The United States invaded Afghanistan to overthrow the Taliban regime, resulting in a long-term war.

>> **Iraq War (2003–2011):** In 2003, the United States–led coalition invaded Iraq to overthrow the government of Saddam Hussein. The conflict continued for much of the next decade as an insurgency emerged to oppose the coalition forces and the post-invasion Iraqi government.

>> **Rise of social media:** Facebook (2004), YouTube (2005), and Twitter (2006) were founded, changing the way people communicate, share, and access information.

>> **Introduction of the iPhone (2007):** A series of smartphones was launched by Apple, integrating the functionality of a mobile phone with internet accessibility.

>> **Election of the first African-American president (2008):** Barack Obama was elected to become the first Black president of the United States.

>> **Great Recession (2008–2009):** The worst financial crisis since the Great Depression occurred in the United States and most of Europe. Multiple overlapping crises were involved, notably, the housing market crisis, a subprime mortgage crisis, soaring oil prices, an automotive industry crisis, and rising unemployment.

>> **Black Lives Matter (2013–present):** A series of nationwide protests took place over the separate shooting deaths of Trayvon Martin, Michael Brown, Eric Garner, Tamir Rice, Breonna Taylor, Georgia Floyd, and other unarmed African Americans by police. Each incident renewed a vigorous debate about racism, police brutality, and the need for criminal justice reform.

>> **Deferred Action for Childhood Arrivals (DACA, 2014–present):** President Obama signed two executive actions which had the effect of delaying deportation for millions of illegal immigrants. The orders apply to parents of U.S. citizens (Deferred Action for Parents of Americans) and young people brought into the country illegally (Deferred Action for Childhood Arrivals). These orders were rescinded in 2018 and restored in 2021. They continue to be key concerns of comprehensive immigration reform.

>> **Islamic State of Iraq and Syria (ISIS, 2014–2017):** ISIS was a terrorist group that seized territory in Iraq and Syria, causing a mass exodus of refugees. Although an international military coalition led by the United States defeated ISIS, many refugees have not yet been resettled.

>> **Marriage Equality (2015):** Same-sex marriage was legalized in all 50 U.S. states.

>> **The 45th president (2016):** Donald Trump won the 2016 presidential election in an upset against Hillary Clinton, the first female to be nominated by a major party. Trump was the first person without prior military or government service to hold the office.

>> **COVID-19 pandemic (2020–present):** COVID-19 is a contagious respiratory disease caused by severe acute respiratory syndrome coronavirus 2 (SARS-CoV-2). As of early 2022, there had been 77.2 million reported cases and 991,000 deaths in the United States alone. Differing responses to COVID-19 prevention and treatment have contributed to the social and political polarization of the American people.

>> **January 6 Insurrection (2021):** Pro-Trump rioters stormed the U.S. Capitol, disrupting the Congressional certification of United States President-elect Joe Biden. This action spurred competing federal and state legislation about voting and election restrictions and reforms.

>> **The 46th President (2021):** Joe Biden, longtime senator and Obama's vice president, was inaugurated as president of the United States. Kamala Harris, sworn in as vice president, became the first woman, first African American, and first Asian American to be vice president.

>> **Fall of Kabul (August 2021):** Following the 2021 Taliban offensive, the Islamic Republic of Afghanistan collapsed, and the country was governed thereafter by the Taliban as the reinstated Islamic Emirate of Afghanistan. The War in Afghanistan thus ended after 20 years, followed by the withdrawal of U.S. and coalition troops and a final airlift of 120,000 people.

>> **Invasion of Ukraine (February 2022):** In 2014, Russia occupied Crimea and supported an ongoing separatist movement in Eastern Ukraine. To thwart Ukraine's pro-western alliances, including potential membership in NATO, Russia invaded Ukraine. People and pundits are horrified by a war in Europe between countries with nuclear arsenals, prompting the worst fears of a second Cold War that could result in further conflict.

IN THIS CHAPTER

» **Forming a new nation**

» **Recognizing the importance of the Declaration**

» **Understanding the Constitution**

» **Getting familiar with the Bill of Rights**

» **Identifying the amendments to the Constitution**

Chapter **11**

The Declaration of Independence and the Constitution

The two most important documents in the United States are the Declaration of Independence and the Constitution. These two documents form the foundation of the U.S. government. The events that led up to their creation were the same events that transformed 13 British colonies into the most powerful country in the world.

If you understand the Declaration of Independence and the Constitution and the history behind them, you'll understand the principles of the U.S. government and you'll know why Americans take their freedoms so seriously. You'll also be prepared for a big part of the civics portion of your citizenship test. In this chapter, we introduce you to both documents, filling you in on their meaning and importance. Information that refers directly to USCIS history and civics questions is followed with "USCIS 100" and the appropriate question number (Example: USCIS 100:59).

Announcing the Birth of a New Nation: The Declaration of Independence

At the time it was written, the Declaration of Independence served as an official notice to the world that a new, independent nation, the United States of America, was born. Like a birth announcement for a new baby, the Declaration notes the exact day when formal separation from England took place: July 4, 1776. We celebrate Independence Day in the United States every July 4 to mark this important anniversary.

In addition to establishing the United States as a new nation, the Declaration of Independence outlines the specific reasons the American colonists wanted to form a free country, separate and independent from England.

Leading up to the Declaration: The colonists' complaints

Between 1689 and 1763, the British kings allowed the American colonies a lot of freedom. They didn't do this because they were particularly nice guys — their energies were just needed elsewhere because England was at war with France at the time. When the war between France and England ended, King George III turned his attention back toward the American colonies. Because the war had left England with a lot of financial debt, King George III thought getting extra revenue from the colonies was a good idea. And, as you may have guessed, the colonists didn't think George's idea was as good as George thought it was.

Of the many grievances the colonists had with the king, the most important problems that led them to declare their freedom and fight the Revolutionary War were the following:

>> **Taxation without representation:** Even though England required the colonists to pay hefty taxes to the British government, the colonies were not allowed to send representatives to the legislature to vote on those taxes or fight for their interests.

>> **Quartering:** Colonists were required by British law to house British soldiers in their homes.

>> **Land policy:** England restricted the colonists to settling only land located east of the Appalachian Mountains.

>> **Trade restrictions:** England forced the colonists to pay high taxes for trading with any country other than England. Of course, England also expected to pay less money for goods than the colonists would have made by trading with the rest of the world.

Needless to say, King George III did not believe in free trade. In fact, trade restrictions had been the cause of several violent confrontations between the colonists and the British. The most famous of these were the Boston Massacre (in which five colonists were killed by British soldiers) and the Boston Tea Party (in which colonists protesting a tax on imported tea dumped all the tea on board ships in Boston Harbor into the sea). These demonstrations only provoked harsher penalties and more taxes from the king.

What the Declaration says

It took Thomas Jefferson 17 days to write the original Declaration of Independence (USCIS 100:62). Benjamin Franklin and John Adams then helped Jefferson revise his first draft. They sent their masterpiece to the Continental Congress on July 2, 1776, and after two days of debate and more changes, the final draft of the Declaration of Independence was adopted. The Declaration of Independence announced our independence from Great Britain (USCIS 100:08a).

TECHNICAL STUFF

A total of 47 revisions were made to the Declaration of Independence before it was presented to the Continental Congress. After voting for independence on July 2, 1776, Congress then continued to improve the document, making 39 additional changes before its final adoption on July 4, 1776 (USCIS 100:63).

The first part of the Declaration declares the break with England and the reasons why the colonists thought they were justified in taking this important action. The second part of the Declaration lists the colonists' complaints against England's King George III. The Declaration of Independence concludes that, because of the king's oppressive acts, the colonies have the right to declare themselves free and independent states.

SEEKING THE ACTUAL DOCUMENTS

Each year, more than a million visitors flock to the Rotunda of the National Archives in Washington, D.C., to view the Declaration of Independence, the Constitution, and the Bill of Rights. You can view the documents online at www.archives.gov.

Aside from the long list of grievances with King George III, Jefferson made two key points in the Declaration of Independence that he said were "self-evident":

>> **That "all men are created equal" and have been given by God certain rights — namely, the right to "Life, Liberty, and the pursuit of Happiness" (USCIS 100:09) — that no one can take away.** This means that anyone who lives in the United States has these rights, regardless of whether they're a U.S. citizen.

>> **That a government exists only by the consent of the governed.** This means that if the citizens of a country feel that their government is not carrying out their wishes, they have the right and the duty to change or do away with that government.

The principles Jefferson set forth in the Declaration of Independence were the ideals the Founding Fathers later incorporated into the Constitution and the Bill of Rights. These ideals appear later in the Declaration of Rights and Sentiments (1848) issued by the first women's rights convention, Abraham Lincoln's Gettysburg Address (1863), and the United Nation's Universal Declaration of Human Rights (1948), and they're enshrined in the manifestos and constitutions of many nations.

VISITING INDEPENDENCE HALL

The Constitution and the Declaration of Independence really come to life when you visit Independence National Historical Park in downtown Philadelphia, Pennsylvania. The park spans approximately 45 acres and includes about 20 buildings open to the public. You can tour Independence Hall, where both the Declaration of Independence and the Constitution were created and where many of our country's most important early events took place. The room is restored to look just as it did in 1787, including original chairs and inkstands.

Congress Hall was the home of the U.S. Congress from 1790 to 1800 and was the location of President George Washington's second inauguration and President John Adams's inauguration. One block to the north of these buildings is the Liberty Bell, which was rung from the belfry of Independence Hall to celebrate the historic events of July 4, 1776.

Administered by the National Park Service, Independence National Historical Park is open every day from 9 a.m. to 5 p.m. Hours for some buildings are extended on weekends in the spring and throughout the week in July and August. For more information, visit the park's website at www.nps.gov/inde.

Adjacent to Independence Hall are the National Constitution Center (constitutioncenter.org), which has special exhibits and programs about the U.S. Constitution and the 27 amendments, and the Philadelphia Mint (www.usmint.gov), which mints coins and medals.

If you are in Washington, D.C., visit the Constitution Gardens and the Memorial to the 56 Signers of the Declaration of Independence in the National Mall near the Washington Memorial.

The Supreme Law of the Land: The Constitution

The most important document in the United States is the U.S. Constitution, which was signed by the delegates to the Constitutional Convention on September 17, 1787 (USCIS 100:66). The Founding Fathers wrote the Constitution (USCIS 100:66) to set up and define our nation's government (USCIS 100:02ab). After fighting so hard to win their freedom in the Revolutionary War, the Founding Fathers wanted to ensure that this nation could never come under tyrannical rule again. They needed a system of government where the citizens had a say in their government at the local, state, and national levels. For this reason, the Constitution was written to protect the essential "self-evident" rights that Thomas Jefferson wrote about in the Declaration of Independence. The Constitution doesn't *give* Americans their freedoms, but rather acts to guarantee or protect those freedoms (USCIS 100:02c).

The U.S. Constitution has lasted for over 200 years, through many changes in the country and the world. The Constitution is known as the "supreme law of the land" for these reasons:

>> No other laws may contradict any of the principles set forth in the Constitution.

>> Everyone must follow the rule of law set forth in the Constitution, including the leaders and government. No one is above the law (USCIS 100:12).

>> The Constitution guarantees the rights and freedoms of all people living in the United States, whether they are U.S. citizens or not.

What the Constitution says

Through the years, the Constitution has been the subject of countless debates. To this day, legal experts fight over the constitutionality of certain laws. People disagree over how to interpret the Constitution when it comes to important issues like gun control, the place of religion in government, and even the immigration and naturalization process. Politicians argue about the Founding Fathers' intent when they wrote the document.

Even though many scholars and legal experts have studied it, the Constitution is essentially quite simple, based on the following principles:

>> **Popular sovereignty:** The Constitution opens with a declaration of self-government: "We the People" (USCIS 100:03). The United States is a government by the people, for the people. The ultimate political authority does not reside in the government or in any single government official; instead, the ultimate political authority rests with the people. The people have the right to change or abolish their government or to amend their Constitution, and no one can take that right away from them. The Founding Fathers thought this principle was important to protect Americans from ever coming under tyrannical rule, like they had been under King George III.

>> **Rule of law:** The U.S. government is guided by a set of laws rather than by any individual or group of people, and the government possesses only the powers that are specifically granted to it in the Constitution. This means that if something isn't in the Constitution, the government doesn't have the authority to do it. Designed to protect individual rights and liberties, the rule of law calls for both individuals and the government to obey the law. In other words, the government is as accountable to the law as any individual. The rule of law prevents any one person or political group from gaining enough power that they can overpower the rights of others.

>> **Separation of powers and a system of checks and balances:** The Constitution establishes that no part of the U.S. government has final authority. The Founding Fathers wanted to make sure that no one branch of government could ever dominate over the other two branches. Although the separation of powers between the executive, legislative, and judicial branches is one of the basic laws of the Constitution, there are many places in which the responsibilities and powers of government branches intentionally overlap. This is known as the system of checks and balances, because one branch is always checking and balancing the activities of the others (USCIS 100:14).

>> **Federalism:** The Constitution created a *federal* system of government, meaning that the government's power is shared between the national government and the individual state governments. Under our Constitution, the federal government reserves for itself specific powers such as the power to print money, to declare war, to create an army, and to make treaties (USCIS 100:41). The Constitution delegates certain powers to the state governments such as to provide schooling and education, to provide protection (police), to provide safety (fire departments), to give a driver's license, and to approve zoning and land use (USCIS 100:42).

>> **Judicial review:** The judicial branch reviews laws, explains laws, resolves disputes (disagreements), and decides if a law goes against the Constitution (USCIS 100:37). Although the Constitution makes no specific references to the power of the Supreme Court to check abuses of the legislative and executive branches, by the early 1800s the court had been called upon to review the constitutionality of both federal and state laws and acts. The right to hold laws unconstitutional actually goes back before the signing of the Constitution; some colonial judges had invalidated state laws on the grounds that they violated that state's constitution.

Through practice, the Supreme Court has become the chief interpreter of the Constitution. The court's job is to examine laws that are challenged on the basis of being unconstitutional. If the Supreme Court finds the law in question to be in accordance with the Constitution, the law stands. If, on the other hand, the Supreme Court rules that the law goes beyond the powers granted to the government by the Constitution, then it cannot be considered a law, because it goes against the supreme law of the land. The court's implied powers became more official in 1803 with the historic *Marbury v. Madison* decision, in which the court assumed the authority to declare acts of Congress and the president unconstitutional.

Constitutional articles

The original body of the United States Constitution consists of seven articles or sections, each of which discuss a different aspect of the government or rules for how the country is to be run. The following list gives an overview of those articles:

>> **Article I:** Establishes the legislative branch of the U.S. government (the House of Representatives and the Senate) and provides rules for how representatives and senators are to be elected, their duties, and the limits of their powers in government. The primary duty of the Congress is to make federal law (USCIS 100:16).

>> **Article II:** Establishes the executive branch of the U.S. government (the presidency) (USCIS 100:15), outlines the requirements for holding office, and provides details on how the president is to be elected and the scope of presidential power. The primary duty of the executive branch is to enforce laws.

>> **Article III:** Establishes the judicial branch of the U.S. government with the forming of the Supreme Court and outlines its judiciary powers. The primary duty of the judicial branch is to explain the laws of the United States (USCIS 100:37).

>> **Article IV:** Deals with matters of the individual states, including how new states can be admitted to the Union, the government's guarantee to states, and rules for how the states should legally interact with one another (USCIS 100:42).

>> **Article V:** Establishes the procedure for amending or changing the constitution (see the upcoming sidebar "Changing the Constitution" for more information) (USCIS 100:04).

>> **Article VI:** Outlines the legal status of the Constitution. This includes the supremacy of federal law over state law; and the oath of service, which binds legislators, executives, and judicial officers of the United States. Article VI also outlines the responsibilities and procedures for paying off financial debts the states accumulated before the signing of the Constitution.

>> **Article VII:** States that ratification by a minimum of nine states is enough to legally establish the Constitution between those states.

The Bill of Rights

Even before the U.S. Constitution was ratified, people began talking about how to improve it. The Founding Fathers believed they had written the document in such a way that individual rights required no express protection. But many people in 1789 were concerned about protecting certain freedoms and rights that the original document neglected to mention. After all, they had just fought the Revolutionary War — they knew what it was like to *not* have rights, and they didn't want to give away the freedoms they had fought so hard for. It was the promise of a Bill of Rights to be added to the Constitution that helped get the document ratified in the first place.

CHECKS AND BALANCES

The executive, legislative, and judicial branches of government check and balance each other in many ways. For instance, the president has the power to appoint federal judges, ambassadors, and other high government officials, but the United States Senate must confirm those appointments before they can go into effect. In this way, the power of the president is "checked" by Congress.

Likewise, the president has the power to *veto* or reject laws that Congress enacts. (*Veto* means "I forbid" in Latin.) Congress may, however, override the president's veto with a two-thirds vote of both houses (the House of Representatives and the Senate).

The Supreme Court retains the right to call the activities of the legislative and/or judicial branches of government unconstitutional or illegal because they violate the principles set forth in the Constitution.

On December 15, 1791, the first ten amendments — also known as the Bill of Rights — were added to the United States Constitution, thereby guaranteeing important rights to both citizens and noncitizens alike (USCIS 100:02c). The Bill of Rights specifically restricts government invasion of certain individual liberties and prohibits the establishment of any official religion. Nearly two-thirds of the Bill of Rights is devoted to safeguarding the rights of those suspected or accused of crimes.

Here's an explanation of the ten amendments that make up the Bill of Rights:

>> **First Amendment:** Guarantees the rights of freedom of speech, religion, press, peaceable assembly, and the right to formally petition the government. This important amendment prevents the government from censoring citizens or the press and allows citizens to peaceably protest government policies and hold their government accountable. It also safeguards freedom from governmental religious persecution (USCIS 100:5, 6, 10, 51).

>> **Second Amendment:** Guarantees the right of the people to bear arms (USCIS 100:51f).

>> **Third Amendment:** States that the government is not allowed to house soldiers in private homes during peacetime without the homeowner's permission (USCID 100:61b).

>> **Fourth Amendment:** Guarantees the right of the people to be secure in their persons, houses, papers, and effects, against unreasonable searches and seizures. In other words, the government cannot search or seize a person's property without a warrant — an official document, issued by a judge, that confirms the government has a legitimate reason to conduct the search.

>> **Fifth Amendment:** States that a person cannot be tried twice for the same crime and cannot be compelled to testify against themself.

>> **Sixth Amendment:** Gives a person charged with a crime the right to a fair and speedy public trial by an impartial jury, to confront witnesses against them, and to have legal representation. This means that even if the accused can't afford a lawyer, one will be provided to them free of charge.

>> **Seventh Amendment:** Guarantees a trial by jury in most federal civil lawsuits (USCIS 100:49a).

>> **Eighth Amendment:** Prohibits excessive or unusual bail or fines or cruel and unusual punishment.

>> **Ninth Amendment:** States that the people have rights other than those specifically mentioned in the Constitution. In other words, just because the Constitution didn't specifically mention it, doesn't mean it's not your right.

>> **Tenth Amendment:** Says that any power not given to the federal government by the Constitution is a power either of the states or of the people.

Constitutional amendments

As time passed, Congress found more reasons to amend the Constitution and adopt new rules for the country to live by. Of all the thousands of amendment proposals put before Congress, only 33 have managed to obtain the necessary two-thirds approval vote. Of those 33, only 27 received approval from at least three-fourths of the state legislatures.

Here's a summary of the rest of the constitutional amendments:

- » **11th Amendment (adopted 1798):** Prevents citizens of a state or foreign country from suing another state in federal court.

- » **12th Amendment (adopted 1804):** The electoral college votes for the president and vice president on the same party ticket (USCIS:46).

- » **13th Amendment (adopted 1865):** Ended slavery in the United States (USCIS 100:60, 74, 75, 76).

- » **14th Amendment (adopted 1868):** Guarantees the citizenship of all people born or naturalized in the United States (N-400 Part 1; Part 12:45–50; Part 18). This amendment also deals with matters of public debt and says that a given state's population determines the number of representatives it can send to Congress (USCIS 100:25).

- » **15th Amendment (adopted 1870):** Guarantees the right to vote to male citizens of any race (USCIS 100:48d).

- » **16th Amendment (adopted 1913):** Gives Congress the right to collect a federal income tax (USCIS 100:56).

- » **17th Amendment (adopted 1917):** Guarantees the people the right to directly elect senators and sets up rules for Senate terms as well as how to fill Senate vacancies that occur in the middle of a senator's term (USCIS 100:18-20).

- » **18th Amendment (adopted 1919):** Made it illegal to produce or sell liquor in the United States. The 18th Amendment holds the distinction of being the only amendment to be repealed (see the 21st Amendment, later in this list).

- » **19th Amendment (adopted 1920):** Guarantees any citizen the right to vote (USCIS 100:48c).

- » **20th Amendment (adopted 1933):** Changed the date the president takes office from March to January, as well as set forth requirements for Senate assembly.

- » **21st Amendment (adopted 1933):** The 21st Amendment repealed the 18th Amendment, which was the prohibition on liquor. (The only way the Constitution provides for repealing an amendment is to pass another amendment.)

>> **22nd Amendment (adopted 1951):** Established a two-term limit for the president (USCIS 100:26).

>> **23rd Amendment (adopted 1961):** Gave residents of the District of Columbia the right to vote in presidential and vice-presidential elections (USCIS 100:50a).

>> **24th Amendment (adopted 1964):** Guarantees citizens the right to vote for president, vice president, and members of Congress without having to pay a voting tax (USCIS 100:48c).

>> **25th Amendment (adopted 1967):** Establishes the presidential line of succession (USCIS 100:30-31).

>> **26th Amendment (adopted 1971):** Gives the right to vote to citizens at least 18 years of age (USCIS 100:48a, 54).

>> **27th Amendment (adopted 1992):** Says that no law that changes the salary of senators or representatives can take effect until an election of representatives has a chance to intervene.

CHANGING THE CONSTITUTION

The main body of the Constitution has remained unchanged since its adoption, but the constitution has been *amended,* or changed. Amendments are the government's way of keeping up with the times and allowing laws to change with the country's needs and circumstances. Article V offers two ways to propose amendments to the Constitution:

- **A vote of two-thirds from both houses of Congress — the Senate and the House of Representatives — is enough to propose a new constitutional amendment.**

- **Two-thirds of the state legislatures can ask Congress to call a national convention to propose amendments.** Although this is a legal and legitimate way of proposing amendments, up to this point in U.S. history, this method has never actually been put into practice.

After an amendment has been proposed, it must be *ratified,* or accepted, by three-fourths of the state legislatures before it can actually become part of the Constitution. In theory, an amendment can also be ratified by special ratifying conventions in three-fourths of the states, although this method has only been used once — to ratify the 21st Amendment, which repealed the *prohibition* (ban) on alcohol.

THE 28TH AMENDMENT?

Currently there are 27 amendments to the U.S. Constitution. There have been several recent proposals for the 28th Amendment:

- Abolish the Electoral College
- Campaign Finance Reform
- Congressional Term Limits
- Expansion of the Supreme Court
- Voting Rights

However, people have been fighting for Equal Rights Amendment (ERA) for almost 100 years! The ERA says: "Equality of rights under the law shall not be denied or abridged by the United States or by any State on account of sex." Here's a brief ERA timeline:

1923: Three years after women won the right to vote, the ERA authored by Alice Paul is introduced in Congress.

1923–1970: The ERA is introduced into each session of Congress.

1971: The ERA is approved by the U.S. House of Representatives in a vote of 354–24.

1972: The ERA is approved by the full Senate in a vote of 84–8.

1972–1982: States vote to ratify the ERA. Some states rescind their vote after approval.

1982: The ERA is stopped three states short of ratification.

1983: The ERA is reintroduced in Congress. The U.S. House of Representatives fails to pass the ERA by a vote of 278 for the ERA and 147 against the ERA, only 6 votes short of the required two-thirds majority for passage.

1985–1992: The ERA is reintroduced into each session of Congress and held in Committee.

2011–present: Resolutions are introduced at state and federal levels to remove the deadline for ratification of the ERA. Recently, Nevada (2017), Illinois (2018), and Virginia (2020) ratified the ERA.

Over the course of American history, the U.S. Constitution has expanded to establish justice and protect civil rights. Despite the lack of ratification, the ERA has influenced federal and state laws and the campaign for women's rights continues.

Chapter **12**

Understanding the United States Federal Government

I n order to pass the citizenship test, you'll need a basic understanding of the United States government. If you've read Chapter 11 on the Declaration of Independence and the Constitution, you already understand the most important principles that shaped the U.S. federal government. The Founding Fathers, in an effort to protect the freedoms they fought so hard for in the Revolutionary War, wanted to make absolutely sure the federal government could never grow strong enough to overthrow the will of the people. They thought long and hard about how best to create a structure of government that would serve the population of the United States without limiting the people's freedom.

In this chapter, we cover the three branches of government, their duties, and the important people responsible for running them. You see how the various branches share duties and check and balance each other to ensure fairness and control government power. The United States government is a huge entity that affects the lives not only of American citizens, but also of people throughout the world. Understanding how it functions is the first step toward getting involved in this government "of the people." Information that refers directly to USCIS history and civics questions is followed with "USCIS 100" and the appropriate question number (Example: USCIS 100:59).

How the U.S. Government Works

The idea of *self-government* is in the first three words of the Constitution: We the People (USCIS 100:03). A government for the people, by the people is a cornerstone principle of the United States Constitution. Nearly everything the Founding Fathers put into the document was designed to protect U.S. citizens from ever having to worry about the government or any branch of the government. It was also designed so that no one individual could ever have the opportunity to overpower the will of the majority. The brilliant insight the Founding Fathers displayed when structuring the United States has allowed the Constitution to last more than 200 years, despite the many changes and transitions the world has gone through during that time.

Problem: How to structure a sound, strong, central government while simultaneously ensuring that no individual or group within that government could ever become powerful enough to overpower the will of the states or the majority of its people.

Solution: A structure of three separate governmental branches (USCIS 100:13), each with its own distinct powers, that operate independently of each other while at the same time interact with each other.

The three-branch system of government outlined in the U.S. Constitution accomplishes three important things:

>> It divides the duties and responsibilities of the federal government.

>> It keeps the federal government from ever gaining enough power to overthrow the will of the individual states.

>> It constantly checks and balances the separation of governmental power (USCIS 100:14).

The power of any one branch cannot grow too large, because the three branches of government are constantly looking over each other's shoulders. Some examples of how governmental power in the United States is checked and balanced include the following:

- » Congress (legislative branch) has the power to impeach the president (executive branch) and federal court justices and judges (judicial branch) if Congress deems it necessary.

- » Although Congress (legislative branch) has the power to pass bills to become law, the president (executive branch) has the power to veto those bills.

- » The Supreme Court (judicial branch) can declare Congressional laws (legislative branch) or presidential actions (executive branch) unconstitutional.

The Duties and Functions of the Executive Branch

Comprised of the president, the vice president, the executive departments, and independent agencies, each part of the executive branch has specific powers and duties, outlined in the following sections.

The president

The president is the leader of the United States. As chief executive office of the executive branch, the president is responsible for enforcing federal laws and treaties. Executive power is administered through the departments and agencies under the presidential cabinet secretaries. The president is the commander-in-chief of the military (USCIS 100:32). The president signs bills passed by Congress into law (USCIS 100:33). If the President vetoes a bill (USCIS 100:35), Congress can vote to override the veto.

In order to become president of the United States, you must be a natural-born citizen, be at least 35 years old by the time you will serve, and have lived in the United States at least 14 years over the course of your life. At publication of this edition of the book, the current president is Joseph R. Biden (USCIS 100:28), who is a member of the Democratic Party (USCIS 100:46).

The vice president

Occupying the second highest office in the United States, the vice president stands ready to assume the duties of president if the current president dies, becomes disabled, or is otherwise unable to serve (USCIS 100:30). The vice president also presides over the Senate and casts the deciding vote in cases of a tie. The office of vice president carries the same age, citizenship, and residency requirements as the president (see the preceding section). The current vice president is Kamala Harris (USCIS 100:29).

The Cabinet and executive departments

The president's Cabinet advises the president (USCIS 100:35). The vice president of the United States and the secretaries (heads) of the fifteen federal departments carry out government policies that affect nearly every aspect of our daily lives. The heads of the executive departments, usually called *secretaries*, make up the president's *Cabinet*, or official group of advisors:

» **Secretary of Agriculture** (www.usda.gov) manages the nation's food supply by, among other duties, helping American farmers and regulating food-safety laws (36a).

» **Secretary of Commerce** (www.commerce.gov) deals with issues of trade, employment, and economic growth (36b).

» **Secretary of Defense** (www.defense.gov) manages the U.S. military and is responsible for protecting the country (36c).

» **Secretary of Education** (www.ed.gov) manages and regulates schools and other educational institutions (36d).

» **Secretary of Energy** (www.energy.gov) oversees matters of energy including conserving energy, protecting America's oil reserves, and planning for future needs (36e).

» **Secretary of Health and Human Services** (www.hhs.gov) advises and protects Americans on matters of health (36f).

» **Secretary of Homeland Security** (www.dhs.gov) protects the country against further terrorist attacks, including managing most components of immigration (36g).

» **Secretary of Housing and Urban Development** (www.hud.gov) helps Americans find housing and regulates fair housing practices (36h).

» **Secretary of Labor** (www.dol.gov) protects America's workforce by enforcing labor laws and regulating wages and benefits (36i).

» **Secretary of State** (www.state.gov) handles matters of international diplomacy, issues visas, and manages U.S. embassies and consulates (36j).

» **Secretary of the Interior** (www.doi.gov) manages publicly held U.S. lands (36k).

» **Secretary of the Treasury** (www.treasury.gov) is responsible for printing currency and managing the country's finances (36l).

- » **Secretary of Transportation** (www.transportation.gov) regulates transportation safety as well as maintains and oversees the nation's transportation systems (36m).

- » **Secretary of Veterans Affairs** (www.va.gov) administers benefits to America's military veterans (36n).

- » **Attorney General** (www.justice.gov) acts as the country's law-enforcement agency (36o).

- » **Vice-President** (www.whitehouse.gov) as the second-highest officer in the executive branch of the U.S. federal government, the Vice President convenes cabinet meetings when the president is unavailable and is a statutory member of the National Security Council (36p).

TECHNICAL STUFF

Although the heads of most of the departments are known as secretaries, like the Secretary of Defense or the Secretary of Agriculture, the head of the Department of Justice is known as the Attorney General.

Independent agencies

Dozens of executive branch independent agencies serve very specific and sometimes even temporary needs the government may have. Examples include the Commission on Civil Rights, the Federal Trade Commission (FTC), the National Labor Relations Board, the Federal Election Commission (FEC), the Small Business Administration (SBA), and the United States Postal Service (USPS). These agencies change according to the country's current needs and circumstances.

HOW AND WHY THE ELECTORAL COLLEGE ELECTS OUR PRESIDENT

Many people are surprised to find out that the president and vice president of the United States are not directly elected by a popular vote but rather by members of the Electoral College — a group of elected officials from the 50 states and the District of Columbia. Confusing as it may be, our Founding Fathers had some tough choices to make when they implemented the idea of the Electoral College in the Constitution.

Some of the framers of the Constitution believed the selection of the president should be left to the U.S. Congress or each state's legislature. These plans were ultimately rejected because they unbalanced the power between the federal and state

(continued)

(continued)

governments. Others thought the average American voter was capable of making wise choices when it came to electing the leader of the land, while still others believed the decision was far too important to leave up to the general populace.

Article II, Section I of the Constitution represents the final compromise — a system in which each state is represented by the same number of electors as the state has U.S. senators and representatives. This gives each state representation based upon the number of people who live there. The distribution of electoral votes among the states can vary every ten years, depending on the results of the census (the official government count of the country's population).

The Electoral College selects a president by majority vote — if no candidate receives a majority of electoral votes, then it's up to the House of Representatives to choose a winner.

No constitutional provision or federal law requires electors to vote according to the results of the popular vote in their states, so a candidate can win the popular vote but lose the electoral vote, as was the case in the 2000 presidential election. Any candidate who wins a majority of the popular vote also has a darned good chance of winning the Electoral College, but there are no guarantees. To reduce the chances of this uncomfortable situation arising, some states require electors to pledge to cast their votes according to the popular vote. These pledges fall into two categories — electors bound by state law and those bound by pledges to political parties. Penalties and fines vary from absolutely nothing, to replacement by another elector, to a fourth-degree felony in New Mexico. The District of Columbia and 26 states all have some type of law governing electors; electors in the remaining states, although expected to vote according to popular vote, are not legally compelled to do so.

For this reason, the Electoral College system remains controversial to this day. Many people believe it should be abolished so that the president can be elected by a direct popular vote. However, a constitutional amendment would need to be passed in order to change the current voting system.

The Duties and Functions of the Legislative Branch

The legislative branch of the U.S. government consists of the Senate and the House of Representatives, collectively known as *Congress* (USCIS 100:17). The Senate and House are primarily responsible for making the federal laws that govern the United States (USCIS 100:16). Sometimes they work separately, although they also share many duties and responsibilities.

The United States Congress

The two houses of Congress have some very specific and separate responsibilities (covered in the following sections). However, the Constitution declares that both the Senate and the House of Representatives share duties related to the following:

>> Regulating money and printing currency

>> Borrowing money on behalf of the government

>> Levying and collecting taxes

>> Regulating trade, both among states and with foreign countries

>> Regulating the system of weights and measures

>> Maintaining the defense of the nation and declaring war

>> Maintaining the U.S. military

>> Making laws regarding naturalization

>> Establishing post offices

>> Passing laws to govern the District of Columbia

The Constitution also lists some things that Congress may *never* do, specifically:

>> Tax exports

>> Pass trade laws that do not treat all the states equally

>> Spend tax money without a law that authorizes that spending

>> Authorize any titles of nobility

>> Pass any law that punishes someone for an act that was legal when the act was committed

>> Pass any law that takes away a person's right to trial in court

Congressional leadership

Elected by the whole of the House of Representatives, the *Speaker of the House* presides over the House, leads the majority party, and represents their congressional district. The business of the House is supported by the Majority Leader, Minority Leader, and party whips. The Speaker of the House is second in line to succeed the President, after the Vice President. The current Speaker of the House is Nancy Pelosi (D-CA) (USCIS 100:47). Find out more about House leadership at www.house.gov/leadership.

Elected by the Senate, the *President Pro Tempore* is the second-highest-ranking official of the United States Senate. During the vice president's absence, the president pro tempore is empowered to preside over Senate sessions. The business of the Senate is supported by the Majority Leader, Minority Leader, and party whips. The President Pro Tempore is third in line to succeed the President, after the Vice President and the Speaker of the House. The current President Pro Tempore is Patrick Leahy (D-VT). Find out more about Senate leadership at www.senate.gov/senators/leadership.htm.

How laws are passed

In spite of all their shared and separate duties, Congress spends most of its time passing laws. New federal laws can start in either the Senate or the House of Representatives. The procedure of getting a law passed may seem complex, but it's all part of the system of checks and balances designed to keep the country fair and democratic. Before a law can pass, a lot of people have the chance to discuss it, ask questions about it and its impact, and change or amend it if they think that's necessary.

The process begins when a senator or representative introduces a bill that they want to become law; the only exception is that only representatives are allowed to introduce tax or budget bills. Of course, long before the bill is introduced in Congress, citizen activists and political groups have usually been hard at work to gain support for their causes, bringing the issue to their representatives' attention.

HOW POLITICAL PARTIES INFLUENCE THE UNITED STATES

A political party is a group of people who have similar ideas about how the government should be run. Political parties distribute information about their candidates and the party platform (views on important issues). Because there is strength in numbers, political parties can accomplish more to further their causes working together as a group to raise funds and get the word out about their candidates. The party also works to promote its platform.

The Democratic and Republican parties are by far the largest political parties in the United States (USCIS 100:45), although many other smaller parties, like the Libertarian Party, the Green Party, and the Reform Party, exist. Some candidates don't belong to any political party at all and are considered independent. You probably won't hear much about independent candidates because it's difficult for an individual to match the economic strength of a party. Likewise, many independent candidates' campaigns get little or no media coverage.

By registering to vote under a political party, a voter can still vote any way they choose on election day. In other words, if you register as a Democrat, you're under no obligation to vote for the Democratic candidate.

Like certain candidates, some voters also prefer to remain independent and not register for any political party. Depending on where you live, however, there may be advantages to registering with a party. Some states restrict voting in primary elections — the elections that determine which candidates will actually run for president — to those who have declared a party affiliation (and sometimes that party must be Democratic or Republican). Some voters get around this loophole by changing their party affiliation just to be able to vote in the primaries, and then changing it back to independent for the general election. For state-by-state party requirements on voting in elections, visit the Federal Election Commission website at www.usa.gov/voting.

Congressional committees

Congressional committees meet regularly to discuss policies, legislation, and funding related to their respective areas. Sub-committees regularly meet under the direction of the standing committee. Select committees are convened temporarily to work on a specific issue. The House and Senate party leadership assigns members to committees. The Chair of each committee is reserved for a member of the majority party. Table 12-1 lists the committees of both the House and Senate.

Meeting your senators

Each state sends two senators to the United States Congress; currently, there are 100 senators (USCIS 100:18). Each senator represents all the people of their state (USCIS 100:24), not any specific district. A senator must be at least 30 years old, be a resident of the state they represent, and have been a U.S. citizen for at least nine years. Elected for six-year terms (USCIS 100:19), as per the 17th Amendment, there is currently no limit to the number of terms a senator may serve.

Duties specifically delegated to the Senate are

>> Determining guilt or innocence in impeachment cases

>> Confirming presidential appointments

>> Ratifying treaties between the United States and foreign governments

TABLE 12-1

Committees of the House and Senate

House of Representatives Committees	Senate Committees
Appropriation	Agriculture, Nutrition, and Forestry
Armed Services	Appropriation
Budget	Armed Services
Education and Labor	Banking, Housing, and Urban Affairs
Energy and Commerce	Budget
Ethics	Commerce, Science, and Transportation
Financial Services	Energy and Natural Resources
Foreign Affairs	Finance
Homeland Security	Foreign Relations
House Administration	Health, Education, Labor, and Pensions
Judiciary	Homeland Security and Governmental Affairs
Natural Resources	Judiciary
Oversight and Reform	Rules and Administration
Rules	Small Business and Entrepreneurs
Science, Space, and Technology	Veterans Affairs
Small Business	
Transportation and Infrastructure	
Veterans' Affairs	
Ways and Means	

Meeting your representatives

The United States census, taken once every ten years, determines the number of congressional representatives a state may send to Congress. Each state, regardless of how small its population, is allowed at least one representative. Most states have more representatives because they have more people (USCIS 100:25b), and these states are divided into districts with each member of the House representing their own district rather than the state as a whole. Currently, 435 voting members serve in the House of Representatives (USCIS 100:21). Elected for a two-year term, there is currently no limit to the number of terms a representative may serve (USCIS 100:22). To qualify to be a representative, a person must be at least 25 years old, be a resident of the state they represent, and have been a U.S. citizen for at least seven years.

NON-VOTING MEMBERS OF THE HOUSE OF REPRESENTATIVES

There are six non-voting members in the House of Representatives: one each representing the District of Columbia and the five U.S. territories: American Samoa, Guam, the Northern Mariana Islands, Puerto Rico, and the U.S. Virgin Islands. A seventh delegate representing the Cherokee Nation has been proposed but not yet seated, and an eighth delegate from the Choctaw Nation is named per the 1830 Treaty of Dancing Rabbit Creek but has not been formally proposed or seated. As with voting members, delegates are elected every two years, while the resident commissioner of Puerto Rico is elected every four years.

Duties of the House include

» Introducing budget and tax bills to Congress

» *Impeaching,* or putting on trial, government officials who may have committed some crime or gross misconduct

REMEMBER

You can really see the Constitution's system of checks and balances at work when you study the separate duties of the Senate and the House of Representatives. Although the House can impeach an official, the Senate must determine final guilt or innocence. Although the president can appoint government officials, the Senate must approve those appointments.

The Duties of the Judicial Branch

Made up of the system of federal courts, the judicial branch of government reviews laws, explains laws, resolves disputes (disagreements), and decides if a law goes against the Constitution (USCIS 100:37). Federal court duties include

» Explaining the meaning of the Constitution, the laws of the United States, and its treaties

» Settling legal disagreements between citizens of different states

» Settling disputes between or among two or more states

» Settling legal questions between the states and the federal government

» Settling legal disputes between individuals and the federal government

>> Settling disagreements between states and foreign governments and/or their citizens

>> Naturalizing U.S. citizens

The federal court system

The entire federal court system makes up the judicial branch. The court system is *hierarchical*, meaning that each court has greater power than, and can overturn decisions made by, the court below it.

The courts in the federal court system include the following:

>> **The Supreme Court:** The highest court of the land. A Supreme Court ruling constitutes the final decision on a case.

>> **Circuit courts of appeals:** The country's 11 circuit courts routinely hear appeals from lower courts when their participants believe the lower courts' decisions to be unjust.

>> **District courts:** The lowest of the federal courts, district courts determine rulings for people accused of breaking federal laws.

>> **Special courts:** Congress has also established some special courts that have very specific and limited jurisdiction: Court of Claims, Customs Court, Court of Customs and Patent Appeals, and Court of Military Appeals.

CONTACTING YOUR ELECTED OFFICIALS

Government representatives are technically employees of the people, so as a citizen, it's important to let them know how you feel about important issues. Each call, fax, letter, or email sent to an elected official's office is recorded. If enough people call a representative about any given issue, it can have a big effect on the way that representative votes. Because representatives depend on their constituents at reelection time, they have a vested interest in keeping the majority of those constituents happy.

Write to the president, the first lady, the vice president, or the wife of the vice president in care of the White House:

The White House
1600 Pennsylvania Ave. NW
Washington, DC 20500

Website: www.whitehouse.gov/contact Email: president@whitehouse.gov or comments@whitehouse.gov.

Social media: @WhiteHouse or WH.gov

You can get contact information for your representative at www.house.gov/representatives/find-your-representative. Put in your zip code; because different congressional districts overlap in some zip codes, you may have to also put in your address. You will be directed to your representative's website that has all of the rep's contact info, including the Washington office, local office, website, email, other social media information, and upcoming meet-and-greet events.

You can also send your representative a letter by addressing envelopes to:

Office of Representative [Name]
United States House of Representatives
Washington, DC 20510

You can get contact information about your senator at www.senate.gov/states/statesmap.htm. Select your state and you will be directed to your two state senators' landing pages. Click their photo. It will take you to the senator's website that has all the senator's contact info, including the Washington office, local office, website, email, other social media information, and upcoming meet-and-greet events. You can also send your senator a letter by addressing envelopes to:

Office of Senator [Name]
United States Senate
Washington, DC 20510

The ultimate constitutional authority: The Supreme Court

Nine judges (or *justices*, as they're called when talking about the Supreme Court) preside over the highest court of the land (39). One of the justices, known as the *Chief Justice*, acts as the court's leader. The current Chief Justice of the Supreme Court is John Roberts (USCIS 100:40). The Supreme Court can overturn decisions made by lower courts as well as declare state or federal laws *unconstitutional* or against the supreme law of the land. If a majority of the justices feel a law disagrees with the Constitution, it must be abolished. The Supreme Court's decision is final.

Most of the Supreme Court's cases are *appellate* cases, meaning the participants are *appealing* a decision made by the lower courts that they believe to be unfair. The only cases that actually originate in the Supreme Court are cases involving foreign diplomats.

IMPORTANT SUPREME COURT CASES

If you want to find out more about the U.S. Supreme Court, I suggest that you check out this excellent resource: VOA Learning English: The U.S. Supreme Court (`learning english.voanews.com/p/6985.html`). This series explains what the Supreme Court is, why it is important (and disputed) in American culture, how the justices ruled on eight important cases in modern U.S. history, and how those cases impact us today:

- Brown v. Board of Education of Topeka, 1954: Is racial segregation legal in public education?

- New York Times v. Sullivan, 1964: Can the media criticize government officials?

- Miranda v. Arizona, 1966: What are your rights if you get arrested?

- Loving v. Virginia, 1967: Is interracial marriage legal in every state?

- Lemon v. Kurtzman, 1971: What does "separation of church and state mean"?

- Roe v. Wade, 1973: Does a woman have a right to an abortion?

- Texas v. Johnson, 1989: Is burning the American flag legal?

- Obergefell v. Hodges, 2015: Is gay marriage legal in every state?

IN THIS CHAPTER

» Understanding the roles of government

» Governing at the state level

» Making sense of local governments

Chapter **13**

Looking at State and Local Governments

T he United States is a *federalist* union, which means that national, state, and even local governments share power. Although some differences exist, the three levels of government represent a *republican* form of government. In a republican form of government, the supreme power lies with the citizens, who have the power to elect their representatives. Obviously, a government like this cannot work without the involvement of an active, informed citizenry, and likewise, citizens have a duty to interact with their government at the local, state, and federal levels.

State and local elections can greatly impact the day-to-day lives of the people who live within their jurisdictions — sometimes in more profound ways than the federal government. You're more likely to have personal interaction with your local or state government — state governments are smaller than the federal government and they have fewer people to interact with, and local governments are even smaller than state governments. The smaller the government entity, the quicker and more efficiently it can respond to the specific needs of its people.

In this chapter, we familiarize you with how state and local governments work in the United States and tell you how you can get involved and be informed about the government actions that directly affect the area where you live. We also get you ready to answer possible questions about your state and local government during your naturalization test. Information that refers directly to USCIS history and civ-ics questions is followed with "USCIS 100" and the appropriate question number (Example: USCIS 100:59).

Capitals and Capitols

There are fifty states in the United States, plus five territories: Puerto Rico, U.S. Virgin Islands, American Samoa, Northern Mariana Islands, and Guam (USCIS 100:91). See Table 13-1 for a complete listing. A *capital* is the city that is the center of the government for a state or territory (USCIS 100:44). A *capitol* is a building in the capital city where the legislature meets. If you ever visit your state or terri-tory's capital city, take the opportunity to check out the capitol building and nearby museum. Your state or territory's website has details about how to tour your capitol and state museum. For state websites, see www.usa.gov/states-and-territories.

TABLE 13-1   ## U.S. States, Territories, and Capitals

State	Abbreviation	Admission	Capital
Alabama	AL	1819	Montgomery
Alaska	AK	1959	Juneau
Arizona	AZ	1912	Phoenix
Arkansas	AR	1836	Little Rock
California	CA	1850	Sacramento
Colorado	CO	1876	Denver
Connecticut	CT	1788	Hartford
Delaware	DE	1787	Dover
Florida	FL	1845	Tallahassee
Georgia	GA	1788	Atlanta
Hawaii	HI	1959	Honolulu
Idaho	ID	1890	Boise
Illinois	IL	1818	Springfield
Indiana	IN	1816	Indianapolis
Iowa	IA	1846	Des Moines
Kansas	KS	1861	Topeka

State	Abbreviation	Admission	Capital
Kentucky	KY	1792	Frankfort
Louisiana	LA	1812	Baton Rouge
Maine	ME	1820	Augusta
Maryland	MD	1788	Annapolis
Massachusetts	MA	1788	Boston
Michigan	MI	1837	Lansing
Minnesota	MN	1858	Saint Paul
Mississippi	MS	1817	Jackson
Missouri	MO	1821	Jefferson City
Montana	MT	1889	Helena
Nebraska	NE	1867	Lincoln
Nevada	NV	1864	Carson City
New Hampshire	NH	1788	Concord
New Jersey	NJ	1787	Trenton
New Mexico	NM	1912	Santa Fe
New York	NY	1788	Albany
North Carolina	NC	1789	Raleigh
North Dakota	ND	1889	Bismarck
Ohio	OH	1803	Columbus
Oklahoma	OK	1907	Oklahoma City
Oregon	OR	1859	Salem
Pennsylvania	PA	1787	Harrisburg
Rhode Island	RI	1790	Providence
South Carolina	SC	1788	Columbia
South Dakota	SD	1889	Pierre
Tennessee	TN	1796	Nashville
Texas	TX	1845	Austin
Utah	UT	1896	Salt Lake City
Vermont	VT	1791	Montpelier
Virginia	VA	1788	Richmond

(continued)

TABLE 13-1 *(continued)*

State	Abbreviation	Admission	Capital
Washington	WA	1889	Olympia
West Virginia	WV	1863	Charleston
Wisconsin	WI	1848	Madison
Wyoming	WY	1890	Cheyenne
U.S. Territory	*Abbreviation*	*Admission*	*Capital*
American Samoa	AS	1899	Pago Pago
Guam	GU	1898	Hagåtña
Northern Mariana Islands	MP	1947	Saipan
Puerto Rico	PR	1898	San Juan
U.S. Virgin Islands	VI	1917	Charlotte Amalie

State Governments

REMEMBER

The United States Constitution gives a great deal of governmental power to the individual states and ensures that the federal government can never grow so strong that it overpowers the will of the states. (For more details on the Constitution, see Chapter 11.)

Even though there were only 13 states when the United States was formed, the Founding Fathers knew the Union would grow. In order for the states to work productively with the federal government, it was important that each state had the same form of government. (For more information on how the federal government is structured, see Chapter 12.)

It helps to think of state governments as the little siblings of the federal government, and like siblings they look a whole lot alike. Here are some ways that the federal government and state governments are similar:

>> All state governments are based upon a constitution. Each state has its own state constitution.

>> All state governments consist of three branches — the executive, legislative, and judicial branches. The three branches of state government check and balance each other's powers, just like the three branches of the federal government do.

State government structure

Most states, even the ones that provide citizens the opportunity for direct democracy (meaning that individual citizens can petition to put initiatives on election ballots), are *representative democracies,* which means that elected officials make the laws and governmental decisions. Although minor details and legal technicalities vary from state to state, all 50 state governments are comprised of an executive branch, a legislative branch, and a judicial branch, just like the federal government. See Table 13-2 for a comparison of federal and state government roles.

TABLE 13-2

Federal versus State Governments

Federal Government	State Government
President	Governor
Vice president	Lieutenant governor
Presidential cabinet; the attorney general, secretary of state, and various federal departments.	Governor's advisors: the attorney general, secretary of state, and the various state departments.
Bicameral Federal Legislature (Congress)	Bicameral State Legislature*
U.S. Senate	State Senate
U.S. House of Representatives	State Assembly
Federal court system	State court system

Forty-nine states have bicameral (two-house) legislatures, usually consisting of a Senate and a House of Representatives (there are slight state-to-state differences in what the houses are called; for example, in New York it's call the State Assembly). Nebraska's unicameral (single-house) legislature is the one exception.

TECHNICAL STUFF

If you're interested in the particular details of your state's government structure, see State, Local, and Tribal Governments at www.usa.gov/state-tribal-governments.

The executive branch

The similarities to the federal government continue even within the three branches of state government. The governor (USCIS 100:43) and their group of advisors are the state level counterpart to the president and their cabinet. A lieutenant governor stands ready to serve in case the governor dies or becomes incapacitated.

Depending on the state, the governor's advisors may be elected officials or they may be people appointed by the governor. Advisors include a secretary of state, an attorney general, and a treasurer or comptroller, as well as other advisors who work on specific issues such as health, labor, education, or public utilities.

The requirements for becoming governor vary slightly from state to state, but most require candidates to be U.S. citizens of a certain age (usually 30 or older) and to have been a resident of the state a designated amount of time. Some states restrict the number of terms a governor may serve; others don't. In either case, a governor's term in office is usually two or four years.

A governor's duties mirror the president's, just at the state level instead of the national level. These duties include

>> Advising the state legislature on needed laws

>> Serving as the head of the state's National Guard, which stands ready to serve and protect the people of the state in times of emergency or crisis

>> Calling special sessions of the state legislature

>> When appropriate, pardoning or reducing the sentences of people convicted in state courts

The state executive branch carries out the laws passed by the state legislature, but unlike the executive branch of the federal government, the state's executive branch also has the power to propose new laws to the state legislature.

NATIONAL GOVERNORS ASSOCIATION

Founded in 1908, the National Governors Association (NGA) is the voice of the leaders of 55 states, territories, and commonwealths. Our nation's governors are dedicated to leading bipartisan solutions that improve citizens' lives through state government. Through NGA, governors identify priority issues and deal with matters of public policy and governance at the state, national, and global levels. Find out more about your governor, contact info, and state websites at www.nga.org/governors.

The legislative branch

Every state except Nebraska has a state *bicameral*, or two-house, legislature — usually a house of representatives and a senate, just like the federal government. (Nebraska makes do with just one house in its legislature.) Each state determines its own legislative structure and requirements for holding office. Most state senate terms cover four years, and the typical house of representatives term spans two years, although the term lengths vary from state to state. Some states base representation on population, others determine the number of representatives by geographic area. Some states have representatives who only represent a specific district, or area, of the state; other states have representatives who represent the state as a whole. To contact your state legislators, go to openstates.org/find_your_legislator.

The main purpose of the legislative branch is to create and carry out laws. The procedure for proposing and passing new laws closely resembles that of the federal government — the senate or house of representatives proposes, debates, and passes a bill to the governor for final approval. To track state and territories bills, go to www.congress.gov/state-legislature-websites.

THEY'VE GOT YOU COVERED: THE NATIONAL GUARD

Authorized by state law to serve as a state's *militia*, or citizens' army, the National Guard stands ready to serve its state's governor in times of statewide emergencies and disasters as well to enforce the state's laws in times of crisis such as riots or civil unrest.

Regionally based and recruited, the National Guard is under control of the state government only during peacetime. The guard does double duty by simultaneously being prepared to serve the federal government in wartime emergencies and other matters of national security. To show its appreciation, the federal government provides 90 percent of the National Guard's funding, although this number only amounts to 8 percent of the total U.S. Department of Defense budget. Find out more about the National Guard and its similarities and differences to U.S. military service and state defense units at www.nationalguard.com/.

The judicial branch

Just like its federal counterpart, the state judicial branch is comprised of a system of courts and judges who decide both *civil cases* (those that deal with a citizen's interaction with the government) and *criminal cases* (where a citizen is accused of breaking the law and committing an actual crime).

State court duties differ somewhat from federal courts in that their jurisdiction only covers state and local laws. State courts explain state laws and how they should be applied in practice, settle disagreements between citizens, determine guilt or innocence in breaking state laws, and, when appropriate, declare state laws unconstitutional.

The responsibilities of state governments

Because the United States Constitution delegates to the individual states any authority not specifically granted to the federal government (USCIS 100:42), your state government provides many important components that help make living in the United States great, including

DISCOVERING YOUR ELECTED REPRESENTATIVES

As a potential U.S. citizen, you could be asked to name your state senators and representatives during your citizenship interview. You can find out who your state representatives are by calling your state capitol building switchboard. Find out about county and city governments by contacting your main governing offices like city hall or the county seat. Visit www.usa.gov/elected-officials for information about representatives on the federal, state, and local levels throughout the country, including the area where you live.

Once you know who your elected officials are, follow them on social media. Take every opportunity to attend town halls or festivals where elected officials come out to meet their constituents. Simply introduce yourself and briefly give the elected official your opinion on an issue (USCIS 100:55f). Join with others to organize phone banks or postcard writing campaigns to publicly support or oppose an issue or policy (USCIS 100:55h). And get on the bus: Every year, large organizations and unions sponsor "Leg Days" (Legislation Days) where their members travel to the capital to meet their elected representatives and petition them to vote on important policies and legislation.

- » Providing schooling and education (USCIS 100:42a)

- » Providing protection (police) (USCIS 100:42b)

- » Providing safety (fire departments) (USCIS 100:42c)

- » Issuing driver's licenses (USCIS 100:42d)

- » Approving zoning and land use (USCIS 100:42e)

In addition, the federal and state governments work together as partners on some programs and services, often in the form of the state receiving federal funding and aid for specific programs such as

- » Healthcare

- » Public assistance for those in need

- » Improvements in living conditions

- » Improvements in working conditions

REMEMBER

Just because the states have lots of power doesn't mean that they can do whatever they want. Article VI of the United States Constitution says that any state or local law can be called *unconstitutional,* or against the supreme law of the land, if it contradicts our nation's most important document (the Constitution) (USCIS 100:37).

TECHNICAL STUFF

The Supreme Court has most often exercised its authority to call state laws unconstitutional in order to protect civil rights. For instance, in 1996, it struck down a Colorado law that deprived persons of protection against discrimination based on sexual orientation under state and local laws.

Citizens' responsibilities to their states

Just as the states exist to protect and serve the people who live within their borders, citizens have the duty to support their state by obeying state laws, paying state taxes, becoming informed about important issues and elections, and exercising their right to vote in all state and local elections.

State constitutions

State governments operate under the authority of their respective state constitutions — the set of rules for how the state government will conduct itself.

(When Americans have a good idea, they stick with it.) Likewise, state constitutions closely resemble the U.S. Constitution and are made up of four sections:

>> **The preamble:** The preamble declares the purpose for the constitution and ensures that the governmental authority comes from and rests with the people of the state.

>> **The bill of rights:** State constitutions typically duplicate much of the U.S. Constitution's Bill of Rights (see Chapter 11), listing fundamental rights like freedom of speech, freedom of religion, and protection against unlawful search and seizure. In addition, the states sometimes guarantee other rights not specifically set forth in the U.S. Constitution. Examples include specific mention of rights for crime victims, accepting or abolishing the death penalty, equal rights for women, or provisions that protect workers from losing their jobs if they don't belong to a union.

>> **An outline for the structure of government:** The outline for the structure of government establishes not only the structure of state government but also the structure for local governments within the state. State governments represent the needs of their citizens to the federal government. In order to effectively serve its population, the state government must be able to productively interact with local governments within the state. The state constitution details the procedures for how state and local governments should work together as well as how new local governments can be created.

>> **Methods for changing the constitution:** Just like the federal government, the states need to keep up with the times, so each state constitution outlines a procedure for amending or changing its constitution in order to best meet the changing needs of the people.

For more information about each state's constitution, law codes, and legal archives, see the Library of Congress's Guide to Law Online: U.S. States and Territories at https://guides.loc.gov/us-states-territories.

Local Governments

Local governments take their form from the detailed guidelines set forth in a state's constitution, but they're usually not based upon a constitution themselves. Different types of local governments include

>> County government

>> City government

>> Township government

>> Village government

In order for a new local government to form, it must receive a *charter*, or official approval from the state legislature. This charter incorporates or creates the new government and county, city, township, or village, and defines its responsibilities, authorities, and governmental structure.

Counties usually operate under the jurisdiction of a board of commissioners or board of supervisors. Some counties also hire a qualified person to work closely with the board of commissioners or board of supervisors and to act as the county manager. In addition, the county may elect certain government officials, such as the sheriff or animal control officer, who fulfill important community duties.

Most cities and towns elect a mayor, who acts as the chief executive. The mayor works together with a city council — a local version of a state legislature — to pass the laws that govern the city. In some cities, an elected commission does double duty as both the executive and legislative branches of government. In still others, an elected council hires a city manager who works in conjunction with the council to run the city.

The duties of local governments include providing services like police and fire protection; ensuring the safety of drinking water; collecting trash; maintaining schools, local courts, and jails; and keeping official records of births, deaths, and marriages. In addition, local governments build and maintain local streets and roads and provide transportation services that benefit residents, such as building bridges or tunnels or providing commuter services.

The citizens of a city or county can have a huge impact on the way their local government runs because they have much greater access to their elected officials at this level of government. Ordinary citizens are invited and encouraged to share their views at city council meetings, school board meetings, county planning meetings, and other official hearings. They can also influence local public policy by starting and circulating petitions, calling and writing to local politicians, and even running for office themselves (USCIS 100:55).

The requirements and terms for city officials vary widely, so check the rules in your local area.

TIP

As a potential U.S. citizen, you're likely to be asked not only about public office holders, but also about your involvement in your local community (USCIS N-400 Part 12:9). A good way to participate in grass-roots democracy is to join a local community or civic group (USCIS 55:d, e). Find the right volunteer opportunity through work, school, the library, a religious group, festivals, the newspaper, social media, or online at www.volunteermatch.org.

REMEMBER

One type of civic activity you should *not* have engaged in while in the United States before becoming a citizen is voting in a U.S. federal election.

Chapter **14**

Celebrating U.S. Holidays and Observances

mericans love to celebrate, and throughout the year they find many reasons to do just that. Some of the celebrations, like the Fourth of July (also known as Independence Day), are joyous. Others, like Memorial Day, serve as solemn reminders of the sacrifices that formed our nation while celebrating the freedom we hold so dear. Still other American holidays, like Halloween, are just for fun.

For the purposes of passing your citizenship test, concentrate on knowing about the patriotic or government holidays and celebrations. But to live your life in the United States to the fullest, check out the traditions, joys, and memories that come with celebrating all the events in this chapter. Information that refers directly to USCIS history and civics questions is followed with "USCIS 100" and the appropriate question number (Example: USCIS 100:59).

Federal Holidays

In the United States, a federal holiday is designated by the federal government of the United States as a national holiday: non-essential federal government offices are closed, stock market trading is usually suspended, and every federal government employee is paid for the holiday. Also, state, county, and city offices are closed as well as banks, schools, and public libraries. Currently, the U.S. government recognizes 11 federal holidays annually (USCIS 100:100).

Although on the surface, designating a day a national holiday may seem like a great idea, it's not as simple as it looks. Holidays have a *huge* financial impact on taxpayers because they give all federal employees a paid day off from work. Countless groups lobby Congress to honor their heroes with a holiday. Elected officials must walk a delicate political balance when choosing who does and does not merit their own special day, and new holidays are very rarely added.

New Year's Day

New Year's is the great equalizer holiday. Regardless of cultural background, ethnicity, religion, or economic stature, the passing of one year and the birth of a new one are cause for revelry.

WHEN TO CELEBRATE?

Sometimes holidays in the United States can be confusing, because only four American holidays are still celebrated on the same calendar day every year:

- New Year's Day (January 1)
- Independence Day (July 4)
- Halloween (October 31)
- Christmas (December 25)

Other holidays occur at the same time each year but not necessarily on the same date:

- Thanksgiving is observed on the fourth Thursday in November.
- Lunar New Year, Passover, Easter, Ramadan, and Diwali vary each year, depending on the lunar calendar.

Most other national holidays were changed so they can be celebrated on a Monday. This comes as a result of the Uniform Holidays Bill, signed in 1968. The bill gives federal employees three-day weekends on Presidents' Day, Memorial Day, Veterans Day, and Columbus Day, regardless of on which day of the week the holiday actually falls.

January 1 marks the official first day of the New Year, but most Americans celebrate the night before, on New Year's Eve, with parties. At the stroke of midnight, everyone toasts the coming year and (usually) kisses the people around them, wishing each other a happy New Year. On the first day of the year, many people make New Year resolutions — including the resolution to apply for U.S. naturalization. Congratulations on taking concrete steps to achieve the lifelong goal of becoming a U.S. citizen! (USCIS 100:53)

Martin Luther King Jr. Day

Reverend Dr. Martin Luther King, Jr., was a leader in the civil rights movement, which protested racial discrimination in federal and state law (USCIS 100:84). He fought for civil rights and worked for equality for all Americans (USCIS 100:85). Although he was committed to nonviolent social change, he was assassinated for his beliefs in 1968. Despite the challenges of creating a new national holiday to honor Dr. King, the Southern Christian Leadership Conference (SCLC) created one of the largest petition drives in history, gathering over 6 million signatures, which culminated in the first Martin Luther King Jr. Day in 1983. In 1994, Congress passed "The King Holiday and Service Act," which dedicated the holiday as "a day on, not a day off; a day of action, not apathy; a day of responding to community needs, not a day of rest." Communities organize volunteers to work on projects to address poverty, crime, and racial injustice. Check http://americorps.gov/ for events near you.

Presidents' Day

Each year, Americans celebrate the third Monday in February as Presidents' Day, a day that honors the accomplishments and contributions of all the past U.S. presidents. But it wasn't always so. Prior to 1971, citizens celebrated George Washington's birthday as a federal holiday in February; Abraham Lincoln's birthday, although never designated a federal holiday, was officially celebrated in several states. All that changed in 1971, when President Richard Nixon renamed the holiday and broadened its scope to honor *all* our past presidents. However, most citizens still think of the day as honoring Washington (USCIS 100:70) and Lincoln (USCIS 100:75).

You usually won't find any major celebrations or parties going on for Presidents' Day, but it does give many folks a much-needed day off from work. It has also become a day when many merchants offer special sales.

TECHNICAL STUFF

If you want to celebrate two of our most important presidents in their own right, George Washington was born on February 22, 1732, in Westmoreland County, Virginia, and Abraham Lincoln was born on February 12, 1809, in Hardin County, Kentucky.

Memorial Day

Memorial Day (the last Monday in May) was originally called "Decoration Day." People honored the soldiers who died during the Civil War (USCIS 100: 73) by decorating their graves with flowers and flags. Many communities claimed that they started the observance, but subsequent U.S. military engagements changed the local observances into a national Day of Remembrance. Memorial Day now honors all service members who have died in the U.S. armed forces (USCIS 100:72, 78).

National cemeteries throughout the land host Memorial Day remembrance ceremonies. The American Legion (http://legion.org) hosts Memorial Day activities in your area.

TECHNICAL STUFF

A lot of people, including many American citizens, don't understand the difference between Memorial Day and Veterans Day. Memorial Day honors and remembers the military men and women who *died* in service to their country. Veterans Day is set aside to honor *everyone* who honorably served in the military, living or dead, in times of war or peace.

Juneteenth

On January 1, 1863, President Abraham Lincoln signed the Emancipation Proclamation, freeing the slaves in most Southern states (USCIS 100:76). Although slaves in Texas had been free since 1863, they did not find out about their emancipation until June 19, 1865, when Union Army General Gordon Granger issued General Order No. 3, proclaiming freedom for slaves in Texas. Galveston's local joyous celebration of emancipation, Juneteenth, was adopted increasingly by more African-American communities over the years. Celebrations include street fairs, concerts, barbeques, family reunions, and public readings of the Emancipation Proclamation. In 2021, Juneteenth was proclaimed as a federal holiday, the first new federal holiday since Martin Luther King Jr. Day was adopted in 1983. Find out more at http://www.juneteenth.com.

Independence Day

Independence Day is the national holiday commemorating the signing of the Declaration of Independence by the Continental Congress on July 4, 1776 (USCIS 100:63) in Philadelphia, Pennsylvania. Also known simply as the Fourth of July (USCIS 100:99), Americans use this day to get together with friends, family, and other members of their communities to celebrate their patriotism.

Because it comes in July when the weather in most of the country is warm and sunny, many people celebrate with picnics and barbecues. Parks as well as backyards across America are filled with the scent of burgers on the grill. American flags fly, and you can see red, white, and blue everywhere — from the decorations in shop windows to the clothing of many revelers.

On the Fourth of July, you'll find that most U.S. communities sponsor large displays of brilliant, noisy fireworks — reminiscent of the guns and bombs of the war for independence. Check your local newspapers around the holiday to find a fireworks display near you. Community Fourth of July festivities, which usually include patriotic music, entertainment, and, of course, fireworks, provide fun for the entire family and are usually free of charge or very low cost.

Labor Day

Labor Day celebrates the achievements of workers and labor unions. Although many countries honor workers on May 1, Labor Day is celebrated in the United States (and Canada) on the first Monday in September. Labor union "brothers and sisters" volunteer tirelessly in our local communities donating their own labor to rally support for a living wage, expanded healthcare, and clean environment initiatives. Because Labor Day is the traditional time to kick-off political campaigns, many union members walk door-to-door to encourage people to vote (USCIS 100:55).

Columbus Day / Indigenous Peoples' Day

Columbus Day honors explorer Christopher Columbus, who "discovered" the New World on October 12, 1492. Because Columbus is widely believed to be of Italian descent, many Italian-American organizations hold Columbus Day celebrations and parades in the explorer's honor. However, many communities across the United States are reclaiming this day as Indigenous Peoples' Day. Native Americans use this time to educate others about who lived in America before the Europeans arrived (USCIS 100:59).

For years, October 12 was celebrated as Columbus Day / Indigenous Peoples' Day, but like so many other holidays, that changed with the Uniform Holiday Bill, when the holiday moved to the second Monday in October.

Veterans Day

The holiday we now celebrate as Veterans Day originally went by another name. In 1938, Congress declared November 11 a day to be dedicated to the cause of world peace and to be known as Armistice Day. In 1954, after World War II, Congress amended the Act of 1938 by substituting the word *Veterans'* for the word *Armistice,* at the urging of several veterans' service organizations. Armistice Day celebrated

World War I veterans. The new holiday, Veterans Day, sets aside time to honor *all* veterans. Although U.S. military service is not currently compulsory, all men must still register for the Selective Service between their 18th and 26th birthdays (USCIS 100:57).

Thanksgiving

On the fourth Thursday in November, Americans throughout the land traditionally sit down with their closest friends and family to a huge feast and give thanks for their blessings. Turkey serves as the traditional main course for this dinner that draws its origins from the Pilgrim and Native American original feast.

REMEMBER

The Pilgrims were one of the earliest groups of English colonists who came to America seeking religious freedom and economic opportunity (USCIS 100:58). Unprepared for their first harsh winter in what is now Massachusetts, only about half survived. A group of the area's original inhabitants, the Wampanoag, helped the remaining Pilgrims learn how to hunt, fish, and farm. Because of the Wampanoag's support, the Pilgrims survived the winter and celebrated Thanksgiving in 1621.

But the Pilgrims never repeated their feast. Customs of celebrating an annual day of Thanksgiving after the autumn didn't get national recognition until the late 1770s when it was suggested by the Continental Congress during the American Revolution. New York officially adopted Thanksgiving Day as an annual custom in 1817, and many other states soon followed suit. But it wasn't until 1863 that President Abraham Lincoln appointed a national day of Thanksgiving. Since then, each president has issued a Thanksgiving Day proclamation.

Today most Americans celebrate by getting together with loved ones for a special dinner and spending a little time reflecting on their blessings.

Christmas

Each year, Christians around the world celebrate the birth of Jesus Christ on December 25, known as Christmas. Although Christian Americans still observe the holiday's religious roots, Christmas in the United States has also taken on a more *secular* (or nonreligious), festive quality, making it a favorite holiday of children and revelers, not to mention storeowners. Undoubtedly the biggest holiday in the United States, the whole country seems to celebrate at this time of year.

TECHNICAL STUFF

Trees and lights are not the only things on display during the holidays — so are our constitutional rights. The First Amendment protects freedom of religion — people can practice any religion, or not practice a religion (USCIS 100:10). On the other hand, displays sponsored by government entities are bound by the First

Amendment's separation of church and state, which the Supreme Court has interpreted to preclude displays of a strictly religious nature. Nativity scenes and menorahs are included in a broader display featuring nonreligious and cultural decorations.

Another display of the religious and cultural diversity is the annual winter holiday stamp collection issued by the United States Postal Service, which includes religious and secular symbols of Christmas, Hannukah, and winter nature scenes. In recent years, the USPS holiday collection has expanded to include Day of the Dead, Diwali, Kwanzaa, Lunar New Year, Eid Mubarak, and Native American Creation stories.

Ten More Important Civic Holidays

You may not get the day off from work or school for the following holidays, but observing them is important nonetheless.

Inauguration Day

The inauguration of the U.S. president takes place on January 20 in the year after an election. During the Inauguration Day ceremony, the newly-elected president takes the presidential Oath of Office for a four-year term (USCIS 100:26). The president solemnly swears to perform the duties of the office and "to preserve, protect, and defend the Constitution of the United States." This oath is witnessed by members of the U.S. Congress, Supreme Court justices, the military, friends, family, media, and the public.

Census Day

As required by the U.S. Constitution (Article I, Section 2), the U.S. census has been conducted every ten years since 1790. The primary goal of the census is to get an accurate count of everyone living in the United States on April 1 of every tenth year to determine the number of seats each state has in the U.S. House of Representatives (USCIS 100:25). To find out more, go to www.census.gov/.

Income Tax Day

The 16th Amendment, ratified in 1913, allows the federal government to tax personal income. As part of the Department of the Treasury, the Internal Revenue Service collects income taxes annually on April 15 (USCIS 100:56) for the federal government to fund Social Security, healthcare, education, defense, and many other federal programs. To file the appropriate tax forms, go to irs.gov and your local state franchise website.

Flag Day

Flag Day commemorates the adoption of the flag of the United States on June 14, 1777: "Resolved, That the flag of the thirteen United States be thirteen stripes, alternate red and white; that the union be thirteen stars, white in a blue field, representing a new constellation." Because the flag retains thirteen stripes for the original colonies (USCIS 100:96) yet adds one star for each state (USCIS 100:97), people display the current and historic U.S. flags to reflect the growth of the United States.

Women's Equality Day

Women's Equality Day commemorates the addition of the 19th Amendment (Amendment XIX) to the U.S. Constitution on August 26, 1920. The 19th Amendment prohibits the states and the federal government from denying the right to vote to citizens of the United States on the basis of sex (USCIS 100:48). Groups such as the League of Women Voters (www.lwv.org) use this day to educate others about voting rights.

State Admissions Day

Soon after the Mexican-American War, California was admitted to the Union on September 9, 1850. More importantly, when and how did your state join the United States? Mark this date on your civics calendar to discover more about your governor (USCIS 100:43) and other famous people, places, and events in your state. Start at your state's website.

9/11

On September 11, 2001, terrorists attacked the United States (USCIS 100:86) resulting in death, destruction, and radical changes in U.S. national security. In response, many people volunteer on this day as a way to honor the victims, first responders, and communities impacted by changes in immigration law. Connect with others at https://americorps.gov/911-day.

Constitution and Citizenship Week

On September 17, 1787, the Founding Fathers signed the U.S. Constitution (USCIS 100:66). During Constitution and Citizenship Week, people study the U.S. Constitution and discuss the rights and responsibilities of U.S. citizenship (USCIS 100:49, 50). Schools, libraries, and communities sponsor public readings of the Preamble and have mock signing ceremonies of the Constitution. USCIS holds special Naturalization Oath Ceremonies during which new citizens promise to defend the Constitution and laws of the United States (USCIS 100:53).

Election Day

Election Day is the Tuesday following the first Monday in the month of November. Election Day is the annual day for the general election of federal public officials such as the president (USCIS 100:27), U.S. senators, U.S. representatives, state officials, and many local officials. Election Day can also include state and local measures. Check the election calendar at https://ballotpedia.org/ Elections_calendar.

Bill of Rights Day

On December 15, 1791, the Bill of Rights (USCIS 100:05) was added to the U.S. Constitution. The Bill of Rights guarantees citizens of the United States basic rights. Bill of Rights Day is often paired with Human Rights Day (December 10).

Heritage Months

The following is a list of month-long observances that celebrate American diversity. Every year, students and scholars uncover and recover more information about the contributions of everyday heroes and their communities.

February: Black History Month

Black History Month was first celebrated in 1970 at Kent State University and was quickly adopted by many schools and communities. In 1976, Black History Month was included as part of the federal celebration of the United States Bicentennial. Every year, more people learn about Martin Luther King, Jr.; Rosa Parks; Malcom X; and the new generation of civil rights workers who try to end racial discrimination (USCIS 100:84). Find out more at https://african americanhistorymonth.gov.

March: Women's History Month

Founded in 1987 and anchored by International Women's Day (March), Women's History Month celebrates the lives and works of women who fought for equal rights such as Susan B. Anthony (USCIS 100:77), Elizabeth Cady Stanton, Alice Paul, Ida B. Wells, Gloria Steinem, and Kamala Harris. Find out more at https://womenshistorymonth.gov.

March: Irish-American Heritage Month

Founded in 1991 and centered on St. Patrick's Day (March 17), Irish-American Heritage Month honors the achievements and contributions of Irish immigrants and their descendants. At least 22 U.S. presidents, notably John F. Kennedy and Joseph R. Biden, are Irish Americans (USCIS 100:28). Find out more at https://archives.gov/news/topics/irish-american-heritage.

April: Arab American Heritage Month

In 2021, Arab American Heritage Month was federally recognized and celebrates the contributions of Arab Americans and Arabic-speaking Americans. Some groups, however, prefer the term MENA (Middle Eastern, North African) to honor the linguistic and cultural diversity of the region. Arab Americans Anna Eshoo (CA-18) and Rashida Tlaib (MI-13) currently serve in the House of Representatives (USCIS 100:23). Discover more at https://ArabAmericanStories.org and watch for further developments of this heritage month.

May: Asian American and Pacific Islander Heritage Month

In 1990, Asian/Pacific American Heritage Week was expanded to a month by presidential proclamation. This month celebrates not only Asians, but the indigenous people and cultures of Hawaii, Guam, American Samoa, and the Northern Marianna Islands. Notable Asian Americans and Pacific Islanders include Wong Kim Ark and Fred Korematsu, who went to the Supreme Court to seek decisions against laws that tried to limit citizenship rights and equal protection under the law (USCIS 100:37). Find out more at https://asianpacificheritage.gov.

May: Jewish American Heritage Month

In 2006, Jewish American Heritage Month was established by presidential proclamation. This month recognizes and celebrates Jewish American's achievements and contributions to the United States. One notable Jewish American is Emma Lazarus, whose poem "The New Colossus" was installed on a plaque in the pedestal of the Statue of Liberty in New York harbor (USCIS 100:95), welcoming all to America. Find out more at https://jewishheritagemonth.gov.

June: Immigrant Heritage Month

Expanding on World Refugee Day (June 20), Immigrant Heritage Month was originally started in 2014 as part of a social media campaign sponsored by FWD.us, a pro-immigration lobbying group. Their stories about DACA dreamers and the struggle for their rights (USCIS 100:51) are especially powerful. Discover more at iamanimmigrant.com.

June: LGBTQI+ Pride Month

The first Pride March in New York City was held on June 28, 1970, on the one-year anniversary of the Stonewall Uprising. Since then, LGBTQI+ individuals have emerged to form families and communities based on life, liberty, and the pursuit of happiness (USCIS 100:09). Notable LGBTQI+ Americans include activist Harvey Milk, poet Audre Lorde, Colonel Margarethe Cammermeyer, U.S. Representative Barney Frank, and Secretary of Transportation Pete Buttigieg. Find out more at https://loc.gov/lgbt-pride-month.

June: Caribbean American Heritage Month

Since 2006, June has been designated as Caribbean American Heritage Month by Presidential Proclamation. Notable Caribbean Americans include Justice Sonia Sotomayor, Secretary of State Colin Powell, and Roberto Clemente, baseball player and humanitarian. Discover more about the unique communities that arose from the intersection of Native American, African, and European peoples on the Atlantic islands off the southeast coast of the United States mainland (USCIS 100:90) at www.archives.gov/news/topics/caribbean-american-heritage.

Mid-September to Mid-October: Hispanic Heritage Month

Hispanic Week was established in 1968 and was expanded to a full month in 1988. Spanish exploration and colonies in California (1542), Florida (1565), and New Mexico (1610) (USCIS 100:93) predate English colonies in what would become the United States. Find out more at https://hispanicheritagemonth.gov.

October: Filipino American History Month

In 2009, Congress recognized October as Filipino American History Month. October was chosen to commemorate the arrival of the first Filipinos who crossed the Pacific Ocean and landed on the West Coast (USCIS 100:89) near Morro Bay, California, on October 18, 1587. Discover more at fanhs-national.org/filam.

October: German American Heritage Month

German-American Day commemorates the founding of Germantown, Pennsylvania (now part of Philadelphia), by German Mennonites on October 6, 1683. It expanded into a month-long celebration to include Oktoberfest and Steuben Day, which honors Baron von Steuben, who trained the soldiers serving under George Washington, the commander-in-chief of the Continental Army (USCIS 100:32). Find out more at https://gahmusa.org.

October: Italian American Heritage Month

In 1989, Congress designated October as Italian American Heritage Month to coincide with Columbus Day, October 12, and to celebrate the Italians' contribution to American culture. Notable Italian Americans include Fiorello La Guardia, who is hailed as one of America's greatest mayors and public servants. While studying law, he worked as an interpreter for the U.S. Bureau of Immigration at the Ellis Island immigration station and went on to serve in a wide variety of public offices. La Guardia worked across party lines with the Roosevelt administration (USCIS 100:45) to implement New Deal programs during the Great Depression and World War II. Discover more at https://museoitaloamericano.org.

November: Native American Heritage Month

In 1990, the month of November was declared as Native American Heritage Month. This month celebrates Native American culture, traditions, arts, religion, and language. Use this time to find out more about your local American Indian tribe (USCIS 100:87). Start at https://nativeamericanheritagemonth.gov and continue on to your local tribe's website. Visit the National Museum of the American Indian (https://americanindian.si.edu) in Washington, D.C., and New York City.

Chapter **15**

Emblems of America

Americans take their patriotic symbols seriously. From the flag to the national anthem, the Great Seal to the national bird, symbols of the United States surround us. This chapter gives you a crash course in symbolic ways to celebrate patriotism. It also prepares you for the questions a BCIS officer may ask during your naturalization interview. Information that refers directly to USCIS history and civics questions is followed with "USCIS 100" and the appropriate question number (Example: USCIS 100:59).

The Flag: Old Glory

More than any other symbol, the American flag — also known as Old Glory — best represents the country and her people. With almost 250 years of history behind it, the flag, like the country it represents, has gone through many important changes through the years.

The symbolism and significance of the flag

For almost a year after the United States first gained its independence from England, the American flag still bore the British Union Jack along with its red and white stripes. On June 14, 1777, the Marine Committee of the Second Continental Congress at Philadelphia changed the look of the American flag by authorizing the first official flag of the United States of America:

Resolved, that the flag of the United States be thirteen stripes, alternate red and white; that the union be thirteen stars, white in a blue field representing a new constellation.

And so it came to be that the American flag was composed of stars and stripes. However, the resolution gave no specific instructions as to how many points the stars should have, or where they should be arranged on the blue union. If you look at historic flags in books or museums, you'll find all kinds of creative variations. Some flags have their stars staggered in rows, others made circles of the 13 stars, while still others opted for completely random placement. On some flags the stars had six points, while others sported eight. The proportion ratio of the blue field to stripes also varied from flag to flag. The matter was never completely resolved until the signing of the Executive Order of June 24, 1912, which outlined specific instructions on how the flag should look.

The 13 stripes represent the 13 original British colonies that formed the United States of America after they gained independence from England after the Revolutionary War. The stars, now 50 in all, represent each of the country's 50 states. The flag's colors also have special significance:

>> Red represents hardiness and valor.

>> White depicts purity and innocence.

>> Blue represents vigilance, perseverance, and justice.

TECHNICAL STUFF

With the addition of Vermont (1791) and Kentucky (1792) to the Union, the original flag of the United States grew to 15 stripes (8 red and 7 white), with 15 white stars in the union of blue. Even though more states were added over the years, the flag remained with 15 stars and 15 stripes until 1818. Congress had a problem. If they continued to add new stripes for each new state, the flag would simply grow too big. They eventually came up with the two-part solution:

>> Return to a flag of 13 stripes, representing the original 13 colonies (USCIS 100:96).

>> Add a new white star for each new state that joined the Union (USCIS 100:97).

Displaying the flag

Many patriotic Americans are enthusiastic about displaying the flag. Unfortunately, a lot of people don't know the proper rules and etiquette of when and how to display the United States flag. Follow these guidelines, excerpted from the National Flag Code, and you'll always display your flag with dignity and pride, no matter what the occasion:

CELEBRATING FLAG DAY

June 14 is the flag's official birthday, commemorated each year in Flag Day ceremonies throughout the country. The Stars and Stripes first flew in Flag Day festivities in 1861 in Hartford, Connecticut, and the first national observance of Flag Day took place on the 100-year anniversary of the flag — June 14, 1877. Although not celebrated as a federal holiday, Americans everywhere continue to honor the flag and the ideals she represents to them through school programs and civic observances on June 14.

- **»** It is the universal custom to display the flag only from sunrise to sunset on buildings and on stationary flagstaffs in the open. However, the flag may be displayed 24 hours a day if properly illuminated during the hours of darkness.

- **»** The flag should not be displayed on days when the weather is inclement, except when an all-weather flag is displayed.

- **»** The flag should be hoisted briskly and lowered ceremoniously.

- **»** To display the flag on a building, hang it on a staff or rope with the stars away from the building.

- **»** When marching, carry the flag on the right in a procession or parade. If there are many other flags, carry the American flag in the front center position.

- **»** No other flag or pennant should be placed above or, if on the same level, to the right of the flag of the United States of America.

- **»** When flags of states, cities, or societies are flown on the same halyard with the Stars and Stripes, the American flag should always be at the peak.

- **»** When the flags of two or more nations are displayed, they are to be flown from separate staffs of the same height. The flags should be of approximately equal size. International usage forbids the display of the flag of one nation above that of another nation in times of peace.

- **»** The U.S. flag should always be on its own right in relation to other flags on adjacent staffs — to the left of the observer.

- **»** On a car, attach the flag to the antenna or clamp the flagstaff to the right fender of a vehicle, but never lay the flag over the vehicle.

- **»** When displayed horizontally or vertically against a wall or in a window, the stars should be uppermost and to the observer's left.

- **»** When carrying the flag, hold it at a slight angle from your body. It is also proper to carry the flag with one hand and rest it on your right shoulder.

>> At a funeral, drape the flag over the casket with the stars at the head and over the left shoulder of the body. Do not lower the flag into the grave or allow it to touch the ground.

Half-staff rules

Flags are flown at half-staff to show respect for the dead. Even so, the practice comes with specific rules for flag etiquette and protocol:

>> By order of the president, the flag shall be flown at half-staff upon the death of principal figures of the United States government or the governor of a state, territory, or possession, as a mark of respect to their memory. In the event of the death of other officials or foreign dignitaries, the flag is to be displayed at half-staff according to presidential instructions or orders, or in accordance with recognized customs or practices not inconsistent with law.

>> When flown at half-staff, the flag should be first hoisted to the peak for an instant and then lowered to the half-staff position. The flag should be again raised to the peak before it is lowered for the day.

>> On Memorial Day, the flag should be displayed at half-staff until noon only, then raised to the top of the staff.

TECHNICAL STUFF

SALUTING THE FLAG

It may seem strange, but the clothing you wear affects how to properly salute the flag. Civilians should place their right hands over their hearts, except when wearing athletic clothing, in which case they should remove their hats and stand at attention; no hand salute is necessary. Civilian men wearing hats should remove the hat and hold it at their left shoulder, with hand over heart. Others should simply stand at attention. Those in uniform should render the military salute.

When the flag is moving, as in a parade, it is proper to salute when it is six paces in front of you and hold the salute until it passes six paces beyond. During the playing of the national anthem, the salute to the flag begins with the first note and continues until the song has ended. Even when a flag is not on display during the playing of the anthem, it is still proper to face the music and salute as if it were actually there.

Caring for the flag: Important etiquette

According to the United States Flag Code, when the flag is lowered, no part of it should touch the ground or any other object — it should be received by waiting hands and arms. The flag should also be cleaned and mended whenever necessary.

When a flag is so worn it is no longer fit to serve as a symbol of our country, it should be destroyed by burning in a dignified manner. Check with your local American Legion Post before Flag Day; most posts conduct flag-burning ceremonies on June 14.

The United States Flag Code provides many rules for how, when, and why the flag may be displayed, but it also warns of some important flag don'ts to avoid:

>> The flag should not be displayed on a float in a parade, except from a staff, and should not be draped over the hood, top, sides, or back of any vehicle, railroad train, or boat.

>> Although it's permissible for the flag to form a distinctive feature of the unveiling ceremony of a statue or monument, it should never be used as the actual covering piece.

>> When it's permissible to use the flag to cover a casket, it should never be lowered into the grave or allowed to touch the ground.

>> When being carried, the flag should not be dipped to any person or thing. Regimental colors, state flags, and organizational or institutional flags are to be dipped to the American flag as a mark of honor.

>> The flag should never be displayed with the union down, except as a signal of dire distress in instances of extreme danger to life or property.

>> The flag should never touch anything beneath it, such as the ground, water, or merchandise.

>> The flag should never be carried flat or horizontally, but always aloft and free.

>> The flag should never be used as wearing apparel, bedding, or drapery. It should never be festooned, drawn back, nor up, in folds, but always allowed to fall free. Bunting of blue, white, and red, always arranged with the blue above, the white in the middle, and the red below, should be used for covering a speaker's desk, draping the front of the platform, and for general decoration.

>> The flag should never be fastened, displayed, used, or stored in such a manner as to permit it to be easily torn, soiled, or damaged in any way.

>> The flag should never be used as a covering for a ceiling.

FOLDING THE FLAG

A properly folded flag ends up in the shape of a tri-cornered hat, symbolic of the hats worn by colonial soldiers during the War for Independence. Here's how to fold the flag:

1. Start by holding the flag waist high with another person so that its surface is parallel to the ground.

2. Fold the flag in half, lengthwise, bringing the lower striped section up to meet the upper field of blue.

3. Fold lengthwise again, keeping the blue field on the outside.

4. Make a triangular fold by bringing the striped corner of the folded edge to meet the top (open) edge of the flag.

5. Fold the outermost point on the right inward, parallel to the top open edge, which forms a second triangle.

6. Continue the triangular folding until the entire length of the flag is folded in this manner. When complete, only a triangular blue field of stars should be visible.

>> The flag should never have placed upon it, nor on any part of it, nor attached to it, any mark, insignia, letter, word, figure, design, picture, or drawing of any nature.

>> The flag should never be used as a receptacle for receiving, holding, carrying, or delivering anything.

>> The flag should never be used for advertising purposes in any manner whatsoever. It should not be embroidered on such articles as cushions or handkerchiefs and the like, or printed or otherwise impressed on paper napkins or boxes or anything that is designed for temporary use and discarded. Advertising signs should not be fastened to a staff or halyard from which the flag is flown.

>> No part of the flag should ever be used as a costume or athletic uniform. However, a flag patch may be affixed to the uniform of military personnel, firemen, policemen, and members of patriotic organizations. The flag represents a living country and is itself considered a living thing. Therefore, the lapel flag pin being a replica, should be worn on the left lapel near the heart.

The Pledge of Allegiance

Today's Pledge of Allegiance reads as follows:

> I pledge allegiance to the flag of the United States of America, and to the Republic for which it stands, one Nation, under God, indivisible, with liberty and justice for all.

Originally written for a public-school program celebrating the 400th anniversary of Columbus's discovery of America, the pledge was developed to encourage loyalty to our country, the United States (USCIS 100:52a). In 1923, "my Flag" was changed to "the Flag of the United States," so that new immigrants would pledge their allegiance to the United States while honoring the heritage of their birth countries (USCIS 100:52b). The pledge didn't receive formal recognition from Congress until it was officially adopted into the U.S. Flag Code on Flag Day of 1942. Even so, the official name "The Pledge of Allegiance" wasn't adopted until 1945.

On Flag Day, June 14, 1954, the words "under God" were added. The wording echoed Lincoln's Gettysburg address (1863), "that this nation, under God, shall have a new birth of freedom." This addition, made during the height of the Cold War, reflected America's main concern about Communist countries' support of atheism and totalitarianism (USCIS 100:83). Several American organizations immediately objected to the addition of "under God" to the pledge, saying that it promoted religion. The courts decided that because the addition of "under God" did not establish a state-sponsored religion, it did not violate freedom of religion (USCIS 100:10). Furthermore, the courts held that people can omit the recitation of the clause "under God" or simply not say the pledge, which is voluntary; no penalties are imposed for noncompliance.

Note the similarities between the Pledge of Allegiance and the detailed promises of the Oath of Allegiance taken during the Naturalization Ceremony. In both the pledge and the oath, people promise to be loyal to the United States, the government, and its laws (USCIS 100:52, USCIS 100:53). Because of freedom of religion, USCIS accommodates those who cannot "swear" oaths or engage in service that supports the military because of their religious beliefs. An individual who takes a modified Oath of Allegiance is a full American citizen.

TECHNICAL
STUFF

The Pledge of Allegiance is now said with the right hand placed over the heart, but it wasn't always so. Prior to 1941, the pledge was said in the so-called *Bellamy Salute* (named for Francis Bellamy, the man credited with writing the pledge) — hand resting outward from the chest, the arm extending out from the body. After Adolf Hitler came to power in Europe, many Americans became concerned that the Bellamy salute too closely resembled the Nazi military salute, so in 1942, Congress established the current practice of reciting the pledge with the right hand over the heart.

The National Anthem

Francis Scott Key wrote the poem, "The Defence of Fort M'Henry," on September 14, 1814. This poem commemorates the Battle of Baltimore, a city where the U.S. government officials had found refuge after the British had burned down the capital, Washington, D.C. (including the White House and the Capitol) three weeks earlier. The enormous 30-x-42-foot historic flag (15 stripes and stars!) that flew over Fort McHenry during the War of 1812 now hangs at the Smithsonian's National Museum of American History in Washington, D.C. The poem became a song, and on March 3, 1931, the Star-Spangled Banner became the national anthem (USCIS 100:98). Find out more about the Star-Spangled Banner flag and song at their online exhibit at https://amhistory.si.edu/starspangledbanner/.

TECHNICAL
STUFF

Technically, our national anthem has four original verses, although you'll almost never hear anything but the first.

Attending a public event and joining in the singing of this proud song can be an uplifting patriotic experience. So you're ready next time you attend a ballgame or other public event, here are the words, so you too can sing proudly along:

> Oh, say can you see by the dawn's early light
> What so proudly we hailed at the twilight's last gleaming
> Whose broad stripes and bright stars thru the perilous fight,
> O'er the ramparts we watched were so gallantly streaming?
> And the rocket's red glare, the bombs bursting in air,
> Gave proof through the night that our flag was still there.
> Oh, say does that star-spangled banner yet wave
> O'er the land of the free and the home of the brave?

More recently, choirs have begun to perform the fifth stanza of the Star-Spangled Banner, which was written during the beginning of the Civil War by Oliver Wendell Holmes, Sr.

> When our land is illumined with Liberty's smile,
> If a foe from within strike a blow at her glory,
> Down, down with the traitor that dares to defile
> The flag of her stars and the page of her story!
> By the millions unchained, who our birthright have gained,
> We will keep her bright blazon forever unstained!
> And the Star-Spangled Banner in triumph shall wave

The "millions unchained" refers to the African American slaves who gained the birthright to "Life, Liberty and the pursuit of Happiness" as promised in the Declaration of Independence (USCIS 100:09). The emancipation of slaves, will protect the "blazon" of the Constitution. People can look deeper into the stanza to see the living promise of the Constitution to protect the basic rights of all Americans (USCIS 100:02).

Other American Anthems

Face it, "The Star-Spangled Banner" is difficult for most Americans to sing. Following are the first verses of other popular American anthems.

America (My Country, 'Tis of Thee)

"America (My Country, 'Tis of Thee)" was written by Samuel Francis Smith in 1832. The melody used is the same as that of the national anthem of the United Kingdom, "God Save the Queen." The song served as one of the anthems of the United States before the adoption of "The Star-Spangled Banner" as the official U.S. national anthem in 1931. Note the reference to the colonial founders (USCIS 100:58).

My country, 'tis of thee,
Sweet land of liberty,
Of thee I sing;
Land where my fathers died,
Land of the pilgrims' pride,
From ev'ry mountainside
Let freedom ring!

America the Beautiful

"America the Beautiful" was written by Katharine Lee Bates in 1895 and adapted into a song in 1911. The song was inspired by a trip to Pike's Peak, Colorado, one of the highest points in the Rocky Mountains. In her song, she imagines that she can see Americans united as one living together in a beautiful, fruitful country.

O beautiful for spacious skies,
For amber waves of grain,
For purple mountain majesties
Above the fruited plain!
America! America!
God shed His grace on thee
And crown thy good with brotherhood
From sea to shining sea!

God Bless America

"God Bless America" was written by Irving Berlin during World War I in 1918 and revised by him in the run-up to World War II in 1938. Since the September 11, 2001, terrorist attacks (USCIS 100:86), "God Bless America" is commonly sung during the seventh-inning stretch in Major League Baseball games, most often on Sundays and holidays.

> God bless America, land that I love
> Stand beside her and guide her
> Through the night with the light from above
> From the mountains to the prairies
> To the oceans white with foam
> God bless America, my home sweet home
> God bless America, my home sweet home

This Land Is Your Land

"This Land Is Your Land" is an American folk song written by Woody Guthrie in 1940. This song of inclusion and protest has been adapted by many musicians who change the lyrics and add verses to express current issues (USCIS 100:51). Here is Guthrie's first verse:

> This land is your land, and this land is my land
> From California to the New York Island,
> From the Redwood Forest, to the Gulf stream waters,
> This land was made for you and me.

Lift Every Voice and Sing

"Lift Every Voice and Sing" — often referred to as the Black national anthem — was written by brothers James and Rosamond Johnson in 1900 to honor President Abraham Lincoln who freed the slaves (USCIS 100:75). The song is a prayer of thanksgiving, full of biblical imagery that refers to the Exodus from slavery to the freedom of the "promised land." Frequently sung during 1950s and 1960s civil rights movement marches, the song came to express the struggle against racial discrimination (USCIS 100:84) and is the highlight of Juneteenth concerts.

> Lift every voice and sing,
> 'Til earth and heaven ring,
> Ring with the harmonies of Liberty;
> Let our rejoicing rise
> High as the listening skies,

Let it resound loud as the rolling sea.
Sing a song full of the faith that the dark past has taught us,
Sing a song full of the hope that the present has brought us;
Facing the rising sun of our new day begun,
Let us march on 'til victory is won.

Investigating American Icons

Although the flag is undoubtedly our most important symbol, there are still more American icons you'll frequently encounter, and their history and symbolism are no less fascinating.

The Great Seal

Our Founding Fathers believed an emblem and national coat of arms would help solidify the identity of the United States as an independent nation of free people. Benjamin Franklin, John Adams, and Thomas Jefferson undertook the task of creating the seal for the United States of America in 1776. Six years later on June 20, 1782, the Great Seal was finalized and approved.

The Secretary of State serves as the official custodian of the Great Seal, and it can only be affixed to certain documents, such as foreign treaties and presidential proclamations. An officer from the department's Presidential Appointments staff does the actual embossing of documents after the Secretary of State has countersigned the president's signature.

The next time you gaze at the Great Seal of the United States, which is rich with patriotic symbolism, keep these points in mind:

» Central to the seal is a bald eagle, our national bird, holding in its beak a scroll inscribed *E pluribus unum* (Latin for "out of many, one," symbolizing how our 13 original colonies came together to form one nation).

» The eagle's right claw clutches an olive branch while the left talon holds 13 arrows, denoting "the power of peace and war."

» A shield with 13 red and white stripes covers the eagle's breast. Supported solely by the eagle, the shield reminds Americans to rely on their own virtue.

» The blue field on the shield represents the president and Congress, being supported by the states, denoted by the red and white stripes.

>> As with our flag, red signifies hardiness and valor; white, purity and innocence; and blue, vigilance, perseverance, and justice.

>> Floating above the eagle's head in a field of blue is a constellation formed of 13 stars. The constellation symbolized that America, a new state, was taking its place among other nations.

On the seal's reverse side, you'll find a familiar image — it's also used on the back of U.S. dollar bills:

>> An unfinished 13-step pyramid symbolizes strength and duration, and once again, the 13 original colonies.

>> Atop the pyramid, the Eye of Providence. The words *Annuit Coeptis* appear above the pyramid, meaning, "God has favored our undertakings."

>> A scroll beneath the pyramid proclaims 1776 as the beginning of the American new era with the Latin words *Novus Ordo Seclorum,* meaning "New Order of the Ages."

The national bird

The bald eagle, our national bird, is the only eagle unique to North America. When America adopted the bird as its national symbol in 1782, as many as 100,000 nesting bald eagles lived in the continental United States, and the bald eagle populated every state in the Union. By 1963, only 417 nesting pairs were counted in the lower 48, although eagle populations in Alaska and Canada have always been healthy. Today, due to efforts by the Interior Department's U.S. Fish and Wildlife Service — in partnership with other federal agencies, tribes, state and local governments, conservation organizations, universities, corporations, and thousands of individual Americans — the number of nesting pairs has risen to an estimated 71,467, and the eagle was removed from the endangered species list in 2007.

TECHNICAL
STUFF

Benjamin Franklin, one of our most respected Founding Fathers, disapproved of the choice of the bald eagle as the national bird. He believed the eagle was a bird of bad moral character because it steals food from weaker animals. Franklin thought the best bird for the job was none other than the humble turkey, which Franklin described as "a bird of courage that would not hesitate to attack a grenadier of the British guards, who should presume to invade his farmyard with a red coat on."

The national motto

Increased religious sentiment during the Civil War spurred Congress to include the national motto "In God We Trust" on United States currency. Despite being barraged with appeals urging then Secretary of the Treasury Salmon P. Chase to recognize God on United States coins, an 1837 Act of Congress specifically prescribed exactly which mottoes and devices could be placed on U.S. currency. Another Act of Congress changed that in 1864, and the words *In God We Trust* were first seen that year on the newly minted two-cent coins. More congressional acts throughout the years have authorized the motto to appear on various other currency denominations. But it wasn't until July 30, 1956, that the words officially became the national motto of the United States.

The national motto comes with a certain degree of controversy because the constitutionality of the words has been challenged on many occasions. Nevertheless, the courts, which tend to favor looking at the motto in a historical rather than religious context, have consistently upheld the legality of the motto's use on the basis that it is not a specific endorsement of religion.

TECHNICAL STUFF

Many people think the Latin words *E pluribus unum* ("out of many, one") form the national motto. You'll hear national figures who should know better make this mistake on television and radio all the time. In fact, you can even find the words labeled as such in some government publications. Although the Latin phrase is used in many patriotic emblems — including the Great Seal of the United States — In God We Trust remains the officially recognized national motto.

American Monuments

Since the beginning of civilization, people have erected a statue, building, or other structure to commemorate a notable person or event. When we visit these monuments, memorials, and parks, their beauty inspires us to more deeply contemplate the life of the person or event, celebrate their legacy, and silently recommit to working for the common good. Here are some key monuments which give deep expression to the American experience.

The Statue of Liberty and Ellis Island

The Statue of Liberty, officially named Liberty Enlightening the World (or Lady Liberty), is a monument that symbolizes the United States. The statue is placed on Liberty Island, in New York City Harbor (USCIS 100:95). The statue commemorates the signing of the United States Declaration of Independence. It was given to the United States by the people of France in 1886 to represent the friendship between the two countries established during the American Revolution. It represents a woman wearing a stola, a crown, and sandals trampling a broken chain, with a torch in her raised right hand and a tablet in her left hand with the date of the Declaration of Independence JULY IV MDCCLXXVI (July 4, 1776) (USCIS 100:63). The statue welcomes visitors, immigrants, and returning Americans traveling by ship.

In 1903, the poem "The New Colossus" by Emma Lazarus, an advocate for Jewish refugees fleeing persecution, was added to the base of the statue. The second stanza celebrates America as a "Nation of Immigrants":

> "Keep, ancient lands, your storied pomp!" cries she
> With silent lips. "Give me your tired, your poor,
> Your huddled masses yearning to breathe free,
> The wretched refuse of your teeming shore.
> Send these, the homeless, tempest-tost to me,
> I lift my lamp beside the golden door!"

North of the Statue of Liberty is Ellis Island, which served as the busiest immigrant inspection station in the United States. From 1892 to 1954, nearly 12 million immigrants arriving at the Port of New York and New Jersey were processed there under federal law. It now hosts the Ellis Island Immigration Museum and Wall of Honor which includes slaves, Native Americans (USCIS 100:59), and immigrants who were not processed on the island. Find out more at the National Park Service's Liberty Island and Ellis Island website: www.nps.gov/stli/index.htm.

The Liberty Bell and the President's House

The Liberty Bell is a famous symbol of American independence, located in Philadelphia, Pennsylvania. The inscription reads "Proclaim Liberty throughout all the land unto all the inhabitants thereof" (Leviticus 25:10). The bell was rung during a public reading of the Declaration of Independence. Abolitionists who fought against slavery adopted it as a symbol of their movement.

Once placed in the bell tower of the Pennsylvania State House (now renamed Independence Hall), the bell today is located across the street in the Liberty Bell Center in Independence National Historical Park. Immediately next to the Liberty Bell Center is the President's House, the site of the former home of Presidents Washington and Adams and at least seven slaves. This memorial serves as a counterbalance to the American fight for independence (USCIS 100:61) by including Africans who were enslaved (USCIS 100:60).

The National Mall

The National Mall & Memorial Parks in Washington, D.C., has some of the oldest protected park lands in the National Park Service (nps.gov). Visitors learn about presidents, honor war veterans, and celebrate the United States commitment to freedom and equality.

In March 2022, USCIs released *A More Perfect Union: The USCIS Civics Test Guide to the Monuments and Memorials on the National Mall*, a series of free downloadable pdfs which connects the monuments and memorials on the National Mall to the naturalization civics test. Each guide describes the monument or memorial, identifies the content that is specifically on the naturalization civics test, and includes the corresponding questions from the 100 Civics Test Questions Study Guide. The guides also serve as a bridge between the USCIS beginning and intermediate civics lessons. There are 13 monuments and memorials included in the series:

» The 56 Signers of Declaration of Independence Memorial

» The Jefferson Memorial

» The Constitution Gardens

» The Washington Monument

» The George Mason Memorial

» The Lincoln Memorial

» The World War I Memorial

» The World War II Memorial

» The Franklin D. Roosevelt Memorial

» The Dwight D. Eisenhower Memorial

» The Korean War Veterans Memorial

» The Vietnam Veterans Memorial

» The Martin Luther King, Jr. Memorial

In order to support multi-generation civics literacy, USCIS plans to develop more virtual civics field trip guides. To extend the content, pair these guides with the memorials' NPS.gov home page, download the official NPS Parks app, and watch videos from YouTube and TikTok. You'll be ready for your own family trip to Washington, D.C., to celebrate our common American heritage.

Chapter **16**

Civic Life

In order to pass the citizenship test, you need a basic understanding of the United States government. In this chapter, we cover the rights and responsibilities of American civic life. In the previous chapters, you read about how the various branches share duties and check and balance each other to ensure fairness and control of government power. The United States government is a huge entity that affects the lives of not only American citizens but also of people throughout the world. Understanding how it functions is the first step toward getting involved in this government "of the people." Information that refers directly to USCIS history and civics questions is followed with "USCIS 100" and the appropriate question number (Example: USCIS 100:59).

The Rights and Duties of Everyone Living in the United States

Thomas Jefferson wrote in the Declaration of Independence (USCIS 100:62) that "all men are created equal" and "are endowed by their Creator with certain unalienable Rights" — namely the right to "Life, Liberty, and the pursuit of Happiness" (USCIS 100:09). The Constitution also protects the basic rights of everyone living in the United States (USCIS 100:02), including freedom of speech, religion, the press, and other important rights outlined in the Constitution's Bill of Rights (USCIS 100:6, 51).

Jefferson's other key point in the Declaration was that a government exists only by the consent of the governed. If the citizens feel that their government is not carrying out their wishes, they have the right and the duty to change or do away with that government.

In order to protect the government that guarantees their inherent rights, all people living in the United States have important duties to their country, including the following:

>> **Obeying laws:** Everyone needs to obey the laws of the community, state, and country in which they live, as well as support the Constitution of the United States (USCIS 100:12, 53c).

>> **Paying taxes:** All persons living in the United States are expected to pay income and other required taxes, honestly and on time, as outlined in the 16th Amendment (USCIS 100:56).

>> **Defending the country:** Males are required to bear arms for the armed forces or otherwise perform noncombatant services for the government when required in times of war or crisis (USCIS 100:53de). Males between their 18th and 26th birthdays who are living in the United States are required to register for the Selective Service (also known as "the Draft") (USCIS 100:57). The U.S. military converted to an all-volunteer system in 1975, but Congress retains the right to reinstate the draft should the country ever need additional military personnel. To learn more, visit the Selective Service System (www.sss.gov/faq/).

Participating in democracy

The United States is a representative democracy. Although our government is elected by citizens, everyone — citizens and noncitizens, young and old — can participate in the democratic process by making their voices heard through individual and communal action.:

>> **Join a political party:** People pool information and resources to develop and promote a common platform or slate of candidates (USCIS 100:55b).

>> **Help with a campaign:** People volunteer to work for a common cause or candidate (USCIS 100:53c).

>> **Join a civic group:** A civic group is sponsored by a governmental entity such as a city council (USCIS 100:53d).

>> **Join a community group:** People volunteer to work for the public good (USCIS 100:53e).

- **Give an elected official your opinion on an issue:** Lawmakers and laws are shaped by public opinion. Elected officials must hear from their constituents so that they can accurately represent their constituents' wants and needs (USCIS 100:53f).

- **Call senators and representatives:** If you support a bill or policy, call Congress at the following numbers: Senate 202-224-3121 or House of Representatives 202-225-3121. Here are a couple of simple phone scripts (USCIS 100:53g):

    Hello, this is (your name) from (your hometown). May I please speak to (Representative/Senator)? I'm calling to ask that they support _____ (policy).

    Or

    I'm calling to ask that they vote (Yes/No) on Bill Number ___. Thank you.

    The operator may ask you for your zip code.

- **Publicly support or oppose an issue or policy:** Demonstrate your support of an issue by attending rallies, marches, and town halls. Or use social media to share your experience and knowledge to influence your network about the issue (USCIS 100:55h).

- **Run for public office:** Who better than you can represent your community? Although you must be a citizen to run for federal office, legal status qualifications vary for local and state offices and advisory boards (USCIS 100:55i).

- **Write to a newspaper:** Educate your local community about a public policy by publishing a letter or short persuasive essay on the editorial page of a local newspaper or media outlet (USCIS 100:55j).

- **Vote:** In most cases, this privilege is reserved for American citizens 18 and older who have registered to vote (see the later section "The Rights and Duties of U.S. Citizens"). However, some school boards and community groups welcome noncitizens to vote in their elections. Check the voting requirements carefully before you cast your ballot (USCIS 100:55a).

Volunteering

If you have a little free time, start looking for volunteer opportunities and resources on http://volunteermatch.org, an online resource to find volunteer opportunities near you. Civic, faith, and community groups such as the Rotary Club, the Lions Club, and the Kiwanis Club also connect children and adults of all ages to volunteer opportunities. Don't forget to include these organizations on the N-400 Part 12:9, because your civic and communal participation will demonstrate your good moral character and commitment to the country. Here are some possibilities:

>> If you're a U.S. citizen, who helped you earn your citizenship? Did you take a citizenship class at an adult school, library, church, or community center? Now that you are a citizen, you can return as a tutor to help people prepare for their interviews. Search USCIS.gov for the online training manual: Adult Citizenship Education Strategies for Volunteers.

>> Visit the U.S. Department of Housing and Urban Development (HUD) for a list of federal and nongovernmental national volunteer programs, including AmeriCorps, the American Red Cross, and Habitat for Humanity. Visit HUD's volunteering web page at www.hud.gov/topics/volunteering for many more opportunities.

>> Ready.gov brings together volunteers to make communities safer and better prepared to respond to emergency situations.

>> You can make America's national parks better by volunteering with the National Park Service (NPS) (www.nps.gov) or with the Girl Scouts of America (www.girlscouts.org) or Boy Scouts of America (www.scouting.org).

>> Celebrate success! USCIS gives the annual Outstanding American by Choice award to naturalized citizens who have made significant contributions to both their communities and their adopted country, America. Read and discuss their stories and share your own! Post pictures and videos to social media with the hashtag #newUScitizen or #newUScitizens.

The Rights and Duties of U.S. Citizens

In order to protect the government that guarantees their inherent rights, all American citizens have important rights and responsibilities to their country, including the following:

>> **Vote in a federal election:** Being a good U.S. citizen begins at the voting booth. Through their votes, citizens can and do have the power to change their government. If an elected official doesn't live up to a majority of their constituents' expectations, those constituents can choose not to reelect that official to another term in office. (*Constituents* are the people who live in an

elected official's district or districts.) Citizens also have the power to elect different representatives, change laws, or change the Constitution itself if a majority of the citizens agree, or even run for federal office (USCIS 100:48-50).

Not only do good citizens need to vote, they need to be informed voters. Being confused about the issues and candidates is easy if you get all your political information from paid political ads that tell only one side of the story. Becoming educated is time consuming, but the stakes are high enough to merit getting the real facts from a variety of sources, such as newspapers, radio and television news sources, websites, and perhaps most important, the words of the candidates themselves.

» **Serve on juries:** The government may call upon citizens to serve on a jury. Jurors perform an essential role in sustaining the U.S. system of justice, so jury duty is an important responsibility of every U.S. citizen. The right to a trial by a jury of your peers is guaranteed in the Constitution, and a jury's fair and honest decisions help protect U.S. citizens' fundamental right to justice for all (USCIS 100:49a).

» **Travel on a U.S. Passport:** An American passport allows U.S. citizens to travel to almost any country in the world, in many instances, without a visa. See U.S Passports at `https://travel.state.gov/content/travel/en/passports.html`.

» **Run for local office:** Lift your voice on behalf of your community. Check out the candidate training resources at `http://candidatebootcamp.com`, `https://emilyslist.org`, `https://runforsomething.net`, and `https://sheshouldrun.org` (USCIS 100:50b, 55i).

» **Run for federal office:** A candidate must be either a natural-born or natural-ized U.S. citizen plus meet office-specific age and residency requirements to serve in a federal office (USCIS 100:50). For example, a candidate for the House of Representatives must (1) be at least 25 years old; (2) have been a citizen of the United States for the past 7 years; and (3) be (at the time of the election) an inhabitant of the state they represent (USCIS 100:13).

» **Apply for a federal job:** Now that you are a U.S. citizen, you meet a major requirement to apply for a federal job. Go to `https://usajobs.gov`, create a profile, and look for a new job! Also check your state, county, and local employment sites; however, they do not post federal jobs, and some local jobs require U.S. citizenship as a condition of employment.

» **Access to education funds:** Education is expensive. U.S. citizens and their children have access to federal scholarships, grants, and loans that are not readily available to noncitizens. Visit `https://studentaid.gov`.

>> **Apply for family members to immigrate to the United States:** One of my proudest moments as a teacher was when I met one of my students at the post office. She had just come from her naturalization oath ceremony and her arms were filled with neat manila envelopes — each one containing a completed USCIS I-130, Petition for Alien Relative for a member of her family. She simply said, "I live to save them," and we both burst into tears. Family reunification is a guiding principle of U.S. immigration power — use your privilege to unify and strengthen you family, thereby building up the American people.

VOTING 101: WHO, WHERE, AND WHEN

Although there are slight variations in voting laws from state to state, all states require voters to be U.S. citizens at least 18 years of age. The states have varying requirements in regard to convicted felons; some do not allow convicted felons to vote, and others do, providing they have paid their debts to society. Most states also require voters to be of sound mental health. Find common answers to voting questions at www.usa.gov/voting

You can obtain a voter-registration application from local election officials in your county or through registration outreach programs at your naturalization oath ceremony. You can also register to vote at state Department of Motor Vehicles (DMV) or drivers' licensing offices, at state offices that provide public assistance or programs for the disabled, and at armed forces recruitment offices. Some states also offer registration opportunities at public libraries, post offices, unemployment offices, and public high schools and universities.

Contact your county Registrar of Voters for sample ballots and voting materials in English and non-English languages. To find out more about the candidates and issues of an election, start with www.Vote411.org, sponsored by the League of Women Voters (www.lwv.org). To learn more about news literacy, visit The Center for News Literacy at www.centerfornewsliteracy.org or check out the Media Bias Chart at www.adfontesmedia.com.

In the U.S., presidential elections are always held on the first Tuesday after the first Monday in November. In non-presidential years, national elections may be held to elect senators and representatives. State and local elections vary, so be sure to keep up with current events in your local community.

4

Practicing for the Citizenship Tests

Brush up on your English skills.

Identify and use key words.

Clarify questions before you answer.

Review exercises for mastering Form N-400, civics questions, and reading and writing sentences.

Chapter **17**

Preparing for the English Test

Part of your citizenship test involves demonstrating that you can read, write, and speak the English language. Many people worry needlessly about the English portion of the test. Relax. The examiner is not expecting you to speak flawless English with perfect pronunciation and precise grammar. Instead, they merely want to know that you have a good basic understanding of the language — that you can converse in and read and write *basic* English. Although this may seem challenging, you can easily practice your skills every day. Before you know it, you'll be holding fluent English conversations with friends, family, co-workers, and your citizenship examiner.

This chapter gives you study hints and tips that should help you easily pass this part of your test.

Building Your Vocabulary

Living in the United States, you'll find opportunities to practice English everywhere — you'll encounter native English speakers in your job or daily activities, and wherever you look you'll see signs in English.

TIP

Every chance you get to speak or read English is an opportunity to improve your skills and add to your *vocabulary* (the group of words you know well enough to use in everyday conversations). Speak and read English whenever possible and you can't help but improve your speaking, reading, and writing abilities. Use some or all the following hints to speed up the process:

>> **Take an English as a Second Language (ESL) course.** Check local adult-education centers and community colleges. Some ESL courses are even geared toward people taking the naturalization test.

>> **Learn English and citizenship online.** USALearns.org has free, online, self-paced citizenship, ESL, and vocational English courses that will really help you pick up English vocabulary. You can also find other ESL/citizenship online courses or video series on YouTube.

>> **Read with your children.** Family time is so precious, especially if you work and go to school. Borrow books from the children's section of your local library. Pick books or videos about the topics you are studying in your citizenship class. You are your children's first teacher: Share what you are learning with your children and strengthen your ability to read and think. A family that reads together, stays together!

>> **Buy a good dictionary.** A good dictionary or dictionary app is essential. Try to find one that's small enough to carry with you wherever you go so that you'll always be able to look up unfamiliar words. A good dictionary can help you master English, and you'll probably find yourself reaching for yours constantly. You can use the frequency of your need to consult your dictionary as a good barometer of your progress — the less you need your dictionary, the more fluent you are in English.

>> **Buy a good thesaurus.** A thesaurus gives you *synonyms* (words with similar meanings) and can help expand your vocabulary. When you become confident with a new vocabulary word, look it up in the thesaurus to find new ways to communicate your precise meaning.

>> **Read USCIS forms.** Reading USCIS forms may be a tough assignment, but if you read and understand every important immigration document, you'll not only understand English very well, but you'll also be a step ahead in preparing for immigration and/or naturalization because you'll know a lot about the requirements and restrictions. Of course, immigration is a complex process, so regardless of how much you read, you should still consult qualified people to help with your unique circumstances. We talk about the USCIS Form N-400 vocabulary later in this chapter.

>> **Enlist help from friends and co-workers.** Tell friends, co-workers, and anyone else who will listen that you're trying to improve your English. Tell them you would appreciate their honest critiques and help. In other words, ask them to tell you about your mistakes so that you can benefit from them. Ask them to orally review papers from your citizenship class, especially material based on USCIS Form N-400.

>> **Each and every day, pick an unfamiliar word from the USCIS Form N-400 or civics questions, look up the word in the dictionary, and find out its meaning.** Play a game with yourself and see how many times that day you can use the word in conversation. If you can handle it, make a conscious effort to practice two, three, or even more words this way every day.

>> **Use flashcards.** You can download citizenship reading, writing, and civics flashcards from USCIS.gov (just enter "flashcards" in the search box). Use a flashcard app or make you own flashcards from index cards. Print the vocabulary word on one side, and on the reverse side print the word's meaning, as well as clues to help you pronounce and use the word properly in conversation. You may even want to go so far as to list a few synonyms from your thesaurus. Try making flashcards for your words of the day. Studying with your flashcards is easy — keep them with you and run through a few flashcards every time you have an extra minute or two.

>> **Find a study-buddy to practice with.** Find a friend who is also trying to improve their English for their own citizenship interview so you can study and practice together. Share new words and flashcards with your friend, and you'll double the speed of building your vocabulary.

>> **Take classes.** Improve your language skills and discover something new by taking a class. Don't limit yourself to English classes — anything you study will require reading and writing (and possibly even speaking) English.

Brushing Up on Your Reading and Writing

Practice by doing — read and write English at every opportunity possible — and you'll see rapid improvement in your comprehension of the English language. Reading on your own allows you the luxury of taking your time — as much time as you need — to really understand the words before you. Keep your dictionary handy to look up any unfamiliar words. You may want to make flashcards to help you remember the new words later.

TIP

Here are some additional tips to help you improve at reading and writing English:

- » **Try to read a newspaper or news site every day.** You'll not only stay up-to-date with civics and current events, but you'll also improve your reading and English-comprehension skills. A good place to begin is with Voice of America's (VOA) websites at VOANews.com or LearningEnglish.VOANews.com

- » **In addition to reading books, magazines, and newspapers, read everything else you can during your daily activities.** Road signs, advertisements, menus, and other pieces of material will all help you get used to reading English. Reviewing job applications, tax forms, and medical forms is a great opportunity to practice the personal info section of USCIS Form N-400.

- » **Play word games such as Scrabble or Boggle.** These fun games will help you in your efforts to write and read in English. Children's versions of these games also exist, so don't be afraid to start there and progress to the adult versions as your skills grow.

- » **Do word puzzles such as crossword puzzles and word searches.** Word puzzles come in all skill levels. Start with easy puzzles and progress. You can even create games from your own vocabulary lists at websites such as Discovery Puzzle Maker (puzzlemaker.discoveryeducation.com) or Quizlet (quizlet.com/create-set).

- » **Rent subtitled movies.** Watching foreign movies with English subtitles will help you to read and comprehend English. Watching these films at home, as opposed to in a movie theater, will allow you to pause the tape when you need to look up unfamiliar words. Clips from movies with closed captions are available on YouTube.

- » **Help your kids with their homework.** You can all improve your skills at the same time (in addition to spending some quality family time together).

Working through USCIS Form N-400

During the interview, the USCIS officer will ask you questions based on your USCIS Form N-400 Application for Naturalization. Although the officer can ask you every single question on your Form N-400, they will focus on the questions most applicable to your case. To be thorough, the officer will ask you questions in sequential order. Form N-400 contains information in roughly chronological order, from your date of birth to recent travel.

Understanding sequence will help you mentally organize and remember not only your personal information but also the special vocabulary. Later, we talk about Part 12, but first we look at the Form N-400 sections.

Getting familiar with the N-400

During your citizenship interview, the USCIS officer will ask your personal information questions in the same order as they appear on your N-400 Application for Naturalization, but they probably won't ask you every single question. Try to remember the order of the N-400 sections so that you can anticipate and correctly answer the questions in the section. In the following exercise, put the N-400 sections in the correct sequence to complete the table:

a. Accommodations

b. Biographic Info

c. Children

d. Contact Info

e. Eligibility

f. Info About You

g. Marital History

h. Parents

i. Residence

j. Travel outside the U.S.

k. Work and School

1		10	
2		11	
3		12	Additional Info
4		13	Applicant's Signature
5		14	Interpreter's Signature
6		15	Preparer's Signature
7		16	Signature at Interview
8		17	Renunciation
9		18	Oath of Allegiance

Answers: 1e. Eligibility; 2f. Info About You; 3a. Accommodations; 4d. Contact Info; 5i. Residence; 6h. Parents; 7b. Biographic Info; 8k. Work and School; 9j. Travel outside the US; 10g. Marital History; 11c. Children

Getting off to a good start

One of the most difficult questions occurs at the very beginning of the interview: "Explain how you are eligible to become a U.S. citizen." Or the officer may ask another question using the word "eligibility," as in, "What is the basis for your eligibility?" The multi-syllabic words "eligible" and "eligibility" are said quickly and can be easily misunderstood as "illegal." The officer is asking about your qualifications for citizenship. Saying that you have lived in the United States for 5 years — or even 50 years — or even that you are married to a U.S. citizen does not answer the officer's question about eligibility. Most applicants meet the qualifications by being a lawful permanent resident for five or more years. Many English language learners simply say, "I have a green card for five years." (*Note:* They must know that a "green card" is a common term for a U.S. Legal Permanent Resident Card and be able to hand over the correct document when the officer asks for it.)

Another common way to talk about eligibility is to say, "I am married to a U.S. citizen." This answers the officer's question partially. It is better to say, "I have been married to a U.S. citizen for three years; they have been a U.S. citizen for three years; I have been a lawful permanent resident for three years; and I have lived in the United States for three years. It is better to give a complete answer rather than a partial one.

What, where, and when?

Part 2 (Info About You) to Part 11 focus on three basic questions: What, Where, or When? "What" is used to ask about information about someone (you!) or something; "Where" is used to ask about a place; and "When" is used to ask about time. Each of the USCIS parts follows the pattern of What, Where, and When. Use Table 17-1 to organize your personal information, and then focus your study and practice on areas that require more explanation such as name changes, lapses in employment, absences longer than 180 days, or multiple marriages. (Part 3 Accommodations, Part 4 Contact Info, and Part 7 Biographic Info do not ask location and time questions and are not included.)

When you are studying for your citizenship interview, identify key words as you study your N-400 and civics questions and listen for the key word when you practice. You don't need to understand every single word in a question, but you do need to know and understand what the key word means. Practice pronouncing multi-syllabic words such as "employment" or "occupation" and giving simple definitions such as "work" or "job." Listening for key words will help you give the correct answer.

TABLE 17-1 **Parts of USCIS Form N-400**

Form N-400 Part	What	Where	When
Part 2: Info About You	Your name (s)	Country of Origin; Country of Nationality	Date of Birth (DOB) Date of Permanent Residence
Part 5: Residence	Home	Address	Date of Residence
Part 6: Parents	U.S. Citizenship	Country of Birth	DOB; Date of U.S. Citizenship
Part 8: Work or School	Work or School Name	Address	Date of Employment or Attendance
Part 9: Travel outside the US	Trips	Destination	Dates you left and returned
Part 10: Marriage	Marital Status Name of spouse(s)	Address; Country of Origin / Nationality	Date of Marriage; DOB; Date of U.S. Citizenship
Part 11: Children	Names of children	Address; Country of Origin / Nationality	DOB

Part 12 Additional Information Subsections

In 2014, Form N-400 doubled in size to include national security questions. Fortunately, the 50 questions are anchored by key words and have been organized into the subsections listed below. To help you get familiar with the subsections, put them in the correct order in the following table.

a. Acts of Violence

b. Affiliations

c. Crime

d. Criminal Records

e. Deportation

f. Gang, Weapons, Child Soldiers

g. Military Groups

h. Work in a Prison

Part 12:01-08	General Questions
Part 12:09–13	1.
Part 12:14	2.
Part 12:15	3.
Part 12:16	4.
Part 12:17–21	5.
Part 12:22–29	6.
Part 12:30	7.
Part 12:31–36	8.
Part 12:37–44	U.S. Military Service
Part 12:45–50	Attachment to the U.S. Constitution

Answers: 1b. Affiliations; 2a. Acts of Violence; 3g. Military Groups; 4h. Work in a Prison; 5f. Gangs, Weapons, Child Soldiers; 6d. Criminal Records; 7c. Crime; 8e. Deportation

Part 12 key words and common concepts

In the N-400 Part 12, the key word is not "Have you ever. . .?" Some applicants hear the beginning of the question and simply say "No," before listening to the entire question. You must listen for the key word to understand what you are affirming (Yes) or denying (No). Furthermore, you must be ready to explain the key word in your own words.

Many key words are linked to both the N-400 and the USCIS civics questions. For example: "Have ever voted in any federal, state, or local elections?"

The key word can be a verb (voted) or a noun (elections). The officer can ask you to define either word. Both words mean "to choose a new leader," but the officer can also ask you, "Why can't you vote yet?" If you respond, "Because I am not a citizen yet," you have demonstrated that you understand the civics material (USCIS 100:27, 28, 49, 50, 51, 54) and are ready to take the rights and responsibilities of citizenship.

For practice, take a look at the following list of key words and the table that follows them. What is the key word (or concept) that links the N-400 Part 12 question and the USCIS civics question?

a. communism

b. hate crimes

c. obey the law

d. military groups

e. Oath of Allegiance

f. religion

g. Selective Service

h. taxes

i. terrorism

j. the Constitution

N-400	Key word	USCIS Civics Questions
Have you ever failed to file your taxes? (N-400 12:7a)	1.	When is the last day you can send in federal income tax forms? (USCIS 100:56)
Have you ever been a member of the Communist Party? (N-400 12:10a)	2.	During the Cold War, what was the main concern of the United States? (USCIS 100:83)
Have you ever been a member of a terrorist organization? (N-400 12:10c)	3.	What major event happened on September 11, 2001, in the United States? (USCIS 100:86)
Have you ever persecuted any person because of race, religion, national origin, member of any particular social group, or political opinion? (N-400 12:11)	4.	What movement tried to end racial discrimination? (USCIS 100:84)
Have you ever stopped someone from practicing their religion? (N-400 12:14f)	5.	What is freedom of religion? (USCIS 100:10)
Have you ever served in a military unit, paramilitary unit, police unit, self-defense unit, vigilante group, rebel group, guerilla group, militia, or insurgent organization? (N-400 12:15)	6.	Name one war fought by the United States in the 1900s. (USCIS 100:78)
Have you ever been arrested or com-mitted a crime? (N-400 12:22, 23)	7.	What is the "rule of law"? (USCIS 100:12)
If you are a male who lived in the U.S. between your 18th and 26th birth-day, did you register for the Selective Service? (N-400 Part 12:44)	8.	When must all men register for the Selective Service? (USCIS 100:57)

N-400	Key word	USCIS Civics Questions
Do you support the U.S. Constitution and the form of government? (N-400 Part 12:45)	9.	What is the supreme law of the land? (USCIS 100:1)
Are you willing to take the full Oath of Allegiance to the U.S. government? (N-400 Part 12:47–50)	10.	What is one promise you make when you become a United States citizen? (USCIS 100:53)

Answers: 1h. taxes; 2a. communism; 3i. terrorism; 4b. hate crimes; 5f. religion; 6d. military groups; 7c. obey the law; 8g. Selective Service; 9j. the Constitution; 10e. Oath of Allegiance

TIP

Build on these common concepts to help you remember unique vocabulary. Take a look at Question 6 and the N-400 Part 12:15 list of every type of military group. Fortunately, these groups are defined clearly in the N-400, but it may be difficult to understand or remember the shades of meaning. You may know how to explain these differences in your native language but may get tripped up explaining them in English. Don't worry; remember the common concept — in this case, "military group." Answer honestly if you participated in a military group or in any group during a war. Also, let the civics questions help you remember the vocabulary. Don't get stuck on vocabulary, though — put your effort into clearly answering the question.

More Part 12 key words

Below are more Part 12 questions with tricky vocabulary. If you remember which section they are part of in Part 12, you are 50 percent closer to understanding the questions. Underline the key word in the question, then match it with its definition.

a. A judge orders a person to leave the United States and return to their home country

b. A person addicted to alcohol

c. A political party that has total control over the people

d. Examples: heroin, cocaine, opium, opioids, fentanyl, meth

e. Mental illness or a patient in a mental hospital

f. To fake marriage to a U.S. citizen to get a green card

g. To give false info to get government support like rent or food

h. To kill many people because of their race, religion, or gender

i. To lie about being a U.S. citizen

j. To use weapons to change the government

	N-400	Definition / Explanation of Key Word
1	Have you ever claimed to be a U.S. citizen? (Part12:1)	
2	Have you been declared legally incompetent or confined to a mental institution? (Part 12:50)	
3	Have you ever been a member of a totalitarian party? (Part 12:10b)	
4	Have you ever advocated the overthrow of any government by either force or violence? (Part 12:11)	
5	Have you ever participated in genocide? (Part 12:14a)	
6	Have you ever been a habitual drunkard? (Part 12:30a)	
7	Have you ever sold or smuggled illegal drugs or narcotics? (Part 12:30c)	
8	Have you ever married someone to get immigration benefits? (Part 12:30e)	
9	Have you ever lied to the U.S. government to get public benefits? (Part 12:30g)	
10	Have you ever been removed, excluded, or deported from the United States? (Part 12:37)	

Answers: 1i. claimed; 2e. legally incompetent; 3c. totalitarian party; 4j. government overthrow; 5h. genocide; 6b. habitual drunkard; 7d. illegal drugs; 8f. married to get immigration benefits; 9g. lied to get public benefits; 10a. deported (removed or excluded)

Part 12:45-50: Attachment to the Constitution

When my students return to class after their Citizenship appointment, they always say that it went so fast! For a well-prepared applicant, the average naturalization appointment takes 10 to 15 minutes. When you answer the question "Do you support the U.S. Constitution and the form of government?" you are moments away from the (successful) completion of your interview! Take a minute to review the final questions, which anticipate your Oath of Allegiance to the United States.

In the following exercise, match the keywords of the Part 12:45–50 questions with the correct definition.

a. A flood, fire, earthquake, or terrorist attack

b. A solemn promise

c. Democracy/Republic

d. I want to fulfill my responsibilities of U.S. citizenship.

e. The supreme law of the land

f. To be loyal

g. To be loyal to the United States

h. To obey non-military safety officers

i. To use a weapon to protect the United States

j. To work in the army without using a weapon

12:45. Do you support the U.S. Constitution and the form of government?

1. U.S. Constitution	
2. U.S. form of government	

12:46. Do you understand the full Oath of Allegiance to the United States?

3. oath	
4. allegiance	
5. the Oath of Allegiance	

12:47. Are you willing to take the full Oath of Allegiance?

6. Are you taking the full Oath freely?	

12:48. If the law requires it, are you willing to bear arms on behalf of the United States?

7. bear arms	

12:49. Are you willing to perform noncombatant services in the U.S. armed forces?

8. noncombatant services	

12:50. Are you willing to perform work of national importance under civilian direction?

9. work of national importance	
10. civilian direction	

Answers: 1e. The supreme law of the land; 2c. Democracy/Republic; 3b. A solemn promise; 4f. To be loyal; 5g. To be loyal to the United States; 6d. I want to fulfill my responsibilities of U.S. citizenship; 7i. To use a weapon to protect the United States; 8j. To work in the army without using a weapon; 9a. A flood, earthquake, or terrorist attack; 10h. To obey non-military safety officers

Understanding Key Words in the Oath of Allegiance

Congratulations! You passed! You have proven your qualifications for U.S. citizenship. On to the Naturalization Ceremony where you will take your Oath of Allegiance along with your fellow new American citizens.

Some of the language dates back all the way to 1795 with additions in 1906 (defend the Constitution/allegiance) and 1950 (bear arms/noncombatant). USCIS has a great resource about the oath at `https://www.uscis.gov/sites/default/files/document/n-400-topic-exercises/The-Oath-Of-Allegiance.pdf`.

Here is a quick review of the key words of the Oath of Allegiance. Match the definitions in the list with the numbered items they correspond to in the table, filling in the blanks in the second column. (*Note:* Some of the blanks in the second column have already been filled in for you.)

a. Leaders of other countries or governments

b. Legal status in my previous country of origin or nationality

c. Loyalty (to other countries or leaders)

d. Loyalty to the United States

e. People inside or outside of the United States who want to hurt or destroy America

f. To do something because I want to do it

g. To promise to do something knowing that I will do only a part of what I promised to do

h. To reject

i. To solemnly promise to do everything I can to fulfill the responsibilities of U.S. citizenship

j. To take on a responsibility or duty because of a law or moral principle

I hereby declare on Oath

that I absolutely and entirely **renounce and abjure** all **allegiance and fidelity** to **any foreign prince, potentate, state, or sovereignty** of whom or which I have **heretofore been a subject or citizen;**

Oath of Allegiance Key Word	Definition
1. renounce and abjure	
2. allegiance and fidelity	
3. foreign prince, potentate, state, or sovereignty	
4. heretofore been a subject or citizen	

that I will support and defend the **Constitution and laws** of the United States of America against **all enemies, foreign and domestic;**

the Constitution and laws	The supreme law of the United States
5. all enemies, foreign and domestic	

that I will bear **true faith and allegiance** to the same;

6. true faith and allegiance	

that I will **bear arms** on behalf of the United States when required by the law;

bear arms	To use a weapon to protect the United States

that I will perform **noncombatant service** in the Armed Forces of the United States when required by the law;

noncombatant service	To work in the United States armed forces without using a weapon

that I will perform **work of national importance under civilian direction** when required by the law;

work of national importance	To do important work for the safety and security of the United States
under civilian direction	To obey non-military safety officers

and that I **take this obligation freely,** without any **mental reservation or purpose of evasion;**

7. take this obligation	
8. freely	
9. mental reservation or purpose of evasion	

So **help me God.**

10. help me God.	

Answers: 1h; 2c; 3a; 4b; 5e; 6d; 7j; 8f; 9g; 10i

1h. To reject; 2c. Loyalty (to other countries or leaders); 3a. Leaders of other countries or governments; 4b. Legal status in my previous country of origin or nationality; 5e. People inside or outside of the United States who want to hurt or destroy America; 6d. Loyalty to the United States; 7j. To take on a responsibility or duty because of a law or moral principle; 8f. To do something because I want to do it. 9g. To promise to do something knowing that I will do only a part of what I promised to do; 10i. To solemnly promise to do everything I can to fulfill the responsibilities of U.S. citizenship.

Here is a paraphrase of the seven promises that you make in the Oath of Allegiance. Match the numbered phrase in the first column with the letter from the following list to which it corresponds. How would you explain the Oath of Allegiance in your own words?

a. to be loyal to the United States

b. to do important work or help in an emergency if needed

c. to follow the laws of the United States

d. to fulfill all the responsibilities of U.S. citizenship

e. to not follow or obey the leader of the country which I came from

f. to use a weapon to protect the United States if needed

g. to work in the U.S. armed forces without using a weapon if needed

I hereby declare on Oath . . .	I publicly and solemnly promise . . .
1. that I absolutely and entirely renounce and abjure all allegiance and fidelity to any foreign prince, potentate, state, or sovereignty of whom or which I have heretofore been a subject or citizen;	
2. that I will support and defend the Constitution and laws of the United States of America against all enemies, foreign and domestic;	
3. that I will bear true faith and allegiance to the same;	
4. that I will bear arms on behalf of the United States when required by the law;	
5. that I will perform noncombatant service in the armed forces of the United States when required by the law;	

6. that I will perform work of national importance under civilian direction when required by the law;	
7. and that I take this obligation freely, without any mental reservation or purpose of evasion;	
8. So help me God.	I promise to do everything I can to be a good U.S. citizen.

Answers: 1e; 2c; 3a; 4f; 5g; 6b; 7d.

1e. to not follow or obey the leader of the country which I came from; 2c. to follow the laws of the United States; 3a. to be loyal to the United States; 4f. to use a weapon to protect the United States if needed; 5g. to work in the U.S. armed forces without using a weapon if needed; 6b. to do important work or help in an emergency if needed; 7d. to fulfill all the responsibilities of U.S. citizenship

Chapter **18**

Preparing for the Civics, Reading, and Writing Tests

How well do you know U.S. history and government? The fun review quizzes in this chapter will help you find out. Here you'll also find the USCIS civics (history and government) questions for the naturalization test, so that you can know what to expect on test day.

TIP

The civics test is part of your naturalization interview. The USCIS officer knows that you are probably anxious about the civics test, so after you are sworn in, the officer will administer an oral civics test, and then move on to the reading and writing tests.

Keeping Current

Although your citizenship examiner will ask you about civics, historical events, and current office holders during the civics test, current events may be mentioned during small talk as you walk with the officer to the exam office. The officer is trying to lessen your tension while trying to gauge your ability to speak and understand English. Don't worry; keeping up with the events and people who shape our world is easy.

Current events

To stay up-to-date with current events, try to read at least one English newspaper or online news site every day. You'll improve your English comprehension and reading skills while keeping current with news and events of local, state, and national importance. A great place to start is Voice of America (VOA) (https://voanews.com or https://learningenglish.voanews.com). VOA also has news in your native language and YouTube channels.

You can also stay informed by listening to radio news or watching the news on TV. Be sure to watch or listen to shows in English in order to improve your language skills at the same time.

History books make great review tools, too. Books like *U.S. History For Dummies* by Steve Wiegand, *Politics For Dummies* by Ann M. DeLaney, and *U.S. Presidents For Dummies* by Marcus A. Stadelmann give you the kind of information you can use to prepare for your citizenship test. They make for fascinating reading and will help you find out about some of history's most important events in easy-to-understand terms. Helpful short articles and cheat sheets from these books and many more are posted regularly to the Dummies website (www.dummies.com).

National, state, and local governments

Your citizenship examiner may ask you about the current representatives in your state government or in the U.S. government — know your senators and representatives in Congress, your state's governor, and your city's mayor. If you read a local newspaper or online news site every day, you should become familiar with the names of your federal, state, and local government officials. You can also follow your elected officials on social media and meet them at town halls and public events.

TIP

You can call or visit your state capitol to find out about your governor and state government representatives or your city hall to find out about your mayor and other local government officials. Or you can locate your state's official website, which will list at least your state's governor and members of your state's legislature; and your city's website, which will list the mayor and other elected city officials. Use a search engine like Google or Safari and search for "State of [insert your state name here]" or search for your city and state (for example, type in "Chicago, Illinois") and you'll find the official website for your city and your state.

TIP

On the national level, you can find out about your state representatives to the United States Congress by going to www.house.gov or calling the U.S. House of Representatives switchboard operator at 202-225-3121. You can find out about your state's U.S. senators by going to www.senate.gov or phoning the United States Capitol switchboard at 202-224-3121. Online, you can identify your state's elected officials in Congress, email elected officials, and stay abreast of current legislation and issues on the national level.

Quizzing Yourself on Civics

After you review all the history and government chapters, get ready to have some fun and test your knowledge about U.S. government and civics at the same time. Try your hand at these quizzes, based on questions that may be asked on your civics test.

As easy as 1, 2, 3

We start off easy by counting from 1 to 10. Match the item to the number.

	How many...?		Item
1		a	amendments in the Bill of Rights
2		b	articles in the U.S. Constitution
3		c	branches of government
4		d	star(s) for each state
5		e	Supreme Court justices
6		f	total years a president can be elected for
7		g	U.S. territories
8		h	voting rights amendments
9		i	years a representative is elected for
10		j	years a senator is elected for

Answers: 1d; 2i; 3c; 4h; 5g; 6j; 7b; 8f; 9e; 10a.

1. star for each state

2. years a representative is elected for

3. branches of government

4. voting rights amendments

5. U.S. territories

6. years a senator is elected for

7. articles in the U.S. Constitution

8. total years a president can be elected for

9. Supreme Court justices

10. amendments in the Bill of Rights

And here's some extra credit:

13		a	2020 census population of the United States
18		b	amendments to the Constitution
26		c	electoral votes to win a presidential election
27		d	minimum age to vote in a federal election
50		e	original colonies
100		f	register for Selective Service before __th birthday
270		g	states in the United States
435		h	total Electoral College electors
538		i	U.S. representatives
331 million		j	U.S. senators

Answers: 13e; 18d; 26f; 27b; 50g; 100j; 270c; 435i; 538h; 331a

It breaks down like this:

13 original colonies

18 minimum age to vote in a federal election

26 register for Selective Service before __th birthday

27 amendments to the Constitution

50 states in the United States

100 U.S. senators

270 electoral votes to win a presidential election

435 U.S. representatives

538 total Electoral College electors

331 million 2020 census population of the United States

Two quizzes about the three branches

Now plug in some of the numbers, terms, and names of your government officials. Complete the following chart about the three branches by choosing the correct letters from the following list to replace the numbers in the chart.

a. Enforce the law

b. Executive Branch

c. Explain the laws

d. four hundred and thirty-five

e. four years

f. House of Representatives

g. representatives

h. Senate

i. six years

j. White House

	Legislative Branch		1	**Judicial Branch**
	Senators	2	President	Justices
Number	one hundred	3	one	nine
Term	4	two years	5	life
Place of Work	6	7	8	Supreme Court
Website	senate.gov	house.gov	wh.gov	supremecourt.gov
Job	Make the laws		9	10
Name of Your Government Official	Senator	Representative	President	Chief Justice

Answers: 1b; 2g; 3d; 4i; 5e; 6h; 7f; 8j; 9a; 10c

1. b Executive Branch

2. g representatives

3. d four hundred and thirty-five

4. i six years

5. e four years

6. h Senate

7. f House of Representatives

8. j White House

9. a Enforce the law

10. c Explain the laws

Now that you have the basics of the three branches squared away, check the branch with its power and responsibility.

Lg	Ex	Ju	Power or Responsibility
			1. The power to conduct foreign policy
			2. The power to confirm presidential appointments
			3. The power to declare laws unconstitutional
			4. The power to introduce tax or budget bills
			5. The power to settle disputes between two or more U.S. states
			6. The power to settle legal disagreements between citizens of different U.S. states
			7. The power to sign bills into law or veto bills before they become law
			8. The responsibility to administer the Federal Election Commission, the Small Business Administration, the United States Postal Service, and the Veterans Administration
			9. The responsibility to maintain the defense of the United States, including the Army, Navy, and Air Force, and the power to declare war
			10. The responsibility to oversee the Department of Labor, the Department of Education, and the Department of the Interior

Answers: 1 Ex; 2 Lg; 3 Ju; 4 Lg; 5 Ju; 6 Ju; 7 Ex; 8 Ex; 9 Lg; 10 Ex

1. **Executive:** The president is responsible for conducting foreign policy (of course, the president's advisors help).

2. **Legislative:** The power to confirm presidential appointments is held by the Senate.

3. **Judicial:** The Supreme Court can declare laws unconstitutional or against the supreme law of the land.

4. **Legislative:** The House of Representatives (although both the House and the Senate can introduce most bills, only the House of Representatives may introduce tax or budget bills).

5. **Judicial:** When states have legal disputes, they look to the federal courts to settle them.

6. **Judicial:** When citizens of different states bring legal action against one another, the federal courts have the authority to decide the outcome.

7. **Executive:** The president has the power to sign bills into law or to veto bills.

8. **Executive:** These independent agencies, which can change according to the country's current needs and circumstances, fall under the authority of the executive branch.

9. **Legislative:** Although the president serves as commander in chief, it is both houses of Congress that must declare war and maintain our military forces.

10. **Executive:** These departments and others like them come under the authority of the executive branch of government.

The important Americans quiz

Our fifth practice quiz! Match the important American in the left column to their description in the right column. Extra credit: Note the political offices and search online for the current office holder. (You'll find the answers at the end of this section.)

	Important American		*Description*
1	Abraham Lincoln	a	1800s civil rights leader; fought for women's rights
2	Alexander Hamilton	b	1900s civil rights leader; worked for equality for all Americans
3	Benjamin Franklin	c	A writer of the Federalist Papers; 1st secretary of the treasury

	Important American		*Description*
4	Dwight D. Eisenhower	d	A writer of the Federalist Papers; 1st Supreme Court chief justice
5	Franklin D. Roosevelt	e	A writer of the Federalist Papers; president during the War of 1812
6	George Washington	f	Declaration of Independence writer; 1st secretary of state; president
7	James Madison	g	First U.S. president; Father of Our Country
8	John Adams	h	President during the Civil War; freed the slaves
9	John Jay	i	President during the Great Depression and World War II
10	Martin Luther King, Jr.	j	President during World War I; founded forerunner of the United Nations
11	Susan B. Anthony	k	U.S. diplomat; 1st vice president; 2nd president
12	Thomas Jefferson	l	U.S. diplomat; started the first free libraries
13	Woodrow Wilson	m	World War II general; president during the early Cold War

Answers: 1h; 2c; 3l; 4m; 5i; 6g; 7e; 8k; 9d; 10b; 11a; 12f; 13j

1. **Abraham Lincoln:** President during the Civil War; freed the slaves

2. **Alexander Hamilton:** A writer of the Federalist Papers; 1st secretary of the treasury

3. **Benjamin Franklin:** U.S. diplomat; started the first free libraries

4. **Dwight D. Eisenhower:** World War II general; president during the early Cold War

5. **Franklin D. Roosevelt:** President during the Great Depression and World War II

6. **George Washington:** First U.S. president; Father of Our Country

7. **James Madison:** A writer of the Federalist Papers; president during the War of 1812

8. **John Adams:** U.S. diplomat; 1st vice president; 2nd president

9. **John Jay:** A writer of the Federalist Papers; 1st Supreme Court chief justice

10. **Martin Luther King, Jr.:** 1900s civil rights leader; worked for equality for all Americans

11. **Susan B. Anthony:** 1800s civil rights leader; fought for women's rights

12. **Thomas Jefferson:** Declaration of Independence writer; 1st secretary of state; president

13. **Woodrow Wilson:** President during World War I; founded forerunner of the United Nations

The citizen responsibilities quiz

True or False: The following are important responsibilities or duties of *all* adult United States citizens, born or naturalized. (You'll find the answers at the end of this section.)

True	False	Responsibilities of U.S. Citizens
		1. Serving in the military
		2. Voting
		3. Serving on a jury
		4. Obeying laws
		5. Paying taxes
		6. Contributing to political campaigns
		7. Allowing their homes to be searched at any time by law enforcement officials
		8. Attending the church of their choice

Answers: 1 False; 2 True; 3 True; 4 True; 5 True; 6 False; 7 False; 8 False

1. **False.** All citizens are not automatically required to serve in the military. Men between the ages of 18 and 26 years old are required, by law, to register with the Selective Service System, an independent agency within the executive branch of the government that works to provide manpower to the armed forces in times of emergency. They may or may not be required to serve (as of this writing, there hasn't been a draft since 1973, when the United States converted to an all-volunteer military).

2. **True.** Although there is no law that compels all citizens to exercise their right to vote, voting nonetheless remains an important citizen responsibility, because those who don't exercise this right lose their voice in government.

3. **True.** Jurors perform an essential role in sustaining the U.S. system of justice. The right to a trial by a jury of one's peers is guaranteed in the Constitution, and a jury's honest and impartial decisions help protect our fundamental rights to fair and efficient justice for all. Although not all citizens will actually serve on a jury, the government has the right to require every citizen to serve periodically.

4. **True.** Everyone living in the United States, whether or not a citizen, is expected to obey the laws of the land.

5. **True.** Everyone who resides in the United States, whether or not a citizen, is required to honestly pay taxes, and the money is used to provide government services that we all benefit from.

6. **False.** U.S. citizens are not compelled to contribute to any political campaigns.

7. **False.** The Constitution guarantees the right of the people against unreasonable searches and seizures of their persons, houses, papers, and effects. The officers must produce a search warrant from the court in order to search your home.

8. **False.** The Constitution guarantees freedom of religion, which also gives citizens the right not to attend church at all, should they choose.

Preparing for Your USCIS Interview: The 100 Questions!

Want to know exactly what kinds of civics questions will be asked during your naturalization interview? The USCIS gives the 100 questions that follow. Does this mean you'll be asked all these questions? No, not by a long shot — the USCIS officer will ask you up to 10 questions from the list of 100 civics test questions. You must answer six questions correctly to pass the civics test.

Two quick questions before you begin

Question: Many questions have multiple correct answers. Does that mean that some answers are "more correct?"

Answer: No, each answer for the correction is equally correct.

Question: Do you need to remember all of the answers?

Answer: If the question asks for one answer, you only need to remember and give one answer.

> **Example:** USCIS 100:06. What is one right or freedom from the First Amendment?
>
> Speech (Other correct answers are religion, assembly, press, petition the government)

If the question asks for two answers, you only need to remember and give two answers.

> **Example:** USCIS 100:09: What are two rights in the Declaration of Independence?
>
> Life and liberty (Other correct answers are "life and the pursuit of happiness" or "liberty and the pursuit of happiness.")

If the question asks for three answers, you only need to remember three answers.

> **Example:** USCIS 100:64. There were 13 original states. Name three.
>
> New York, New Jersey, and New Hampshire (or more combos such as North Carolina, South Carolina, Georgia)

REMEMBER

The more you try to remember, the better prepared you will be.

If you are 65 years old or older and have been a legal permanent resident of the United States for 20 or more years, you may study just the questions that have been marked with an asterisk (*).

TIP

American Government

A: Principles of American Democracy

1. What is the supreme law of the land?

the Constitution

2. What does the Constitution do?

sets up the government

defines the government

protects basic rights of Americans

3. **The idea of self-government is in the first three words of the Constitution. What are these words?**

We the People

4. **What is an amendment?**

a change (to the Constitution)

an addition (to the Constitution)

5. **What do we call the first ten amendments to the Constitution?**

the Bill of Rights

6. **What is one right or freedom from the First Amendment?***

speech

religion

assembly

press

petition the government

7. **How many amendments does the Constitution have?**

twenty-seven (27)

8. **What did the Declaration of Independence do?**

announced our independence (from Great Britain)

declared our independence (from Great Britain)

said that the United States is free (from Great Britain)

9. **What are two rights in the Declaration of Independence?**

life

liberty

pursuit of happiness

10. **What is freedom of religion?**

You can practice any religion, or not practice a religion.

11. **What is the economic system in the United States?***

capitalist economy

market economy

12. What is the "rule of law"?

Everyone must follow the law.

Leaders must obey the law.

Government must obey the law.

No one is above the law.

B: System of Government

13. Name one branch or part of the government.*

Congress

legislative

President

executive

the courts

judicial

14. What stops one branch of government from becoming too powerful?

checks and balances

separation of powers

15. Who is in charge of the executive branch?

the president

16. Who makes federal laws?

Congress

Senate and House (of Representatives)

(U.S. or national) legislature

17. What are the two parts of the U.S. Congress?*

the Senate and House (of Representatives)

18. How many U.S. senators are there?

one hundred (100

19. We elect a U.S. senator for how many years?

six (6)

20. Who is one of your state's U.S. senators now?*

Answers will vary. (District of Columbia residents and residents of U.S. territories should answer that D.C. [or the territory where the applicant lives] has no U.S. senators.)

21. The House of Representatives has how many voting members?

four hundred thirty-five (435)

22. We elect a U.S. representative for how many years?

two (2)

23. Name your U.S. representative.

Answers will vary. (Residents of territories with nonvoting delegates or resident commissioners may provide the name of that delegate or commissioner. Also acceptable is any statement that the territory has no [voting] representatives in Congress.)

24. Who does a U.S. senator represent?

all people of the state

25. Why do some states have more representatives than other states?

(because of) the state's population

(because) they have more people

(because) some states have more people

26. We elect a President for how many years?

four (4)

27. In what month do we vote for President?*

November

28. What is the name of the president of the United States now?*

Joseph R. Biden (at the time of this publication).

29. What is the name of the vice president of the United States now?

Kamala Harris (at the time of this publication).

30. If the president can no longer serve, who becomes President?

the vice president

31. If both the president and the vice president can no longer serve, who becomes president?

the Speaker of the House

32. **Who is the Commander in Chief of the military?**

the president

33. **Who signs bills to become laws?**

the president

34. **Who vetoes bills?**

the president

35. **What does the president's Cabinet do?**

advises the president

36. **What are two Cabinet-level positions?**

[Any two of the following are correct.] Secretary of Agriculture, Secretary of Commerce, Secretary of Defense, Secretary of Education, Secretary of Energy, Secretary of Health and Human Services, Secretary of Homeland Security, Secretary of Housing and Urban Development, Secretary of the Interior, Secretary of Labor, Secretary of State, Secretary of Transportation, Secretary of the Treasury, Secretary of Veterans Affairs, Attorney General, Vice President

37. **What does the judicial branch do?**

reviews laws

explains laws

resolves disputes (disagreements)

decides if a law goes against the Constitution

38. **What is the highest court in the United States?**

the Supreme Court

39. **How many justices are on the Supreme Court?**

9 (at the time of this publication).

40. **Who is the Chief Justice of the United States now?**

John Roberts (at the time of this publication).

41. **Under our Constitution, some powers belong to the federal government. What is one power of the federal government?**

to print money

to declare war

to create an army

to make treaties

42. **Under our Constitution, some powers belong to the states. What is one power of the states?**

provide schooling and education

provide protection (police)

provide safety (fire departments)

give a driver's license

approve zoning and land use

43. **Who is the governor of your state now?**

Answers will vary. (District of Columbia residents should answer that D.C. does not have a Governor.)

44. **What is the capital of your state?***

Answers will vary. (District of Columbia residents should answer that D.C. is not a state and does not have a capital. Residents of U.S. territories should name the capital of the territory.)

45. **What are the two major political parties in the United States?***

Democratic and Republican

46. **What is the political party of the president now?**

Democratic Party (at the time of this publication).

47. **What is the name of the Speaker of the House of Representatives now?**

Nancy Pelosi (at the time of this publication).

C: Rights and Responsibilities

48. **There are four amendments to the Constitution about who can vote. Describe one of them.**

Citizens eighteen (18) and older (can vote).

You don't have to pay (a poll tax) to vote.

Any citizen can vote. (Women and men can vote.)

A male citizen of any race (can vote).

49. **What is one responsibility that is only for United States citizens?***

serve on a jury

vote in a federal election

50. **Name one right only for United States citizens.**

vote in a federal election

run for federal office

51. **What are two rights of everyone living in the United States?**

freedom of expression

freedom of speech

freedom of assembly

freedom to petition the government

freedom of religion

the right to bear arms

52. **What do we show loyalty to when we say the Pledge of Allegiance?**

the United States

the flag

53. **What is one promise you make when you become a United States citizen?**

give up loyalty to other countries

defend the Constitution and laws of the United States

obey the laws of the United States

serve in the U.S. military (if needed)

serve (do important work for) the nation (if needed)

be loyal to the United States

54. **How old do citizens have to be to vote for President?***

eighteen (18) and older

55. **What are two ways that Americans can participate in their democracy?**

[Any two of the following are correct.] Vote, join a political party, help with a campaign, join a civic group, give an elected official your opinion on an issue, call senators and representatives, publicly support or oppose an issue or policy, run for office, write to a newspaper

56. **When is the last day you can send in federal income tax forms?***

April 15

57. **When must all men register for the Selective Service?**

at age eighteen (18)

between eighteen (18) and twenty-six (26)

American History

A: Colonial Period and Independence

58. **What is one reason colonists came to America?**

freedom

political liberty

religious freedom

economic opportunity

practice their religion

escape persecution

59. **Who lived in America before the Europeans arrived?**

American Indians

Native Americans

60. **What group of people was taken to America and sold as slaves?**

Africans

people from Africa

61. **Why did the colonists fight the British?**

because of high taxes (taxation without representation)

because the British army stayed in their houses (boarding, quartering)

because they didn't have self-government

62. **Who wrote the Declaration of Independence?**

(Thomas) Jefferson

63. **When was the Declaration of Independence adopted?**

July 4, 1776

64. **There were 13 original states. Name three.**

[Any three of the following are correct.] New Hampshire, Massachusetts, Rhode Island, Connecticut, New York, New Jersey, Pennsylvania, Delaware, Maryland, Virginia, North Carolina, South Carolina, Georgia

65. **What happened at the Constitutional Convention?**

The Constitution was written.

The Founding Fathers wrote the Constitution.

66. When was the Constitution written?

1787

67. The Federalist Papers supported the passage of the U.S. Constitution. Name one of the writers.

(James) Madison

(Alexander) Hamilton

(John) Jay

Publius

68. What is one thing Benjamin Franklin is famous for?

U.S. diplomat

oldest member of the Constitutional Convention

first Postmaster General of the United States

writer of *Poor Richard's Almanac*

started the first free libraries

69. Who is the "Father of Our Country"?

(George) Washington

70. Who was the first president?*

(George) Washington

B: 1800s

71. What territory did the United States buy from France in 1803?

the Louisiana Territory

Louisiana

72. Name one war fought by the United States in the 1800s.

War of 1812

Mexican-American War

Civil War

Spanish-American War

73. Name the U.S. war between the North and the South.

the Civil War

the War between the States

74. **Name one problem that led to the Civil War.**

slavery

economic reasons

states' rights

75. **What was one important thing that Abraham Lincoln did?***

freed the slaves (Emancipation Proclamation)

saved (or preserved) the Union

led the United States during the Civil War

76. **What did the Emancipation Proclamation do?**

freed the slaves

freed slaves in the Confederacy

freed slaves in the Confederate states

freed slaves in most Southern states

77. **What did Susan B. Anthony do?**

fought for women's rights

fought for civil rights

C: Recent American History and Other Important Historical Information

78. **Name one war fought by the United States in the 1900s.***

World War I

World War II

Korean War

Vietnam War

(Persian) Gulf War

79. **Who was President during World War I?**

(Woodrow) Wilson

80. **Who was President during the Great Depression and World War II?**

(Franklin) Roosevelt

81. **Who did the United States fight in World War II?**

Japan, Germany, and Italy

82. Before he was President, Eisenhower was a general. What war was he in?

World War II

83. During the Cold War, what was the main concern of the United States?

Communism

84. What movement tried to end racial discrimination?

civil rights (movement)

85. What did Martin Luther King, Jr. do?*

fought for civil rights

worked for equality for all Americans

86. What major event happened on September 11, 2001, in the United States?

Terrorists attacked the United States.

87. Name one American Indian tribe in the United States.

[USCIS Officers will be supplied with a list of federally recognized American Indian tribes. Any of the following are correct.] Apache, Arawak, Blackfeet, Cherokee, Cheyenne, Chippewa, Choctaw, Creek, Crow, Hopi, Huron, Inuit, Iroquois, Lakota, Mohegan, Navajo, Oneida, Pueblo, Seminole, Shawnee, Sioux, Teton.

Integrated Civics

A: Geography

88. Name one of the two longest rivers in the United States.

Missouri (River)

Mississippi (River)

89. What ocean is on the West Coast of the United States?

Pacific (Ocean)

90. What ocean is on the East Coast of the United States?

Atlantic (Ocean)

91. Name one U.S. territory.

Puerto Rico

U.S. Virgin Islands

American Samoa

Northern Mariana Islands

Guam

92. **Name one state that borders Canada.**

[Any of the following are correct.] Alaska, Idaho, Maine, Michigan, Minnesota, Montana, New Hampshire, New York, North Dakota, Ohio, Pennsylvania, Vermont, Washington

93. **Name one state that borders Mexico.**

California

Arizona

New Mexico

Texas

94. **What is the capital of the United States?***

Washington, D.C.

95. **Where is the Statue of Liberty?***

New York (Harbor)

Liberty Island

(Also acceptable are New Jersey, near New York City, and on the Hudson [River].)

B: Symbols

96. **Why does the flag have 13 stripes?**

because there were 13 original colonies

because the stripes represent the original colonies

97. **Why does the flag have 50 stars?***

because there is one star for each state

because each star represents a state

because there are 50 states

98. **What is the name of the national anthem?**

"The Star-Spangled Banner"

REMEMBERING FACTS

You can memorize facts easier by using mnemonics or other memory techniques. A *mnemonic* is a word, rhyme, abbreviation, or similar verbal shorthand that you create to help trigger your memory. You can trick yourself into remembering facts in many different ways. For example, if you're trying to remember the names of the 13 original colonies of the United States (Connecticut, Delaware, Georgia, Maryland, Massachusetts, New Hampshire, New Jersey, New York, North Carolina, Pennsylvania, Rhode Island, South Carolina, and Virginia), you can just remember the first letters of their names — C, D, G, two Ms, four Ns, P, R, S, and V in alphabetical order. If you set those letters to a familiar tune such as the "Alphabet Song," it'll be even easier to remember.

The trick is to do whatever works for you. Try out several different techniques and see which one works best for you.

C: Holidays

99. When do we celebrate Independence Day?*

July 4

100. Name two national U.S. holidays.

[Any two of the following are correct.] New Year's Day, Martin Luther King Jr. Day, Presidents' Day, Memorial Day, Independence Day, Labor Day, Columbus Day, Veterans Day, Thanksgiving, Christmas

ONLINE PRACTICE FOR THE CIVICS TEST

You can find the civics questions in different formats and translations at this website:

```
www.uscis.gov/citizenship/find-study-materials-and-resources/
study-for-the-test
```

USCIS has translations of the English civics test in Arabic, Chinese, Korean, Spanish, Tagalog, and Vietnamese. Go to USCIS Citizenship Resource Center: Study for the Test at this website:

```
www.uscis.gov/citizenship/find-study-materials-and-resources/
study-for-the-test.
```

(continued)

(continued)

USCIS has civics lesson plans for beginning and intermediate English learners. Go to Citizenship Resource Center: Educational Products for Educators and Program Administrators here:

```
www.uscis.gov/citizenship/resources-for-educational-programs/
educational-products-for-educators-and-program-administrators
```

USCIS officers "star" in USCIS civics playlists — 102 videos of real USCIS officers asking and answering the civics questions. Check out the USCIS YouTube channel (playlist tab). These videos also pop up on USCIS social media accounts on Facebook, Instagram, and Twitter.

USCIS has an official mobile app: "USCIS: Civics Test Study Tools." Go to your favorite app store and download the "Torch."

Warning: There are many apps that claim to be from the USCIS — make sure that USCIS is the developer. Also, there are apps that claim they can manage your case — these apps are collecting and selling your personal data! If you need to check your case status and such, use the USCIS tools:

```
www.uscis.gov/tools/uscis-tools-and-resources/
uscis-tools-and-resources
```

USCIS and the National Museum of American History (NMAH) collaborated on "Preparing for the Oath," which are videos and activities for each civics question, explained in clear English and illustrated by beautiful historical items from the Smithsonian collections. Find "Preparing for the Oath" here:

```
americanhistory.si.edu/citizenship/
```

CLINIC has collected translations of the English civics test in 20 more languages from Albanian to Urdu. Go to "Translation of Civics Questions and Answers for the Naturalization Test" by Community Organizations:

```
https://cliniclegal.org/resources/citizenship-and-naturalization/
citizenship-test-preparation/translation-civics-questions
```

The Reading and Writing Tests

Although there is no official list of USCIS reading sentences, USCIS does provide a reading test vocabulary list for the naturalization test (www.uscis.gov/sites/default/files/document/guides/reading_vocab.pdf). The officer will ask you to read a simple question out loud. Typical questions may be, "Who was the second president?" or "What is the largest state?" You must read one out of three sentences correctly to pass the reading test.

The officer will then dictate a sentence for you to write. Frequently the sentence is a response to the question that you just read, but don't jump ahead! Listen carefully to the complete sentence — the officer can only repeat it once. Although there is no official list of USCIS reading sentences, USCIS does provide a writing test vocabulary list for the naturalization test (www.uscis.gov/sites/default/files/document/guides/writing_vocab.pdf) that complements the reading vocabulary list. Typical questions may be, "Adams was the second president," or "Alaska is the largest state." You must write one out of three sentences correctly to pass the reading test.

People seldom fail the civics and reading tests, but they do fail the writing tests for two reasons: First, they are not used to people with different accents dictating sentences in English. Second, they never learned how to write the English alphabet — instead they "draw" the words. Learning how to listen, write, and take dictation requires practice, practice, practice! Listen to English speakers with a variety of accents. Take notes during conversations. Ask different people to dictate numbers, prices, words, messages, and finally sentences to you. Build up your handwriting skills by copying the numbers, letters, words, and sentences. Some of my own students re-copy their class exercises and notes when they get home. Other students write five citizenship questions and answers five times every day that they are studying for the test. Still others do civics-themed word search puzzles and other games. It will help you build up muscle memory and keep your brain happy and active. Although there is no official USCIS list of the reading and writing sentences, here is a list of example sentences based on the USCIS reading and writing vocabulary lists that complement the civics knowledge you gained by preparing for the civics test:

	Read the Question	Write the Answer
1	Who was the second president?	Adams was the second president.
2	What is the largest state?	Alaska is the largest state.
3	Who lived here first?	American Indians lived here first.
4	What state has the most people?	California has the most people.
5	What country is north of the United States?	Canada is north of the United States.
6	Who can vote?	Citizens can vote.
7	When is Columbus Day?	Columbus Day is in October.

	Read the Question	Write the Answer
8	What does Congress do?	Congress makes laws.
9	Where does Congress meet?	Congress meets in Washington, D.C.
10	What was the first U.S. state?	Delaware was the first state.
11	When is Flag Day?	Flag Day is in June.
12	Name one right in the Bill of Rights.	Freedom of speech is a right.
13	When is Independence Day?	Independence Day is in July.
14	When is Labor Day?	Labor Day is in September.
15	Who was Abraham Lincoln?	Lincoln was the president during the Civil War.
16	When is Memorial Day?	Memorial Day is in May.
17	What country is south of the United States?	Mexico is south of the United States.
18	What was the first U.S capital?	New York City was the first capital.
19	Why do people come to America?	People come here to be free.
20	Which president is on the one-dollar bill?	President Washington is on the one-dollar bill.
21	When is Presidents' Day?	Presidents' Day is in February.
22	When is Thanksgiving?	Thanksgiving is in November.
23	What are the colors of the flag?	The colors of the flag are red, white, and blue.
24	Who elects Congress?	The people elect Congress.
25	Who lives in the White House?	The president lives in the White House.
26	Where is the White House?	The White House is in Washington, D.C.
27	How many states are in the United States?	There are 50 states in the United States.
28	How many U.S. senators are there?	There are one hundred U.S. senators.
29	Why do people want to live in America?	They want to live in a free country.
30	Why do people want to be citizens?	They want to vote.

	Read the Question	Write the Answer
31	Who is the Father of Our Country?	Washington is the Father of Our Country.
32	Who was George Washington?	Washington was the first U.S. president.
33	What is the capital of the United States?	Washington, D.C., is the capital of the United States.
34	What do we pay to the government?	We pay taxes.
35	When do we vote for president?	We vote for the president in November.

5

The Part of Tens

Review some advice to help you pass your interview.

Avoid common mistakes that can hurt your naturalization case.

Read up on ten great Americans.

Chapter **19**

Ten Tips to Help You Pass Your Naturalization Interview

U se this chapter as a checklist of items to put into practice before going to your naturalization interview. Each of the ideas in the following pages can actually improve your chances of successfully passing the interview and becoming a naturalized citizen of the United States.

Be On Time

Get to the interview on time. That means on USCIS time, which means that if you have an 8 a.m. interview, you should arrive at the building at least 15 minutes early to allow time to get into the building and go through a security screening. After going through the security screening, you may be directed to the reception-ist, who will check your appointment letter again and direct you to the appropriate waiting room, where you will give your appointment letter to a clerk. Sit down, take some calming breaths, and wait for your name to be called.

REMEMBER

Security procedures at government buildings may significantly increase the amount of time it takes to even enter the building. Allow plenty of extra time so that you don't risk being late. Naturalization interview appointments are a high priority — if there is a long line to get into the building, approach the security guard calmly, holding your appointment letter and state issued ID in front of you. The officer will quickly review your letter and will let you in.

TIP

Before the day of your interview, take a trip to the building where your interview will be held, leaving at the same time of day as you'll need to leave for the real thing. This way, you can time how long it takes you to get to the building, allowing for traffic or other delays. Then allow even more time than that on the day of your interview, in case something unexpected comes up. Also, arrange for child care — you cannot bring your children into the interview with you.

Present Yourself Favorably

You only get one chance to make a first impression. Dress like you're going to a job interview and be polite to everyone you meet. Even if you have to wait three hours before being called in, wait with a calm heart and clear mind. Use the time to review your N-400, civics questions, and other documents one more time. If your application is based on marriage to a U.S. citizen, ask your spouse to wait with you in case the officer has any questions about your marriage. Present yourself favorably from the time you enter the building until the time you leave.

Listen Carefully

Listen carefully to the questions the examiner asks you. Furthermore, the examiner may ask you to define a word. (For example, What does "vote" mean? To choose a new leader or law.) Or the examiner may ask you to explain a basic law. (For example, Why can't you vote? I can't vote because I am not a citizen.) If, for any reason, you don't understand a question, do not answer the question until you do! Politely ask to have it repeated, rephrased, or the unfamiliar vocabulary explained until you do. You're better off getting clarification on the question than answering it incorrectly.

Answer the Right Questions

When you're sure you understand the question, take care to answer the question the officer asks you. Be alert for key words and wait for the examiner to finish asking the question before you respond. For example, if the examiner asks, "What do the stripes on the flag mean?" don't say, "Red." Answer that the stripes on the flag represent our 13 original colonies. And limit your response to the question asked (there are no extra points for showing off, and it will only lengthen the interview).

Know Your Application

Be familiar with your naturalization application. Knowing that there is a mistake on your application and asking the officer to correct it is much easier than having the officer ask you to explain a discrepancy or inconsistency (for instance, you correctly recall your dates of travel out of the United States as being less than six months, corroborated by your passport, but the dates are wrong on the application, stating a much longer trip).

Before the interview begins, the examiner will ask you if you have any questions or concerns about the interview. Briefly tell the officer which part of the N-400 form (for example, travel) and question number needs to be corrected. The officer will note the section and start the interview. When the interview comes to the N-400 section that needs to be corrected, the officer will then ask you about the details and may ask to see the documents (for example, your passport) to support the correction. Most corrections can be made during the interview.

Be Prepared

If something in your application requires an explanation, such as an extended trip abroad, past membership in the Communist Party, or a criminal record, don't let your interview be the first time you try to explain it to someone. If you have issues like this, you should have already included an explanatory affidavit with your naturalization application, and ideally, you would have consulted with a knowledgeable immigration lawyer or accredited representative before filing. Practice explaining these potential problems simply and clearly — long or confusing explanations can lead to more problems.

Know Your Stuff

If you're required to take the English and history/civics tests, which you most likely will be, remember, they are called *tests* for a reason. Study, practice, and be prepared. Yes, you can get another chance if you fail this portion of the interview, but why delay things and have to come back? Study hard the first time.

Bring What You Need

Bring your green card, passport, state-issued identification, and appointment letter. You may want to prepare a binder with original documentation such as marriage certificates, divorce decrees, children's birth certificates, travel documentation, affidavits, court records, and so on. Include the documentation that clarifies potential problems and supports your N-400 application.

Do not punch holes or staple your original copies! Instead, slip them into plastic page protectors and then put the protected original copies in your binder. During the interview, the examiner may need to make a copy of your original document. Upon request, simply open your binder, remove the original document from the binder, and hand over the document in its plastic sleeve to the officer. Don't worry! The officer will review, copy, and return the original document immediately.

TIP

Before the interview, copy or scan these original documents and keep the copies in a secure place. After the interview, return the original documents to a secure place (like, for example, a safety deposit box) and keep the copies in a secure yet accessible place (such as a locked cabinet).

Be Honest and Honorable

This may seem obvious, but don't lie, cheat, steal, or attempt to bribe your examining officer. Any of these can and probably will get you immediately disqualified from naturalization. If you cry, get upset, or become angry, the examiner will stop the interview and ask you to leave the office. In some cases, you may have to reapply for naturalization and pay the fee again! You have been preparing for this interview for a long time — stay calm and do the best you can.

Treat Immigration Officers with Respect

USCIS adjudicators deal with huge caseloads. You aren't the only applicant your adjudicator will see that day. To ensure fair and prompt treatment of your application, try to make their job easier. Limit your discussions in the interview to the topics covered by the USCIS officer.

Note that this information should not make you feel compelled to tolerate inappropriate behavior by a USCIS officer. If you think the officer is acting inappropriately or asking inappropriate questions, you should ask to speak with a supervisor immediately to report the incident. You can report the misconduct to the USCIS Office of Investigations (OI) oiintake@uscis.dhs.gov and include details about the date, time, location, name of the USCIS employee, and description of the incident. USCIS hold its employees to the highest standards of professional behavior and will investigate accusations of investigate misconduct thoroughly.

Chapter **20**

Ten Things That Can Hurt Your Naturalization Case

Just as there are things you can do to help your immigration chances, there are also some definite immigration don'ts. If any of the items on this list apply to you, we strongly urge you to seek the help of a qualified immigration attorney — long before you ever get to the stage of interviewing with the USCIS. Information that refers directly to USCIS history and civics questions is followed with "USCIS 100" and the appropriate question number (Example: USCIS 100:59).

Some of the items here can prevent you from ever becoming a U.S. citizen; others present temporary problems. Again, a qualified attorney can best advise you on how to deal with the situation. For a list of pro bono legal service providers, go to www.justice.gov/eoir/list-pro-bono-legal-service-providers.

Perpetrating Fraud

Fraud encompasses lying on your naturalization application as well as seeking immigration benefits that you know you aren't entitled to by putting forth a fraudulent claim. For example, claiming to be a U.S. citizen to vote or get a federal government job; denying your legal permanent residence status to avoid paying taxes; lying to obtain public benefits; or marrying a U.S. citizen solely to gain legal permanent residence (USCIS N-400 Part 12:1–3, 8, 30e, 31–32).

Participating in Subversive Activities

You can't expect to be welcomed as a citizen if you devote yourself to opposing the ideals upon which that citizenship is based. Anarchists, recent willful communists, supporters of totalitarian governments, and those who advocate for the overthrow of the U.S. government by force are barred from naturalization. And besides, if you're so opposed to the ideals of the United States, why become a citizen anyway? (USCIS N-400 Part 12:10–13)

Supporting Violence, Terror, and Participating in War Crimes

Individual or group participation in violent activities such as persecution, genocide, torture, sexual assault, severe violations of religious freedom, or terrorism are permanent bars to naturalization. Also excluded are those who support terrorism, financially or otherwise. If a person who legally resides in the United States is shown to have engaged in violent crime, they will be arrested, their residence status or U.S. citizenship will be rescinded, and they will be extradited (deported) for criminal prosecution (USCIS N-400 Part 12:9, 10c, 14–21).

Committing a Crime

Murder, along with aggravated felonies such as human trafficking, child pornography, or immigration fraud committed on or after November 29, 1990, constitutes a *permanent bar to naturalization*. Other crimes present *temporary bars,* meaning you must wait a designated period of time before applying for citizenship. Furthermore, the USCIS can and will take your criminal record into consideration when determining whether you have good moral character. You will need to submit court and rehabilitation records about your case to USCIS. The bottom line: Obey the law, and you'll have a lot less to worry about (USCIS N-400 Part 12:22–29).

Doing Drugs

Violating any controlled-substance law of the United States, any state, or any foreign country can get your application bounced on grounds of a lack of good moral character. Translation: In order to protect your immigration chances, don't use, sell, traffic, or otherwise be involved with illegal drugs or other controlled substances of any kind, anywhere (USCIS N-400 Part 12:30c).

Behaving Poorly (Even If You're Not Breaking a Law)

Criminal convictions are not the only criteria upon which a negative determination of good moral character can be made. Other transgressions can include failing to provide child support; committing adultery that destroys a viable marriage, affects minor children, or is otherwise scandalous; having practiced polygamy; having been or being a habitual drunkard; or committing other unlawful acts that undermine moral character (USCIS N-400 Part 12:30).

Unlawfully Staying in the United States

Being caught illegally in the United States can seriously impact your immigration and naturalization goals in a negative way. Make sure that your immigration status is legal and up-to-date, and never stay in the United States beyond the date stamped on your I-94. If you have recently been ordered to leave the country, you aren't eligible for citizenship. If you're currently in removal proceedings, you may not apply for citizenship until the proceedings are complete and you've been allowed to remain in the country as a lawful permanent resident (USCIS N-400 Part 12:30e, 31–36).

Failing to Register with the Selective Service (If You're a Male)

The Selective Service provides personnel to the Department of Defense during a national emergency while at the same time providing for an Alternative Service Program for conscientious objectors. By registering, a young man remains eligible for jobs, state-based student aid in 31 states, federally funded job training, and U.S. citizenship for immigrant men. All male legal permanent residents between their 18th and 26th birthdays must register with the Selective Service. Failure to register can be found to undermine good moral character (USCIS N-400 Part 12:44). To check your registration status, go to www.sss.gov. Related to military service, desertion from the U.S. armed forces during a time of war may subject an applicant to a permanent bar to naturalization (USCIS N-400 Part 12:43).

Failing to Meet Deadlines

Immigration proceedings come with strict time deadlines. From knowing when you're eligible to apply to knowing how long you have to file an appeal, you need to monitor the calendar to make sure you don't miss out.

Remember the following:

» You can file your N-400 three months before your naturalization eligibility date (five years; three years for spouses of U.S. citizens).

» You must have lived within the USCIS district in which you file at least three months before the filing date.

» You must have been physically present in the United States for at least half the required residence time (30 months out of five years; 18 months out of three years).

Don't forget to keep track of your absences from the United States — absences of more than six months require an explanation, and those over a year break the continuity of residence. After you've filed your application, be sure to read all government correspondence carefully.

REMEMBER

Make sure you follow all instructions carefully and that you provide the USCIS with any paperwork and documentation that they need within the time period that they specify. Failing to meet deadlines will cause the USCIS to think you've abandoned your application; your application will be thrown out, and you'll have to start the process all over again.

Abandoning Your Application

You must follow up on your application, make and meet appointments, and deliver necessary forms and documents to the appropriate immigration authorities in a timely manner.

The USCIS takes deadlines seriously, and missing them can result in your application being denied and your having to start the entire process all over again (complete with all the fees involved).

Also, make sure you notify the USCIS each and every time you change your address, so they'll always know where to send you information or get in touch when needed. If mail sent to you is returned to the USCIS, they will assume you've abandoned your application. Failure to keep the USCIS informed of changes of address is a crime and can be grounds for removal.

Chapter **21**

Ten Important American Heroes

The United States would be nothing without its heroes. Americans owe their national heroes a debt of gratitude because their contributions helped shape this nation into the strong, freedom-loving, democratic country it is today. These ambitious people saw problems and were not afraid to get involved and work to create change and a better world for us all.

Learning about the people covered in this chapter will provide you with a stronger understanding of American history and better prepare you to take your citizenship test. Information that refers directly to USCIS history and civics questions is followed with "USCIS 100" and the appropriate question number (Example: USCIS 100:59).

George Washington

The man who became the first president of the United States was born February 22, 1732, in Westmoreland County, Virginia, to a family of planters. Washington's love of farming remained consistent throughout his life, although he became much better known for his military and political accomplishments.

Washington was commissioned a lieutenant colonel in 1754, where he fought the first fights of what grew into the French and Indian War. At the Second Continental Congress in 1775, Washington was elected commander in chief of the Continental Army.

From 1759 until the start of the Revolutionary War, Washington managed his lands around his home in Virginia, called Mount Vernon. He also served in the Virginia *House of Burgesses,* the colony's seat of government.

After the war, Washington planned to retire, but he was troubled by the problems the new nation faced being governed by the Articles of Confederation (you can find out more about the Articles in Chapter 9). He soon began to work toward establishing a Constitutional Convention.

After ratifying the Constitution, the delegates unanimously elected Washington the first president of the United States (USCIS 100:70). He took the oath of office on April 30, 1789, standing on the balcony of Federal Hall on Wall Street in New York City with John Adams serving as his vice president.

By the end of his first term in office, Washington was disappointed that two political parties were developing in the United States. In his farewell address, he urged his countrymen to forego political-party spirit and geographical distinctions between the states. He also warned against long-term foreign alliances; the United States was largely able to maintain a position of neutrality in foreign affairs until World War I. Despite his personal beliefs, Washington never infringed upon the policy-making powers the Constitution gave Congress.

After leaving office, Washington retired to Mount Vernon, his beloved home. Unfortunately, he was only able to enjoy it for about three years. George Washington died of a throat infection on December 14, 1799. He is hailed as the "Father of Our Country" (USCIS 100:69) and is honored along with Abraham Lincoln on Presidents' Day (USCIS 100:100c).

Benjamin Franklin

An inventor, statesman, and philosopher, Benjamin Franklin was one of the most influential of our Founding Fathers, despite the fact that he never held the presidential office. A printer by trade, Franklin's book *Poor Richard's Almanac* (USCIS 100:68d) became the best-selling book in the colonies, selling over 10,000 copies a year. In addition to publishing the *Pennsylvania Gazette,* he helped establish newspapers in New York, Connecticut, and two islands in the West Indies. In 1731 Benjamin Franklin started the Library Company of Philadelphia, the first public library (USCIS 100:68e). In 1737, he was appointed postmaster of Philadelphia. One of his main jobs was to survey the roads to determine the best routes and schedule to deliver the mail. In 1775, the Second Continental Congress appointed him the first Postmaster General of the new United States (USCIS 100:68c).

During the fight for independence, he traveled to Europe as a U.S. diplomat (USCIS 100:68a), negotiating with the French to help the colonial cause by securing guns, ammunition, and other provisions for the army as well as volunteer troops. He also helped negotiate the peace treaty with England after America won its independence from England. At 81, Franklin was the oldest delegate to the Constitutional Convention (USCIS 100:68b).

Franklin had many inventions to his credit, including swim fins, bifocal eyeglasses, glass harmonica, watertight bulkheads for ships, lightning rod, odometer, and a style of wood stove that came to be known as the Franklin stove.

Franklin's experiments led to the discovery that lightning is actually a form of electricity (and not a punishment from God, as was thought at the time). He was knocked unconscious several times during his experiments, which entailed flying a kite in an electrical storm with a piece of metal at one end and a metal key at the other. His experiments with lightning led him to invent the lightning rod, which protected buildings from lightning fires and damage, and opened the door for many important advances in electricity that came later. Although he received much recognition for his inventions, Franklin didn't profit from them, choosing instead to give them freely to the world.

TECHNICAL
STUFF

Benjamin Franklin is the only Founding Father to have signed all five documents that established American independence: the Declaration of Independence, the Treaty of Amity and Commerce with France, the Treaty of Alliance with France, the Treaty of Peace with Great Britain, and the Constitution of the United States of America.

Thomas Jefferson

Thomas Jefferson, our third president, was born on April 13, 1743, in Virginia, but even before he became the commander in chief, he made major contributions to the country. With the help of Benjamin Franklin and John Adams, Jefferson wrote the original Declaration of Independence (USCIS 100:62) at the age of 33. He was elected to Congress in 1783 and succeeded Benjamin Franklin as minister to France in 1785. George Washington chose Jefferson as his Secretary of State in 1789. But this was the dawn of political parties in the United States. Sharp differences between Federalist Alexander Hamilton and Democratic-Republican Thomas

Jefferson prompted Jefferson to resign his position a few years later. Sympathetic toward the French Revolution, Jefferson also opposed a strong central government, believing most of the power of government should remain with the states.

Jefferson ran for president in 1796, losing by three votes to his opponent, John Adams. Although Jefferson was vice president, he simply retired to his home to wait for the next election.

REMEMBER

Before the adoption of the 12th Amendment, the candidate with the most electoral votes became president, and the candidate with the second-highest number of votes became vice president.

By the time Jefferson became president, the revolution in France was over. He was able to cut taxes and reduce the national debt, as well as buy the Louisiana Territory in 1803 from France (USCIS 100:71), probably the most notable act of his administration. But war between England and France was raging in Europe, with both countries interfering with American merchant ships. In an attempt to keep the United States neutral in the European conflicts, Jefferson placed an *embargo* (a government order prohibiting shipping) on merchant ships. The embargo was wildly unpopular, ending Jefferson's presidency on a low note.

After retiring to Monticello, his mountaintop home, Jefferson founded the University of Virginia. He died on July 4, 1826.

James Madison

Our fourth president, James Madison, was born in 1751 in Virginia. Perhaps more important than his role as president, however, was the impact he had on preparing and ratifying the country's most important document, the Constitution. Madison didn't just prepare the Bill of Rights; his influence had a great impact on getting the Constitution ratified in the first place.

Madison believed that a strong central government would provide the order and stability needed to make our young country strong. The Federalist Papers, which he authored with Alexander Hamilton and John Jay (USCIS 100:65), convinced many colonists of the importance of ratifying the Constitution. He also helped frame the Bill of Rights, the first ten amendments to the Constitution (USCIS 100:5), and enacted the United States' first revenue legislation. The development of the Republican, or Jeffersonian, party evolved out of his leadership, which opposed Hamilton's financial proposals.

Madison became president while Thomas Jefferson's unpopular embargo acts were still in force, but in 1810, Congress authorized trade with both England and France, providing they accepted the United States' neutral foreign policy. Napoleon pretended to accept the conditions, and Madison declared that the United States would trade with France, but not with England — a decision that led to the United States entering the War of 1812. This decision was strongly opposed by the Federalists.

Our young country was not prepared for war and sustained great losses. The British even managed to invade and burn most of Washington, D.C., setting fire to the White House and the Capitol. But a few notable military victories made many Americans believe that the War of 1812 had been successful. An increase in nationalism followed, resulting in the end of the Federalist political party.

Even after he had retired from political life, James Madison, the Father of the Constitution, continued to speak out against states' rights, which threatened to undermine the strength of the federal union. He died in 1836.

Alexander Hamilton

Born a British subject on the island of Nevis in the West Indies on January 11, 1755, Alexander Hamilton was a highly influential and controversial figure in the early formative years of the United States. He first traveled to Boston near the beginning of the Revolutionary War. Hamilton quickly established a reputation for patriotism, writing newspaper articles and pamphlets and delivering speeches attacking British policies. His military accomplishments and bravery in fighting the British brought him to the attention of General George Washington, and he served four years as Washington's personal secretary and aide.

Hamilton began his legal and political career after the war and remained politically active for the rest of his life. He served in Congress from 1782 to 1783, was elected to the Continental Congress, and founded the Bank of New York in 1784.

Hamilton fought for the adoption of the Constitution, writing about 75 percent of the Federalist Papers — the remaining 25 percent was penned by James Madison and John Jay (USCIS 100:65).

REMEMBER

The Federalist Papers remain an important commentary on the Constitution to this day because they illustrate the thoughts and frame of mind of two of our most important Founding Fathers, Madison and Hamilton.

Hamilton holds the honor of being the United States' first Secretary of the Treasury under our first president, George Washington. He was largely responsible for securing credit for the new nation. He advocated the need for a private bank that promoted public interests, patterned after the British model of national finance. Although many questioned the constitutionality of such a national bank, Hamilton argued that the authority to create such a system was implied in the Constitution; Washington agreed. Hamilton is largely credited with creating the financial stability the United States needed in order to grow into the powerful country it is today.

A brilliant and ambitious man, Hamilton was known to frequently overstep his authority. Hamilton and Jefferson entered into a bitter conflict over the question of foreign affairs. When the French Revolution turned into a war against all of Europe, Hamilton called for a U.S. policy of strict neutrality.

Even after he resigned his position of Secretary of the Treasury and returned to practice law in New York in 1795, he remained one of George Washington's chief advisors. Hamilton even wrote Washington's farewell address.

After George Washington's death, the leadership of the Federalist Party became divided between John Adams and Alexander Hamilton. But Hamilton was too arrogant, opinionated, and uncompromising to become popular enough to actually win the office of president. While Adams was in office, Hamilton constantly sought to undermine his authority. In 1800, on the eve of the presidential election, Hamilton wrote a bitter attack on President Adams. Although he intended the pamphlet to be private — only meant for the eyes of a few high-ranking government officials — Aaron Burr, one of Hamilton's political and legal rivals, published it. This made the feud between the two men even worse, and Hamilton made it his duty to prevent Burr, whom he thought had poor character, from ever gaining political power. Hamilton's influence with other Federalists cost Burr elections for the presidency and the governorship of the state of New York.

In retaliation, Burr challenged Hamilton to a duel. In the duel, which took place on July 12, 1804, Burr shot and killed Hamilton, who was only 47 years old. It was reported that Hamilton never intended to fire at his enemy. Nonetheless, Burr fired, and one of the nation's most influential men was gone.

Abraham Lincoln

Our 16th president was born on February 12, 1809, to a poor family in Hardin County, Kentucky. Despite his humble beginnings, Lincoln was ambitious. He worked and studied hard throughout his life.

Lincoln served eight years in the Illinois state legislature. He ran for state senator in 1858 against Stephen Douglas. Although he lost this election, his spirited debates against Douglas earned him national attention and the 1860 Republican nomination for president.

The first Republican president, Lincoln helped grow the party into a strong organization and even managed to get most Northern Democrats to preserve the Union during the Civil War (USCIS 100:45, 73, 75). In 1863, his Emancipation Proclamation declared all slaves (in the Confederacy) to be free (USCIS 100:75, 76).

A great speaker, Lincoln is perhaps most famous for his Gettysburg Address, given November 19, 1863, on the battlefield near Gettysburg, Pennsylvania. The address, one of the most famous American speeches ever, officially dedicated the cemetery at Gettysburg and honored the soldiers who died in the fight. More important, the Gettysburg Address brought better understanding of the Civil War to many Americans and confirmed again that "government of the people, by the people, for the people, shall not perish from the earth."

Lincoln won reelection in 1864, as the Civil War was coming to an end. In an effort to rebuild the damage done by the war, Lincoln encouraged the South to lay down arms and rejoin the Union. His efforts were not popular with everyone. On Good Friday, April 14, 1865, Lincoln was assassinated while attending a play at Ford's Theatre in Washington. It is thought that Lincoln's assassin, actor John Wilkes Booth, was trying to help the cause of the South. In fact, his terrible deed had the opposite effect, and the entire country united in grief for the slain president.

Susan B. Anthony

One of American history's most influential women, Susan B. Anthony was born February 15, 1820, in Adams, Massachusetts. Anthony's Quaker background put her in the perfect position to champion the cause for women's rights. One of the first groups to practice equality between men and women, the Quakers based their religion on the belief that priests and churches are not necessary for a person to experience God.

After completing her education, Anthony worked as a schoolteacher in New York, one of the few "respectable" jobs a woman of the time could hold. Unfortunately, she was paid about one-fifth of what her male counterparts earned. When she protested this inequality, she was fired from her job. She found a better position and taught for about ten more years, although she eventually became disheartened by the lack of career opportunities for women.

WOMEN ON CURRENCY

Susan B. Anthony's image was chosen to decorate the new U.S. dollar coin in 1979, making her the first woman to be depicted on U.S. currency. The coins proved unpopular with the general public, however, probably because they were so close in size to the quarter. The Anthony dollar was replaced in 1999 with another dollar coin, this one depicting the image of Sacagawea, a female Shoshone Native American guide who helped Lewis and Clark explore the Louisiana Territory from 1804 to 1806 (USCIS 100:71).

In 2005, the United States Mint started a series that honors our nation's first spouses by issuing one-half ounce $10 gold coins featuring their images in the order they served as first spouse.

In 2016, the U.S. Treasury Department announced that it would redesign the $20 bill as part of the currency modernization process and feature a portrait of the abolitionist Harriet Tubman on the front of the bill. Although it has been delayed, look for it to be dispensed by your bank's ATM in the not-too-distant future.

In 2017, the U.S. Mint released a gold coin with a hundred-dollar face value depicting Lady Liberty as an African-American woman.

Beginning in 2022, the U.S. Mint will issue five American Women Quarters annually to celebrate their accomplishments.

The 2022 American Women Quarters honor

- **Maya Angelou,** celebrated writer, performer, and social activist
- **Dr. Sally Ride,** physicist, astronaut, educator, and first American woman in space
- **Wilma Mankiller,** first female principal chief of the Cherokee Nation
- **Nina Otero-Warren,** a leader in New Mexico's suffrage movement and the first female superintendent of Santa Fe public schools
- **Anna May Wong,** first Chinese American film star in Hollywood

The 2023 American Women Quarter features

- **Bessie Coleman,** first African American and first Native American woman pilot
- **Edith Kanaka'ole,** indigenous Hawaiian composer, chanter, dancer, teacher, and entertainer

She turned her attention to social and political causes. As a Quaker, Anthony didn't believe in the use of alcohol and she founded the Daughters of Temperance, the first women's temperance organization, after being denied the chance to speak at a Sons of Temperance meeting because she was a woman.

Anthony had a fateful meeting with women's rights leader Elizabeth Cady Stanton at a temperance meeting. From that point on, she worked tirelessly for the woman's *suffrage* (right-to-vote) movement, organizing state and national conventions on the issue. She helped to found the American Equal Rights Association in 1866 (USCIS 100:77b).

Anthony and other women's rights activists also worked toward the *emancipation* (freeing) of slaves during the Civil War. They hoped to link women's rights to those of freed slaves. Unfortunately, the plan didn't work, and when the 15th Amendment to the Constitution passed in 1870, it extended the right to vote only to males of any race (USCIS 100:48e), particularly African-American men.

Anthony challenged the Constitution on the basis of the 14th Amendment, which stated that *all* people born in the United States were citizens and that no legal privileges could be denied them (USCIS 100:49, 50). As such, she argued on that basis that women could not be denied the right to vote. She and 15 other women voted in the presidential election of 1872 in Rochester, New York. Days later, the women were all arrested, although only Anthony was actually brought to trial. The judge, who opposed women's right to vote, found her guilty and fined her $100,000. She refused to pay, and no further action was taken.

Undaunted, Anthony continued to fight for women's rights (USCIS 100:77a), and her efforts resulted in new career opportunities for women. At the time of her death in 1906, only four states — Colorado, Idaho, Utah, and Wyoming — had granted women the right to vote. But the cause she fought so hard for continued even after she was gone. In 1920, Congress finally passed the 19th Amendment, giving women the right to vote (USCIS 100:48c).

Woodrow Wilson

Woodrow Wilson (December 28, 1856–February 3, 1924) was an American politician and academic who served as the 28th president of the United States from 1913 to 1921. A member of the Democratic Party, Wilson served as the president of Princeton University and as the governor of New Jersey before winning the 1912 presidential election. As president, Wilson changed the nation's economic policies and led the United States into World War I in 1917 (USCIS 100:78, 79).

During his administration, two amendments were added to the Constitution: the 18th Amendment and the 19th Amendment. The 18th Amendment made the production, sale, and consumption of alcohol illegal. Wilson vetoed the bill (USCIS 100:34), but Congress overrode his veto. Although Wilson personally did not approve of women's suffrage, he pressured Congress to pass the 19th Amendment. He knew that signing the bill thereby giving women the right to vote (USCIS 100:33,48c) was key to women's support on the home front during World War I in Europe.

After World War I, he supported international peace efforts and helped found the League of Nations, for which he was awarded the Nobel Peace Prize. When he sent the League of Nations treaty to the Senate for confirmation, they rejected it (USCIS 100:41d). The league still formed, but it was weakened by the lack of American support and was unable to resolve the issues that ultimately led to World War II. The idea of a peace-keeping organization was revived after World War II as the United Nations.

In 1919, he had a severe stroke. Although he never did physically recover, his mind was clear, and he continued as president with the help of his wife and inner circle. His vice president did not assert himself to take over Wilson's presidency as would be expected (USCIS 100:30). Wilson completed his second term in office and died three years later.

Franklin Delano Roosevelt

Born in 1882 in Hyde Park, New York, Franklin Delano Roosevelt (often referred to as FDR), like his fifth cousin Theodore Roosevelt (our 26th president) before him, went into politics. He was elected a New York state senator in 1910 and was the Democratic nominee for vice president in 1920.

FDR was elected our 32nd president in November 1932, while the country was feeling the terrible effects of the Great Depression (USCIS 100:81). Unemployment reached record numbers, and nearly every bank was closed. In response to the desperate times, Roosevelt enacted changes that had been previously unheard of in American policy.

The Constitution severely limited the areas where the government could get involved. The tough financial times of the Depression made people interpret the Constitution more loosely, and the scope of constitutional powers has not been taken as literally since.

Roosevelt proposed and Congress enacted the New Deal, a series of new laws and programs that supported a market economy (USCIS 100:11) while expanding social services. The New Deal helped businesses and agriculture recover, as well as brought relief to the unemployed and to those in danger of losing farms and homes. Although popular with the people, Roosevelt's policies drew strong criticism, especially from bankers and businessmen. Roosevelt responded to the criticism by creating more new programs, including Social Security, which supplements American citizens' retirement incomes. He also enacted stricter controls over banks and public utilities, and America's wealthy saw an increase in their federal tax bills under FDR (USCIS 100:56).

Roosevelt also prompted legislation to enlarge the Supreme Court (USCIS 100:39) in order to increase support for his New Deal policies — the Supreme Court had previously been less than receptive. Although he lost the bid for more justices, a revolution in constitutional law followed, after which the government was legally allowed to regulate the economy (USCIS 100:37).

Roosevelt also radically changed the policy of American neutrality in foreign affairs, pledging the country to the *Good Neighbor Policy*, which called for mutual action against aggressors. Although he tried to remain neutral, he did send aid to the Allied powers in World War II, and when the Japanese attacked the United States at Pearl Harbor, the country was ready for war. On December 8, 1941, the United States joined the Allies: Britain, France, Russia, China, and many other countries and colonies to fight against the Axis Powers: Japan, Germany, and Italy (USCIS 100:81).

By the end of the war, Roosevelt's health had worsened, and he died of a cerebral hemorrhage on April 12, 1945. A month later, World War II in Europe came to an end. Four months later, World War II ended in the Pacific.

Dwight David "Ike" Eisenhower

Dwight David "Ike" Eisenhower (October 14, 1890–March 28, 1969) was an American military officer and statesman who served as the 34th president of the United States from 1953 to 1961. During World War II, he served as Supreme

Commander of the Allied Expeditionary Force in Europe and achieved the rare five-star rank of General of the Army (USCIS 100:82). He was responsible for planning and supervising the invasion of North Africa in 1942–1943 and the successful invasion of Normandy in 1944–1945, which ultimately led to the end of World War II in Europe. He also served as the first Supreme Commander of NATO (1951–1952).

As president, Eisenhower signed the Civil Rights Act of 1957 and sent Army troops to enforce federal court orders that integrated schools in Little Rock, Arkansas. The courage of nine Little Rock students, more than 1957 act, led to a nationwide fight against racial discrimination in education and empowered the civil rights movement (USCIS 100:84). Eisenhower also signed into law the Interstate Highway System, a massive infrastructure project, which was key to the modernization of American society.

Although he signed a treaty (armistice) to end the Korean War (USCIS 100:41, 78), Eisenhower still had grave concerns about the escalation of the Cold War (USCIS 100:83) at home and abroad. He used his influence to stop politicians seeking to gain power by falsely accusing people of being secret communists. In his farewell address to the nation, this former general and president expressed his concerns about the dangers of massive military spending, particularly deficit spending and government contracts to private military manufacturers, which he dubbed "the military–industrial complex."

Eisenhower was honored on a U.S. one-dollar coin, minted from 1971 to 1978. His centenary was honored on a commemorative dollar coin issued in 1990.

Martin Luther King, Jr.

Our nation's most important civil rights leader was born on January 15, 1929, at his family's home in Atlanta, Georgia. King entered Morehouse College at the age of 15 and graduated in 1948 with a BA degree in sociology. During his academic career, he won numerous honors and earned several degrees, including a PhD in theology.

At the age of 19, King was ordained a minister at the Ebenezer Baptist Church in Atlanta. Although he left this post for periods of time throughout his life, he returned from 1960 until his death in 1968, serving as co-pastor with his father.

Arrested 30 times for his participation in the civil rights movement (USCIS 100:84), King was instrumental in effecting change through peaceful, nonviolent means, such as boycotts, protests, and *civil disobedience,* a form of protest in which demonstrators intentionally (but nonviolently) resisted racial discrimination and unjust laws and risked arrest in order to have a more democratic society (USCIS 100:84, 55).

In 1964, at the age of 35, King's efforts in the fight for civil rights (USCIS 100:85a) earned him the prestigious Nobel Peace Prize. He was the youngest man ever, the second American, and the third Black man to be awarded this honor.

In 1968, Dr. King traveled to Memphis, Tennessee, to help lead sanitation workers there in a protest against low wages and unsavory working conditions. While in Memphis, he was shot down by an assassin's bullet. The president of the United States, Lyndon Johnson, proclaimed a national day of mourning, and flags throughout the country were flown at half-staff.

Today, the King Center, established in Atlanta, Georgia, by Dr. King's widow, Coretta Scott King, continues Martin Luther King, Jr.'s work of equality, civil rights, and nonviolent social change. Over 600,000 visitors make the trip to Atlanta annually to honor the work of this great civil rights leader and pay their respects at his final resting place.

His work for equity and equality for all Americans continues (USCIS:85b)! On Martin Luther King Jr. Day, we join together in a "day of service" to work on local community issues and civic projects (USCIS 100:55).

Appendixes

Appendix A

The Declaration of Independence

WHEN in the Course of human Events, it becomes necessary for one People to dissolve the Political Bands which have connected them with another, and to assume among the Powers of the Earth, the separate and equal Station to which the Laws of Nature and of Nature's God entitle them, a decent Respect to the Opinions of Mankind requires that they should declare the causes which impel them to the Separation.

WE hold these Truths to be self-evident, that all Men are created equal, that they are endowed by their Creator with certain unalienable Rights, that among these are Life, Liberty, and the Pursuit of Happiness—That to secure these Rights, Governments are instituted among Men, deriving their just Powers from the Consent of the Governed, that whenever any Form of Government becomes destructive of these Ends, it is the Right of the People to alter or to abolish it, and to institute new Government, laying its Foundation on such Principles, and organizing its Powers in such Form, as to them shall seem most likely to effect their Safety and Happiness. Prudence, indeed, will dictate that Governments long established should not be changed for light and transient Causes; and accordingly all Experience hath shewn, that Mankind are more disposed to suffer, while Evils are sufferable, than to right themselves by abolishing the Forms to which they are accustomed. But when a long Train of Abuses and Usurpations, pursuing invariably the same Object, evinces a Design to reduce them under absolute Despotism, it is their Right, it is their Duty, to throw off such Government, and to provide new Guards for their future Security. Such has been the patient Sufferance of these Colonies; and such is now the Necessity which constrains them to alter their former Systems of Government. The History of the present King of Great-Britain is a History of repeated Injuries and Usurpations, all having in direct Object the Establishment of an absolute Tyranny over these States. To prove this, let Facts be submitted to a candid World.

HE has refused his Assent to Laws, the most wholesome and necessary for the public Good.

HE has forbidden his Governors to pass Laws of immediate and pressing Importance, unless suspended in their Operation till his Assent should be obtained; and when so suspended, he has utterly neglected to attend to them.

HE has refused to pass other Laws for the Accommodation of large Districts of People, unless those People would relinquish the Right of Representation in the Legislature, a Right inestimable to them, and formidable to Tyrants only.

HE has called together Legislative Bodies at Places unusual, uncomfortable, and distant from the Depository of their public Records, for the sole Purpose of fatiguing them into Compliance with his Measures.

HE has dissolved Representative Houses repeatedly, for opposing with manly Firmness his Invasions on the Rights of the People.

HE has refused for a long Time, after such Dissolutions, to cause others to be elected; whereby the Legislative Powers, incapable of Annihilation, have returned to the People at large for their exercise; the State remaining in the mean time exposed to all the Dangers of Invasion from without, and Convulsions within.

HE has endeavoured to prevent the Population of these States; for that Purpose obstructing the Laws for Naturalization of Foreigners; refusing to pass others to encourage their Migrations hither, and raising the Conditions of new Appropriations of Lands.

HE has obstructed the Administration of Justice, by refusing his Assent to Laws for establishing Judiciary Powers.

HE has made judges dependent on his Will alone, for the Tenure of their Offices, and the Amount and Payment of their Salaries.

HE has erected a Multitude of new Offices, and sent hither Swarms of Officers to harrass our People, and eat out their Substance.

HE has kept among us, in Times of Peace, Standing Armies, without the consent of our Legislatures.

HE has affected to render the Military independent of and superior to the Civil Power.

HE has combined with others to subject us to a Jurisdiction foreign to our Constitution, and unacknowledged by our Laws; giving his Assent to their Acts of pretended Legislation:

FOR quartering large Bodies of Armed Troops among us:

FOR protecting them, by a mock Trial, from Punishment for any Murders which they should commit on the Inhabitants of these States:

FOR cutting off our Trade with all Parts of the World:

FOR imposing Taxes on us without our Consent:

FOR depriving us, in many Cases, of the Benefits of Trial by Jury:

FOR transporting us beyond Seas to be tried for pretended Offences:

FOR abolishing the free System of English Laws in a neighbouring Province, establishing therein an arbitrary Government, and enlarging its Boundaries, so as to render it at once an Example and fit Instrument for introducing the same absolute Rule into these Colonies:

FOR taking away our Charters, abolishing our most valuable Laws, and altering fundamentally the Forms of our Governments:

FOR suspending our own Legislatures, and declaring themselves invested with Power to legislate for us in all Cases whatsoever.

HE has abdicated Government here, by declaring us out of his Protection and waging War against us.

HE has plundered our Seas, ravaged our Coasts, burnt our Towns, and destroyed the Lives of our People.

HE is, at this Time, transporting large Armies of foreign Mercenaries to compleat the Works of Death, Desolation, and Tyranny, already begun with circumstances of Cruelty and Perfidy, scarcely paralleled in the most barbarous Ages, and totally unworthy the Head of a civilized Nation.

HE has constrained our fellow Citizens taken Captive on the high Seas to bear Arms against their Country, to become the Executioners of their Friends and Brethren, or to fall themselves by their Hands.

HE has excited domestic Insurrections amongst us, and has endeavoured to bring on the Inhabitants of our Frontiers, the merciless Indian Savages, whose known Rule of Warfare, is an undistinguished Destruction, of all Ages, Sexes and Conditions.

IN every stage of these Oppressions we have Petitioned for Redress in the most humble Terms: Our repeated Petitions have been answered only by repeated Injury. A Prince, whose Character is thus marked by every act which may define a Tyrant, is unfit to be the Ruler of a free People.

NOR have we been wanting in Attentions to our British Brethren. We have warned them from Time to Time of Attempts by their Legislature to extend an unwarrantable jurisdiction over us. We have reminded them of the Circumstances of our Emigration and Settlement here. We have appealed to their native justice and Magnanimity, and we have conjured them by the Ties of our common Kindred to disavow these Usurpations, which, would inevitably interrupt our Connections and Correspondence. They too have been deaf to the Voice of Justice and of Consanguinity. We must, therefore, acquiesce in the Necessity, which denounces our Separation, and hold them, as we hold the rest of Mankind, Enemies in War, in Peace, Friends.

WE, therefore, the Representatives of the UNITED STATES OF AMERICA, in GENERAL CONGRESS, Assembled, appealing to the Supreme Judge of the World for the Rectitude of our Intentions, do, in the Name, and by Authority of the good People of these Colonies, solemnly Publish and Declare, That these United Colonies are, and of Right ought to be, FREE AND INDEPENDENT STATES; that they are absolved from all Allegiance to the British Crown, and that all political Connection between them and the State of Great-Britain, is and ought to be totally dissolved; and that as FREE AND INDEPENDENT STATES, they have full Power to levy War, conclude Peace, contract Alliances, establish Commerce, and to do all other Acts and Things which INDEPENDENT STATES may of right do. And for the support of this Declaration, with a firm Reliance on the Protection of divine Providence, we mutually pledge to each other our Lives, our Fortunes, and our sacred Honor.

Appendix B

The United States Constitution

We the People of the United States, in Order to form a more perfect Union, establish Justice, insure domestic Tranquility, provide for the common defence, promote the general Welfare, and secure the Blessings of Liberty to ourselves and our Posterity, do ordain and establish this Constitution for the United States of America.

Article. I.

Section. 1.

All legislative Powers herein granted shall be vested in a Congress of the United States, which shall consist of a Senate and House of Representatives.

Section. 2.

Clause 1: The House of Representatives shall be composed of Members chosen every second Year by the People of the several States, and the Electors in each State shall have the Qualifications requisite for Electors of the most numerous Branch of the State Legislature.

Clause 2: No Person shall be a Representative who shall not have attained to the Age of twenty five Years, and been seven Years a Citizen of the United States, and who shall not, when elected, be an Inhabitant of that State in which he shall be chosen.

Clause 3: Representatives and direct Taxes shall be apportioned among the several States which may be included within this Union, according to their respective Numbers, which shall be determined by adding to the whole Number of free Persons, including those bound to Service for a Term of Years, and excluding Indians not taxed, three fifths of all other Persons. The actual Enumeration shall be made within three Years after the first Meeting of the Congress of the United States, and within every subsequent Term of ten Years, in such Manner as they shall by Law direct. The Number of Representatives shall not exceed one for every thirty Thousand, but each State shall have at Least one Representative; and until such enumeration shall be made, the State of New Hampshire shall be entitled to chuse three, Massachusetts eight, Rhode-Island and Providence Plantations one, Connecticut five, New-York six, New Jersey four, Pennsylvania eight, Delaware one, Maryland six, Virginia ten, North Carolina five, South Carolina five, and Georgia three.

Clause 4: When vacancies happen in the Representation from any State, the Executive Authority thereof shall issue Writs of Election to fill such Vacancies.

Clause 5: The House of Representatives shall chuse their Speaker and other Officers; and shall have the sole Power of Impeachment.

Section. 3.

Clause 1: The Senate of the United States shall be composed of two Senators from each State, chosen by the Legislature thereof, for six Years; and each Senator shall have one Vote.

Clause 2: Immediately after they shall be assembled in Consequence of the first Election, they shall be divided as equally as may be into three Classes. The Seats of the Senators of the first Class shall be vacated at the Expiration of the second Year, of the second Class at the Expiration of the fourth Year, and of the third Class at the Expiration of the sixth Year, so that one third may be chosen every second Year; and if Vacancies happen by Resignation, or otherwise, during the Recess of the Legislature of any State, the Executive thereof may make temporary Appointments until the next Meeting of the Legislature, which shall then fill such Vacancies.

Clause 3: No Person shall be a Senator who shall not have attained to the Age of thirty Years, and been nine Years a Citizen of the United States, and who shall not, when elected, be an Inhabitant of that State for which he shall be chosen.

Clause 4: The Vice President of the United States shall be President of the Senate, but shall have no Vote, unless they be equally divided.

Clause 5: The Senate shall chuse their other Officers, and also a President pro tempore, in the Absence of the Vice President, or when he shall exercise the Office of President of the United States.

Clause 6: The Senate shall have the sole Power to try all Impeachments. When sitting for that Purpose, they shall be on Oath or Affirmation. When the President of the United States is tried, the Chief Justice shall preside: And no Person shall be convicted without the Concurrence of two thirds of the Members present.

Clause 7: Judgment in Cases of Impeachment shall not extend further than to removal from Office, and disqualification to hold and enjoy any Office of honor, Trust or Profit under the United States: but the Party convicted shall nevertheless be liable and subject to Indictment, Trial, Judgment and Punishment, according to Law.

Section. 4.

Clause 1: The Times, Places and Manner of holding Elections for Senators and Representatives, shall be prescribed in each State by the Legislature thereof; but the Congress may at any time by Law make or alter such Regulations, except as to the Places of chusing Senators.

Clause 2: The Congress shall assemble at least once in every Year, and such Meeting shall be on the first Monday in December, unless they shall by Law appoint a different Day.

Section. 5.

Clause 1: Each House shall be the Judge of the Elections, Returns and Qualifications of its own Members, and a Majority of each shall constitute a Quorum to do Business; but a smaller Number may adjourn from day to day, and may be authorized to compel the Attendance of absent Members, in such Manner, and under such Penalties as each House may provide.

Clause 2: Each House may determine the Rules of its Proceedings, punish its Members for disorderly Behaviour, and, with the Concurrence of two thirds, expel a Member.

Clause 3: Each House shall keep a Journal of its Proceedings, and from time to time publish the same, excepting such Parts as may in their Judgment require Secrecy; and the Yeas and Nays of the Members of either House on any question shall, at the Desire of one fifth of those Present, be entered on the Journal.

Clause 4: Neither House, during the Session of Congress, shall, without the Consent of the other, adjourn for more than three days, nor to any other Place than that in which the two Houses shall be sitting.

Section. 6.

Clause 1: The Senators and Representatives shall receive a Compensation for their Services, to be ascertained by Law, and paid out of the Treasury of the United States. They shall in all Cases, except Treason, Felony and Breach of the Peace, be privileged from Arrest during their Attendance at the Session of their respective Houses, and in going to and returning from the same; and for any Speech or Debate in either House, they shall not be questioned in any other Place.

Clause 2: No Senator or Representative shall, during the Time for which he was elected, be appointed to any civil Office under the Authority of the United States, which shall have been created, or the Emoluments whereof shall have been encreased during such time; and no Person holding any Office under the United States, shall be a Member of either House during his Continuance in Office.

Section. 7.

Clause 1: All Bills for raising Revenue shall originate in the House of Representatives; but the Senate may propose or concur with Amendments as on other Bills.

Clause 2: Every Bill which shall have passed the House of Representatives and the Senate, shall, before it become a Law, be presented to the President of the United States; If he approve he shall sign it, but if not he shall return it, with his Objections to that House in which it shall have originated, who shall enter the Objections at large on their Journal, and proceed to reconsider it. If after such Reconsideration two thirds of that House shall agree to pass the Bill, it shall be sent, together with the Objections, to the other House, by which it shall likewise be reconsidered, and if approved by two thirds of that House, it shall become a Law. But in all such Cases the Votes of both Houses shall be determined by yeas and Nays, and the Names of the Persons voting for and against the Bill shall be entered on the Journal of each House respectively. If any Bill shall not be returned by the President within ten Days (Sundays excepted) after it shall have been presented to him, the Same shall be a Law, in like Manner as if he had signed it, unless the Congress by their Adjournment prevent its Return, in which Case it shall not be a Law.

Clause 3: Every Order, Resolution, or Vote to which the Concurrence of the Senate and House of Representatives may be necessary (except on a question of Adjournment) shall be presented to the President of the United States; and before the Same shall take Effect, shall be approved by him, or being disapproved by him, shall be repassed by two thirds of the Senate and House of Representatives, according to the Rules and Limitations prescribed in the Case of a Bill.

Section. 8.

Clause 1: The Congress shall have Power To lay and collect Taxes, Duties, Imposts and Excises, to pay the Debts and provide for the common Defence and general Welfare of the United States; but all Duties, Imposts and Excises shall be uniform throughout the United States;

Clause 2: To borrow Money on the credit of the United States;

Clause 3: To regulate Commerce with foreign Nations, and among the several States, and with the Indian Tribes;

Clause 4: To establish an uniform Rule of Naturalization, and uniform Laws on the subject of Bankruptcies throughout the United States;

Clause 5: To coin Money, regulate the Value thereof, and of foreign Coin, and fix the Standard of Weights and Measures;

Clause 6: To provide for the Punishment of counterfeiting the Securities and current Coin of the United States;

Clause 7: To establish Post Offices and post Roads;

Clause 8: To promote the Progress of Science and useful Arts, by securing for limited Times to Authors and Inventors the exclusive Right to their respective Writings and Discoveries;

Clause 9: To constitute Tribunals inferior to the supreme Court;

Clause 10: To define and punish Piracies and Felonies committed on the high Seas, and Offences against the Law of Nations;

Clause 11: To declare War, grant Letters of Marque and Reprisal, and make Rules concerning Captures on Land and Water;

Clause 12: To raise and support Armies, but no Appropriation of Money to that Use shall be for a longer Term than two Years;

Clause 13: To provide and maintain a Navy;

Clause 14: To make Rules for the Government and Regulation of the land and naval Forces;

Clause 15: To provide for calling forth the Militia to execute the Laws of the Union, suppress Insurrections and repel Invasions;

Clause 16: To provide for organizing, arming, and disciplining, the Militia, and for governing such Part of them as may be employed in the Service of the United States, reserving to the States respectively, the Appointment of the Officers, and the Authority of training the Militia according to the discipline prescribed by Congress;

Clause 17: To exercise exclusive Legislation in all Cases whatsoever, over such District (not exceeding ten Miles square) as may, by Cession of particular States, and the Acceptance of Congress, become the Seat of the Government of the United States, and to exercise like Authority over all Places purchased by the Consent of the Legislature of the State in which the Same shall be, for the Erection of Forts, Magazines, Arsenals, dock-Yards, and other needful Buildings; — And

Clause 18: To make all Laws which shall be necessary and proper for carrying into Execution the foregoing Powers, and all other Powers vested by this Constitution in the Government of the United States, or in any Department or Officer thereof.

Section. 9.

Clause 1: The Migration or Importation of such Persons as any of the States now existing shall think proper to admit, shall not be prohibited by the Congress prior to the Year one thousand eight hundred and eight, but a Tax or duty may be imposed on such Importation, not exceeding ten dollars for each Person.

Clause 2: The Privilege of the Writ of Habeas Corpus shall not be suspended, unless when in Cases of Rebellion or Invasion the public Safety may require it.

Clause 3: No Bill of Attainder or ex post facto Law shall be passed.

Clause 4: No Capitation, or other direct, Tax shall be laid, unless in Proportion to the Census or Enumeration herein before directed to be taken.

Clause 5: No Tax or Duty shall be laid on Articles exported from any State.

Clause 6: No Preference shall be given by any Regulation of Commerce or Revenue to the Ports of one State over those of another: nor shall Vessels bound to, or from, one State, be obliged to enter, clear, or pay Duties in another.

Clause 7: No Money shall be drawn from the Treasury, but in Consequence of Appropriations made by Law; and a regular Statement and Account of the Receipts and Expenditures of all public Money shall be published from time to time.

Clause 8: No Title of Nobility shall be granted by the United States: And no Person holding any Office of Profit or Trust under them, shall, without the Consent of the

Congress, accept of any present, Emolument, Office, or Title, of any kind what-ever, from any King, Prince, or foreign State.

Section. 10.

Clause 1: No State shall enter into any Treaty, Alliance, or Confederation; grant Letters of Marque and Reprisal; coin Money; emit Bills of Credit; make any Thing but gold and silver Coin a Tender in Payment of Debts; pass any Bill of Attainder, ex post facto Law, or Law impairing the Obligation of Contracts, or grant any Title of Nobility.

Clause 2: No State shall, without the Consent of the Congress, lay any Imposts or Duties on Imports or Exports, except what may be absolutely necessary for exe-cuting it's inspection Laws: and the net Produce of all Duties and Imposts, laid by any State on Imports or Exports, shall be for the Use of the Treasury of the United States; and all such Laws shall be subject to the Revision and Controul of the Congress.

Clause 3: No State shall, without the Consent of Congress, lay any Duty of Ton-nage, keep Troops, or Ships of War in time of Peace, enter into any Agreement or Compact with another State, or with a foreign Power, or engage in War, unless actually invaded, or in such imminent Danger as will not admit of delay.

Article. II.

Section. 1.

Clause 1: The executive Power shall be vested in a President of the United States of America. He shall hold his Office during the Term of four Years, and, together with the Vice President, chosen for the same Term, be elected, as follows

Clause 2: Each State shall appoint, in such Manner as the Legislature thereof may direct, a Number of Electors, equal to the whole Number of Senators and Repre-sentatives to which the State may be entitled in the Congress: but no Senator or Representative, or Person holding an Office of Trust or Profit under the United States, shall be appointed an Elector.

Clause 3: The Electors shall meet in their respective States, and vote by Ballot for two Persons, of whom one at least shall not be an Inhabitant of the same State with themselves. And they shall make a List of all the Persons voted for, and of the

Number of Votes for each; which List they shall sign and certify, and transmit sealed to the Seat of the Government of the United States, directed to the President of the Senate. The President of the Senate shall, in the Presence of the Senate and House of Representatives, open all the Certificates, and the Votes shall then be counted. The Person having the greatest Number of Votes shall be the President, if such Number be a Majority of the whole Number of Electors appointed; and if there be more than one who have such Majority, and have an equal Number of Votes, then the House of Representatives shall immediately chuse by Ballot one of them for President; and if no Person have a Majority, then from the five highest on the List the said House shall in like Manner chuse the President. But in chusing the President, the Votes shall be taken by States, the Representation from each State having one Vote; A quorum for this Purpose shall consist of a Member or Members from two thirds of the States, and a Majority of all the States shall be necessary to a Choice. In every Case, after the Choice of the President, the Person having the greatest Number of Votes of the Electors shall be the Vice President. But if there should remain two or more who have equal Votes, the Senate shall chuse from them by Ballot the Vice President.

Clause 4: The Congress may determine the Time of chusing the Electors, and the Day on which they shall give their Votes; which Day shall be the same throughout the United States.

Clause 5: No Person except a natural born Citizen, or a Citizen of the United States, at the time of the Adoption of this Constitution, shall be eligible to the Office of President; neither shall any Person be eligible to that Office who shall not have attained to the Age of thirty five Years, and been fourteen Years a Resident within the United States.

Clause 6: In Case of the Removal of the President from Office, or of his Death, Resignation, or Inability to discharge the Powers and Duties of the said Office, the Same shall devolve on the Vice President, and the Congress may by Law provide for the Case of Removal, Death, Resignation or Inability, both of the President and Vice President, declaring what Officer shall then act as President, and such Officer shall act accordingly, until the Disability be removed, or a President shall be elected.

Clause 7: The President shall, at stated Times, receive for his Services, a Compensation, which shall neither be encreased nor diminished during the Period for which he shall have been elected, and he shall not receive within that Period any other Emolument from the United States, or any of them.

Clause 8: Before he enter on the Execution of his Office, he shall take the following Oath or Affirmation: — "I do solemnly swear (or affirm) that I will faithfully execute the Office of President of the United States, and will to the best of my Ability, preserve, protect and defend the Constitution of the United States."

Section. 2.

Clause 1: The President shall be Commander in Chief of the Army and Navy of the United States, and of the Militia of the several States, when called into the actual Service of the United States; he may require the Opinion, in writing, of the principal Officer in each of the executive Departments, upon any Subject relating to the Duties of their respective Offices, and he shall have Power to grant Reprieves and Pardons for Offences against the United States, except in Cases of Impeachment.

Clause 2: He shall have Power, by and with the Advice and Consent of the Senate, to make Treaties, provided two thirds of the Senators present concur; and he shall nominate, and by and with the Advice and Consent of the Senate, shall appoint Ambassadors, other public Ministers and Consuls, Judges of the supreme Court, and all other Officers of the United States, whose Appointments are not herein otherwise provided for, and which shall be established by Law: but the Congress may by Law vest the Appointment of such inferior Officers, as they think proper, in the President alone, in the Courts of Law, or in the Heads of Departments.

Clause 3: The President shall have Power to fill up all Vacancies that may happen during the Recess of the Senate, by granting Commissions which shall expire at the End of their next Session.

Section. 3.

He shall from time to time give to the Congress Information of the State of the Union, and recommend to their Consideration such Measures as he shall judge necessary and expedient; he may, on extraordinary Occasions, convene both Houses, or either of them, and in Case of Disagreement between them, with Respect to the Time of Adjournment, he may adjourn them to such Time as he shall think proper; he shall receive Ambassadors and other public Ministers; he shall take Care that the Laws be faithfully executed, and shall Commission all the Officers of the United States.

Section. 4.

The President, Vice President and all civil Officers of the United States, shall be removed from Office on Impeachment for, and Conviction of, Treason, Bribery, or other high Crimes and Misdemeanors.

Article. III.

Section. 1.

The judicial Power of the United States, shall be vested in one supreme Court, and in such inferior Courts as the Congress may from time to time ordain and establish. The Judges, both of the supreme and inferior Courts, shall hold their Offices during good Behaviour, and shall, at stated Times, receive for their Services, a Compensation, which shall not be diminished during their Continuance in Office.

Section. 2.

Clause 1: The judicial Power shall extend to all Cases, in Law and Equity, arising under this Constitution, the Laws of the United States, and Treaties made, or which shall be made, under their Authority; — to all Cases affecting Ambassadors, other public Ministers and Consuls; — to all Cases of admiralty and maritime Jurisdiction; — to Controversies to which the United States shall be a Party; — to Controversies between two or more States; — between a State and Citizens of another State; — between Citizens of different States, — between Citizens of the same State claiming Lands under Grants of different States, and between a State, or the Citizens thereof, and foreign States, Citizens or Subjects.

Clause 2: In all Cases affecting Ambassadors, other public Ministers and Consuls, and those in which a State shall be Party, the supreme Court shall have original Jurisdiction. In all the other Cases before mentioned, the supreme Court shall have appellate Jurisdiction, both as to Law and Fact, with such Exceptions, and under such Regulations as the Congress shall make.

Clause 3: The Trial of all Crimes, except in Cases of Impeachment, shall be by Jury; and such Trial shall be held in the State where the said Crimes shall have been committed; but when not committed within any State, the Trial shall be at such Place or Places as the Congress may by Law have directed.

Section. 3.

Clause 1: Treason against the United States, shall consist only in levying War against them, or in adhering to their Enemies, giving them Aid and Comfort. No Person shall be convicted of Treason unless on the Testimony of two Witnesses to the same overt Act, or on Confession in open Court.

Clause 2: The Congress shall have Power to declare the Punishment of Treason, but no Attainder of Treason shall work Corruption of Blood, or Forfeiture except during the Life of the Person attainted.

Article. IV.

Section. 1.

Full Faith and Credit shall be given in each State to the public Acts, Records, and judicial Proceedings of every other State. And the Congress may by general Laws prescribe the Manner in which such Acts, Records and Proceedings shall be proved, and the Effect thereof.

Section. 2.

Clause 1: The Citizens of each State shall be entitled to all Privileges and Immunities of Citizens in the several States.

Clause 2: A Person charged in any State with Treason, Felony, or other Crime, who shall flee from Justice, and be found in another State, shall on Demand of the executive Authority of the State from which he fled, be delivered up, to be removed to the State having Jurisdiction of the Crime.

Clause 3: No Person held to Service or Labour in one State, under the Laws thereof, escaping into another, shall, in Consequence of any Law or Regulation therein, be discharged from such Service or Labour, but shall be delivered up on Claim of the Party to whom such Service or Labour may be due.

Section. 3.

Clause 1: New States may be admitted by the Congress into this Union; but no new State shall be formed or erected within the Jurisdiction of any other State; nor any State be formed by the Junction of two or more States, or Parts of States, without the Consent of the Legislatures of the States concerned as well as of the Congress.

Clause 2: The Congress shall have Power to dispose of and make all needful Rules and Regulations respecting the Territory or other Property belonging to the United States; and nothing in this Constitution shall be so construed as to Prejudice any Claims of the United States, or of any particular State.

Section. 4.

The United States shall guarantee to every State in this Union a Republican Form of Government, and shall protect each of them against Invasion; and on Application of the Legislature, or of the Executive (when the Legislature cannot be convened) against domestic Violence.

Article. V.

The Congress, whenever two thirds of both Houses shall deem it necessary, shall propose Amendments to this Constitution, or, on the Application of the Legislatures of two thirds of the several States, shall call a Convention for proposing Amendments, which, in either Case, shall be valid to all Intents and Purposes, as Part of this Constitution, when ratified by the Legislatures of three fourths of the several States, or by Conventions in three fourths thereof, as the one or the other Mode of Ratification may be proposed by the Congress; Provided that no Amendment which may be made prior to the Year One thousand eight hundred and eight shall in any Manner affect the first and fourth Clauses in the Ninth Section of the first Article; and that no State, without its Consent, shall be deprived of its equal Suffrage in the Senate.

Article. VI.

Clause 1: All Debts contracted and Engagements entered into, before the Adoption of this Constitution, shall be as valid against the United States under this Constitution, as under the Confederation.

Clause 2: This Constitution, and the Laws of the United States which shall be made in Pursuance thereof; and all Treaties made, or which shall be made, under the Authority of the United States, shall be the supreme Law of the Land; and the Judges in every State shall be bound thereby, any Thing in the Constitution or Laws of any State to the Contrary notwithstanding.

Clause 3: The Senators and Representatives before mentioned, and the Members of the several State Legislatures, and all executive and judicial Officers, both of the United States and of the several States, shall be bound by Oath or Affirmation, to support this Constitution; but no religious Test shall ever be required as a Qualification to any Office or public Trust under the United States.

Article. VII.

The Ratification of the Conventions of nine States, shall be sufficient for the Establishment of this Constitution between the States so ratifying the Same.

Attest William Jackson Secretary

Done in Convention by the Unanimous Consent of the States present the Seventeenth Day of September in the Year of our Lord one thousand seven hundred and Eighty seven and of the Independence of the United States of America the Twelfth In witness whereof We have hereunto subscribed our Names,

G°. Washington
Presidt and deputy from
Virginia

Delaware

Geo: Read
Gunning Bedford jun
John Dickinson
Richard Bassett
Jaco: Broom

Maryland
James McHenry
Dan of St Thos. Jenifer
Danl. Carroll.

Virginia
John Blair
James Madison Jr.

North Carolina
Wm. Blount
Richd. Dobbs Spaight.
Hu Williamson

South Carolina
J. Rutledge
Charles Cotesworth Pinckney
Charles Pinckney
Pierce Butler

Georgia
William Few
Abr Baldwin

New Hampshire
John Langdon
Nicholas Gilman

Massachusetts
Nathaniel Gorham
Rufus King

Connecticut
Wm. Saml. Johnson
Roger Sherman

New York
Alexander Hamilton

New Jersey
Wil: Livingston
David Brearley.
Wm. Paterson
Jona: Dayton

Pennsylvania
B Franklin
Thomas Mifflin
Robt. Morris
Geo. Clymer
Thos. FitzSimons
Jared Ingersoll
James Wilson
Gouv Morris

Appendix C

Document Checklist

Department of Homeland Security
U.S. Citizenship and Immigration Services

M-477

Document Checklist

All applicants must send the following 3 items with their N-400 application:

1. ☐ A photocopy of both sides of your Permanent Resident Card (formerly known as the Alien Registration Card or "Green Card"). If you have lost the card, submit a photocopy of the receipt of your Form I-90, Application to Replace Permanent Resident Card; **and**

2. ☐ A check or money order for the application fee and the biometric services fee, as stated in the M-479, Current Naturalization Fees, enclosure in the *Guide*.(Applicants 75 years of age or older are exempted from the biometrics services fee). Write your A-Number on the back of the check or money order.

   You may also pay using a credit card. There is no additional fee when you do so. The N-400 is the only form that you can pay for by credit card using the G-1450, Authorization for Credit Card Transaction. Check www.uscis.gov for more specific information.

3. ☐ If you reside outside the United States, **2** identical color photographs, with your name and Alien Registration Number (A-Number) written lightly in pencil on the back of each photo. For details about the photo requirements, see **Part 5** of Form M-476, A Guide to Naturalization, and the Form N-400, Application for Naturalization instructions. If your religion requires you to wear a head covering, your facial features must still be exposed in the photo for purposes of identification.

Send copies of the following documents, unless we ask for an original.

If an attorney or accredited representative is acting on your behalf, send:

☐ A completed <u>original</u> Form G-28, Notice of Entry of Appearance as Attorney or Representative.

If your current legal name is different from the name on your Permanent Resident Card, send:

☐ The document(s) that legally changed your name (marriage certificate, divorce decree, or court document).

If you are applying for naturalization on the basis of marriage to a U.S. citizen, send the following 4 items:

1. ☐ Evidence that your spouse has been a U.S. citizen for the last 3 years:

   a. Birth certificate (if your spouse never lost citizenship since birth); **or**

   b. Certificate of Naturalization; **or**

   c. Certificate of Citizenship; **or**

   d. The inside of the front cover and signature page of your spouse's current U.S. passport; **or**

   e. Form FS-240, Report of Birth Abroad of a Citizen of the United States of America; **and**

2. ☐ Your current marriage certificate; **and**

3. ☐ Proof of termination of all prior marriages of your spouse (divorce decree(s), annulment(s), or death certificate(s)); **and**

4. ☐ Documents referring to you and your spouse:

   a. Tax returns, bank accounts, leases, mortgages, or birth certificates of children; **or**

   b. Internal Revenue Service (IRS)-certified copies of the income tax forms that you both filed for the past 3 years; **or**

   c. An IRS tax return transcript for the last 3 years.

If you were married before, send:

☐ Proof that **all** earlier marriages ended (divorce decree(s), annulment(s), or death certificates(s)).

If you are currently in the U.S. military service and are seeking citizenship based on that service, send:

☐ A completed <u>original</u> Form N-426, Request for Certification of Military or Naval Service.

Form M-477 (Rev. 11/21/2016 N)

If you have taken any trip outside the United States that lasted 6 months or more since becoming a Lawful Permanent Resident, send evidence that you (and your family) continued to live, work and/or keep ties to the United States, such as:

☐ An IRS tax return "transcript" or an IRS-certified tax return listing tax information for the last 5 years (or for the last 3 years if you are applying on the basis of marriage to a U.S. citizen).

☐ Rent or mortgage payments and pay stubs.

If you have a dependent spouse or child(ren) who do not live with you, send:

☐ Any court or government order to provide financial support; and

☐ Evidence of your financial support (including evidence that you have complied with any court or government order), such as:

    a. Cancelled checks;

    b. Money and receipts;

    c. A court or agency printout of child support payments;

    d. Evidence of wage garnishments;

    e. A letter from the parent or guardian who cares for your child(ren).

If you have ever been arrested or detained by any law enforcement officer for any reason, and <u>no charges were filed</u>, send:

☐ An <u>original</u> official statement by the arresting agency or applicant court confirming that no charges were filed.

If you have ever been arrested or detained by any law enforcement officer for any reason, and <u>charges were filed</u>, send:

☐ An <u>original</u> or court-certified copy of the complete arrest record and disposition for each incident (dismissal order, conviction record **or** acquittal order).

If you have ever been convicted or placed in an alternative sentencing program or rehabilitative program (such as a drug treatment or community service program), send:

☐ An <u>original</u> or court-certified copy of the sentencing record for each incident; **and**

☐ Evidence that you completed your sentence:

    a. An <u>original</u> or certified copy of your probation or parole record; **or**

    b. Evidence that you completed an alternative sentencing program or rehabilitative program.

If you have ever had any arrest or conviction vacated, set aside, sealed, expunged or otherwise removed from your record, send:

☐ An <u>original</u> or court-certified copy of the court order vacating, setting aside, sealing, expunging or otherwise removing the arrest or conviction, **or** an <u>original</u> statement from the court that no record exists of your arrest or conviction.

    NOTE: If you have been arrested or convicted of a crime, you may send any countervailing evidence or evidence in your favor concerning the circumstances of your arrest and/or conviction that you would like U.S. Citizenship and Immigration Services to consider.

If you have ever failed to file an income tax return since you became a Lawful Permanent Resident, send:

☐ All correspondence with the IRS regarding your failure to file.

If you have any Federal, state or local taxes that are overdue, send:

☐ A signed agreement from the IRS or state or local tax office showing that you have filed a tax return and arranged to pay the taxes you owe; **and**

☐ Documentation from the IRS or state or local tax office showing the current status of your repayment program.

    NOTE: You may obtain copies of tax documents and tax information by contacting your local IRS offices, using the Blue Pages of your telephone directory, or through its Web site at **www.irs.gov**.

If you are applying for a disability exception to the testing requirement, send:

☐ An <u>original</u> Form N-648, Medical Certification for Disability Exceptions, completed less than 6 months ago by a licensed medical or osteopathic doctor or licensed clinical psychologist.

If you did not register with the Selective Service and you (1) are male, (2) are 26 years old or older, and (3) lived in the United States in a status other than as a lawful nonimmigrant between the ages of 18 and 26, send:

☐ A "Status Information Letter" from the Selective Service (Call **1-847-688-6888** for more information).

Form M-477 (Rev. 11/21/2016 N) Page 2

Index

G

O

About the Author

Jennifer Gagliardi has been teaching ESL/Citizenship at Milpitas Adult School since 2002. In 2007, she launched *US Citizenship Podcast* (uscitizenpod.com), which distributes citizenship resources and immigration news. She regularly presents workshops on the intersection between citizenship and technology at national, state, and regional adult education conferences.

Jennifer has worked on many citizenship projects, most notably coordinating the Santa Clara County Library District Citizenship outreach project (2015–2016), which partnered with local affiliates of IRC (International Rescue Committee) and SIREN (Services, Immigrant Rights, and Education Network) to help naturalize over 200 new U.S. citizens. She has also helped register young immigrants for DACA. She has published *US Citizenship Bootcamp: Exercises and Quizzes to Pass the Naturalization Interview* (2017; updated 2021).

Dedication

To you who come, welcome! I know that you will be great American citizens.

Author's Acknowledgments

I want to thank the outstanding team at Wiley. As usual, their expertise, support, and guidance were of immeasurable help. Thank you to Greg Tubach, Michelle Hacker, and Grace Freedson for their encouragement during the initial planning for the book. Project manager extraordinaire, Tim Gallan, answered questions and kept the content on point. Thank you also to Christy Pingleton for her particularly insightful input.

Special thanks goes out to the students, staff, and families of Milpitas Adult Education and the Milpitas Unified School District. Thanks also to OTAN.us techs, CASAS/EL Civics assessors, COABE/CCAE adult educators, and TESOL/CATESOL members.

Publisher's Acknowledgments

Acquisitions Editor: Greg Tubach

Development Editor: Tim Gallan

Copy Editor: Christine Pingleton

Technical Reviewers: Susan Burgess
    and Dale Kubicki (previous edition)

Production Editor: Tamilmani Varadharaj

Cover Image: © Hill Street Studios/Getty Images